THE GOVERNMENT
OF MANITOBA

CANADIAN GOVERNMENT SERIES

General Editors

R. MacG. DAWSON, 1946–58

J. A. CORRY, 1958–61

C. B. MACPHERSON, 1961–

The Govern- ment of Manitoba

M. S. Donnelly

UNIVERSITY OF
TORONTO PRESS

© UNIVERSITY OF TORONTO PRESS 1963
REPRINTED IN PAPERBACK 2015

SCHOLARLY REPRINT SERIES
ISBN 978-0-8020-7063-0 (CLOTH)
ISBN 978-1-4426-3123-6 (PAPER)
LC 63-23544

TO MY PARENTS

PREFACE

MANY HAVE CONTRIBUTED to this book and it is a pleasure to record my thanks to those who supplied information and offered helpful criticism of the manuscript in its earlier stages. The book began, as have several others in this series, as a doctoral thesis under the supervision of the late R. MacG. Dawson and all who have been through this process will know how much I owe to him. A host of individuals in the Public Archives at Ottawa, in the Legislative Library and Provincial Archives in Winnipeg, and in the Manitoba Civil Service have supplied information and answered innumerable questions. Many, particularly in the Civil Service, have had to answer queries twice, for, after submission as a Ph.D. dissertation, the manuscript was allowed to lie fallow for several years and then updated to June 1960. The editors of the University of Toronto Press have been very helpful and efficient. My most helpful critic has been my wife who not only read the manuscript twice but also made the index. Publication has been made possible by a grant from the Canada Council through the Social Science Research Council of Canada and by assistance from the Publications Fund of the University of Toronto Press. To all I extend my thanks as well as the customary absolution from responsibility for what follows.

M. S. D.

University of Manitoba,
April 1963.

CONTENTS

THE GOVERNMENT
OF MANITOBA

INTRODUCTION

1

THE SYSTEM OF GOVERNMENT in the eastern provinces of the Canadian federation was well established before union. Confederation produced no basic changes in the institutions of representative and responsible government that had grown up there; it meant only that the area of legislative competence was restricted by the British North America Act of 1867 to matters of local interest. The case of Manitoba, the first new province, was completely different. When it was admitted to the union on July 15, 1870, its system of government had to be created. The residents, and there were only 11,000 of them, had not even the most elementary experience with local government—words such as franchise, assembly, cabinet, or civil service were scarcely in their vocabulary. Only two institutions of government had existed before 1870: the Council of Assiniboia, an offshoot of the Hudson's Bay Company, and the provisional government of Louis Riel which resulted from the insurrection of 1869 and 1870.

The Council of Assiniboia grew out of the settlement which Thomas Douglas, Earl of Selkirk, created in 1812 near the present site of Winnipeg. Selkirk had acquired a grant of land called Assiniboia in what is now Manitoba, Saskatchewan, North Dakota, and Minnesota. The legal basis for his colony, and for the powers that the first governor, Miles Macdonnell, exercised, was the charter of the Hudson's Bay Company granted by Charles II in 1670. The governor and committee of this trading company were at that time given full and complete authority "to make ordain and constitute such and so many laws constitutions orders and ordinances as to them or the greater part of them being then and

there present shall seem necessary and convenient for the good government of the said company and of its colonies forts and plantations."[1]
They were also given the power "to judge all persons belonging to the
said Governor and Company or that shall live under them in all causes
whether civil or criminal according to the laws of this kingdom. . . ."[2]

The power that the British monarch conferred on the central committee of the company was delegated to overseas governors, including
Macdonnell, but this power meant little in the face of the overwhelming
difficulties encountered by the settlement from the start. The open hostility of the North West Company and dissension within the settlement
made government of any kind nearly impossible. The North West Company looked upon the creation of the settlement as a threat to its trade
routes and as a pawn in its cutthroat war with the Hudson's Bay Company.[3] Internal dissensions led Governor Macdonnell to write to Selkirk:
"No government is so fit for such an establishment . . . as a military one.
I imagine that once in possession of the Royal Commission, martial law
might be established by proclamation . . . in support of this some coer-
sive force will be necessary—a Company of 50 men would be sufficient
in the first outset . . . if we are to have Glasgow weavers, or others of
similar principles among us, instead of being formidable to the Indians,
or other external enemies, we may be all overturned by one tumultuous
onset of our own people."[4] The suggestion of martial law was vetoed by
Selkirk and, at his insistence, councillors and a sheriff were appointed in
1814. He eventually ceased writing about the necessity for strict consti-
tutionalism and legality, however, and in 1818 advised the Governor "to
set aside certain days upon which four or five of the principal persons
. . . should meet in the manner of Justices of Peace . . . if an individual
refuses to submit to the judgement of his neighbours . . . he is fair game
to anyone who is not afraid to make a prey of him."[5]

Open hostility ceased with the amalgamation of the North West and
Hudson's Bay companies in 1821 but gave way only to contempt and
ridicule. For a time the Red River Settlement, and its council and resident governor, became the butt of many a joke and the subject of deri-
sive letters. "The Council meetings," wrote Sir George Simpson, "usually
open with the bottle and end with a boxing match between the Colonial

---

[1]*Charters, Statutes, Orders in Council, etc. Relating to the Hudson's Bay Company*, p. 12.

[2]*Ibid.*, p. 18.

[3]For a full account of the struggle between these two companies see Douglas
MacKay, *The Honourable Company*.

[4]P.A.C., Selkirk Papers, pp. 358–9.

[5]*Ibid.*, p. 959.

Governor and a burly settler, while the sage councillors stand by to see fair play."[6] Two factors produced a gradual change in the attitude of the Company, however. It became obvious to its officers that they had to make the best of a bad bargain and, more important, they began to find in the Council of Assiniboia a mechanism for enforcing fur-trade regulations. Such enforcement became particularly significant when American traders began to appear in considerable numbers.

The Company liquidated the interest of the Selkirk heirs by re-purchase in 1834 and in 1835 reorganized the council. Sir George Simpson was present for the occasion and his speech is evidence of the nature of government up to that time. He said, in part:

The population of this Colony is become so great [3,679] . . . that the personal influence of the Governor and Council . . . which, together with the good feeling of the public, have heretofore been its principal safeguard, are no longer sufficient to maintain the tranquillity and good government of the Settlement, so that although rights of property have of late been frequently invaded and other serious offences been committed, I am concerned to say we are under the necessity of allowing them to pass unnoticed because we really have not the means at command of enforcing obedience and due respect to the law.[7]

In the reorganization the area within the jurisdiction of the council was defined as that within a fifty-mile radius of the junction of the Red and Assiniboine rivers. The Company broadened the council's representative base by adding a member of the clergy and an independent merchant, and allocated to it a small revenue which was raised by an import duty. The ordinances of the council reflected the primitive nature of the isolated community it governed. The great bulk of its statutes dealt with such things as the protection of hay stacks, and of the settlement in general, against fire, the responsibility for stray animals, hay privileges on the commons, the distillation of alcohol, and the intoxication of Indians. The small revenue—in 1848 £50 was voted—was spent on essential public works. Education was carried on by the Church and supported, in the main, by the direct benevolence of the Company.

There is no doubt that in its legislative and executive capacity the council served the community very well. However, it was also the judiciary, and the administration of justice was a continuous source of friction and difficulty. The arrangements were simple enough. The settlement was divided into four districts and a magistrate or justice of the peace was appointed in each to hold court four times a year. An appeal

[6]*Ibid.*, p. 7600, Simpson to Colvile, May 20, 1822. (Simpson was Governor-in-Chief of the whole overseas area.)

[7]E. H. Oliver, ed., *The Canadian North West*, I, 267.

to the governor-in-council sitting as a court was provided in criminal cases "of a serious nature" and in any case involving a sum of more than £10. The procedures of the court were regularized in 1839 by the appointment of Adam Thom[8] as recorder of Rupert's Land[9] and Assiniboia. Thom's position became most important since he was, at that time, the only person in Red River trained in law and frequently was not just recorder but judge and attorney as well. He came to the colony with a solid and well-deserved reputation for hostility to the French. In Montreal he had assisted Charles Buller in the preparation of the Durham report and in the settlement he was given full credit for the recommendation that the French be anglicized. His well-known *Anti-Gallic Letters* had been published three years before his appointment as recorder.[10] The Métis and the French thus found it easy to hate him while the English merchants suspected him of protecting the interests of the Company in every suit.[11]

Even the staunch defenders of the system had to admit that the term "judiciary" could scarcely be applied to a court whose officers were paid by a commercial company and were subject to dismissal at any time. It was, in fact, little more than a tool of the Company and many of its proceedings were a travesty of justice. For example, the Quarterly Court Records of the case of *Foss* v. *Pelly* in 1850 begin with the following remarkable statement: "The defendant Mr. Pelly stated that he objected to the present formation of the Court as Mr. Thom was allowed to sit as Judge in a case where he had already acted as Attorney for the plaintiff."[12] The following entry recorded that the objection had been overruled by Thom. Alexander Ross, an early settler and the best contemporary observer of Red River affairs, wrote: "As might have been expected, Thom's charge was almost uniformly echoed by the verdict: and yet this uniformity of success, which elsewhere would be reckoned as proof of the truth and reasonableness of a judge's views, tended here

[8]Adam Thom was born in Aberdeen, Scotland. He emigrated to Canada in 1832 and settled in Montreal where he became editor of the *Settler* and in 1836 of the *Montreal Herald*. He read law and in 1837 was admitted to the Bar of Upper Canada.

[9]Rupert's Land was the name given to all the Company's possessions in North America and included the area that is now Manitoba, those portions of the present provinces of Ontario and Quebec north of the Laurentian watershed and west of the Labrador boundary, all of Saskatchewan, the southern half of Alberta, and a large part of the Northwest Territories.

[10]Adam Thom, *Anti-Gallic Letters addressed to His Excellency the Earl of Gosford* (Montreal, 1836.)

[11]Testimony to this effect is found in the *Report from the Select Committee on the Hudson's Bay Company* (1857), items 4808–4986 and throughout the report.

[12]P.A.M., Records of the General Quarterly Court of Assiniboia, 1850, p. 181.

to inspire the multitude with a notion, that Mr. Thom could turn black into white, and white into black."[13]

Protests, which centred around use of the court to enforce the fur-trade regulations, took two forms. A group of English and Scottish settlers, led by merchants, addressed a memorial and petition to the British government in 1846.[14] This petition, signed by nearly one thousand people, was taken to London by James Sinclair, an independent merchant, and presented to the Colonial Secretary. An interesting feature of it is that it made no demands for representative government, asking only for the end of the trading monopoly in furs. This was refused. On the other hand, many of the French and English half-breeds openly and successfully defied the regulations.[15] In 1849 Pierre Guillame Sayer and three accomplices were brought to trial charged with violating fur-trade regulations. The records of the trial begin: "On the Defendant being called to answer the charges against him a considerable time elapsed before he could be found . . . and the Sheriff left the bench in search of him but in place of the defendant . . . James Sinclair, Peter Garriock, and many others presented themselves as Delegates from a great number of Armed Half-Breeds who were outside the court."[16] The decision of the court was that Sayer was guilty but the sentence was never carried out and charges against the other three were dropped. Effective government had clearly ceased, if indeed it had ever begun.

The resistance of the half-breed population was only one of several forces that brought about a change in the status of the Red River Settlement. Many politicians in Britain were beginning to realize that the monopoly of the Company was an anachronism; in the Province of Canada there was a growing interest in the territory and both Britain and Canada feared that eventual annexation of the Northwest by the United States would be the inevitable result of inactivity. The British government made an attempt to settle the future of the Hudson's Bay Company domain in 1857 by appointing a parliamentary committee to inquire and recommend. The claims of the Province of Canada were put by Chief Justice Draper who attempted to cast doubt on the validity of the Company's character and urged that Canada be given a free hand in surveying the territory and putting in settlers wherever possible. In

[13]Alexander Ross, *The Red River Settlement*, p. 384.
[14]A copy of this document and evidence submitted with it may be found in *Papers Relating to the Red River Settlement* (1819), p. 227A.
[15]For more details on the English and French half-breeds see W. L. Morton, ed., *Alexander Begg's Red River Journal*; Ross, *The Red River Settlement*, chap. viii; and Marcel Giraud, *Le Métis canadien*.
[16]Records of the General Quarterly Court, 1849, p. 151.

this he was supported by Gladstone who, although unwilling to discuss the validity of the charter, moved that land suitable for settlement be withdrawn from the jurisdiction of the Company and opened up as rapidly as possible. The motion was lost on the deciding vote of the chairman with the result that official action was delayed for more than a decade.

But Canadian influence continued to make itself felt by steady if ineffective pressure on the Company, through parties[17] sent out to explore the hinterland and through a few adventurous immigrants who went to seek their fortune. About 1860 a small but very vocal Canadian party arose in Winnipeg led by Mr. John Schultz of Kingston. Schultz acquired control of the *Nor'Wester*, the only newspaper in the settlement, and turned it into an advocate of Canadian annexation of the Northwest and a vehicle for violent attacks on the Company. The Company, of course, defended itself and insisted on full compensation before surrender of its rights, but it had recognized some years before that the old order was about to end.

Three-cornered negotiations between Canada, the Colonial Office, and the Hudson's Bay Company began in earnest shortly after Confederation. The Colonial Office acted as auctioneer and on occasion as referee. The provision made in the British North America Act[18] for admitting Rupert's Land into the union was by-passed and the governor and committee were shielded from direct dealings with Canada by a British statute. Once terms had been settled the area was to be formally repossessed by the Crown and then transferred to its new owner at a date to be agreed upon. A large part of the negotiation over terms was a more or less dignified exchange of insults between Canada's delegates and the officers of the Company through the medium of the Colonial Secretary. The official Canadian attitude to compensation was that it was tantamount to bribery—a method of getting a squatter to move off one's land without legal action. Eventually the Colonial Secretary sent both parties an ultimatum stating what he considered reasonable terms and forced their acceptance.

[17]The main one was the Canadian Exploring Expedition of 1857 under the leadership of S. J. Dawson and Henry Youle Hind. Hind wrote an account called *Narrative of the Canadian Red River Exploring Expedition of 1857.*

[18]Section 146 reads: "It shall be lawful for the Queen . . . on Addresses from the Houses of Parliament of Canada . . . to admit Rupert's Land and the North-Western Territory, or either of them, into the Union, on such Terms and Conditions in each Case as are in the Addresses expressed and as the Queen thinks fit to approve. . . ."

When negotiations for purchase of the territory were complete, Canadian officials began to give some thought to organizing a government. The main problem, so they thought, was not the form of government or the rights of the inhabitants, but the assertion of ownership and sovereignty in terms that would be clearly understood in the United States. Accordingly, in 1869 the Canadian Parliament passed the Act for the Temporary Government of Rupert's Land.[19] Its terms were simple. The whole area was to be constituted as one vast territory under a lieutenant governor and council. The powers of this body were not defined but were to be conferred as the need arose. In less than a year this plan was scrapped and Canada's first new province was created. This sudden about-face in policy was the result of the Riel insurrection which occurred at a time when sentiments of manifest destiny were very strong in the United States. In the interval between an agreement to purchase the territory and the successful assertion of Canadian authority the Red River Settlement was first in a state of confusion and anarchy, then under martial law imposed by Riel, and, for a few months, under the provisional government which he organized.

Since the details of and reasons for the Riel insurrection have been completely accounted for by Canadian historians[20] a very brief recapitulation of the main events will suffice. Shortly after the passage of the Act for the Temporary Government of Rupert's Land, Ottawa appointed William McDougall[21] to be lieutenant governor of the Northwest with headquarters in Winnipeg. In the interval between his departure from the capital and his arrival in Winnipeg a small band of Métis, led by Louis Riel, took over the Hudson's Bay Company headquarters at Fort Garry. McDougall was refused admittance and because quiet possession could not be given, the Canadian cabinet refused to accept responsibility for the territory and postponed the date (December 1, 1869) previously agreed upon for transfer. Before their decision could be communicated to McDougall he issued two proclamations of his own—one asserting that Rupert's Land had been transferred to Canada and the other authorizing the raising of a force to quell the insurrection. Ottawa repu-

[19] *Statutes of Canada*, 1869, c. 105.

[20] See in particular: W. L. Morton, *Manitoba: A History*, and G. F. G. Stanley, *The Birth of Western Canada: A History of the Riel Rebellions*.

[21] William McDougall, a prominent pre-Confederation politician, was Commissioner of Crown Lands in the Macdonald-Sicotte and Macdonald-Dorion administrations of 1862–64, and Provincial Secretary in the coalition of 1864. In 1868 he went to England with Sir George Etienne Cartier to arrange for transfer of the Hudson's Bay territories to Canada. He had always been interested in the Northwest and was a logical choice for lieutenant governor.

diated the Lieutenant Governor and sent in his place emissaries of peace to placate the insurgents.[22]

Riel and his armed band were left as the *de facto* authority. Four days after he had seized Fort Garry Riel gave public notice of the formation of a council to consist of representatives from all the parishes. This council, composed of twelve English or Scots and twelve French or Métis, met for the first time on November 9, 1869. At this stage the English and Scots participated in the hope of overturning or at least restraining Riel. Alexander Begg's diary, the best eye-witness account of the time, provides positive evidence of the hostility between "loyalists" and "rebels."[23] Riel strove, with eventual success, to bring unity between the two groups. His authority was, of course, greatly strengthened by McDougall's illegal acts and subsequent repudiation. Even so he appears to have ruled by martial law for nearly two months.

Riel's authority, although it originated in armed force, came within a few months to be based on the majority will of the community. He secured two specific endorsements for the provisional government which he proclaimed on December 8, 1869. When Donald A. Smith, the Commissioner from Canada, arrived in late December a committee of forty prominent citizens was formed to consider his proposals and explanations. This convention, at the insistence of Riel and after considerable debate, formally recognized the provisional government and struck a subcommittee to draw up a working constitution. A short time later, elections, in the form of previously announced public meetings, were held to return members for the assembly. Every English parish participated and many passed resolutions similar to that of St. Clement's, which read: "Resolved that the inhabitants of St. Clement's do acknowledge and hereby declare ourselves subject to the Provisional Government about to be formed under Louis Riel."[24] Riel's government was illegal in the sense that it was never recognized by the Crown, but it

---

[22]The Very Reverend Grand Vicar Thibault and Colonel de Salaberry were sent immediately. Both had lived in Red River and were thought to have the confidence of the Métis but neither carried with them any specific proposals. Later (December 10, 1869) Donald A. Smith, the chief representative of the Hudson's Bay Company in Canada, was appointed as a special commissioner "to enquire into and report upon the causes and extent of the armed obstruction offered at Red River" and to "explain to the inhabitants the principles on which the Government of Canada intends to govern the country, and to remove any misapprehensions that may exist on the subject. And also to take such steps . . . as may seem most proper for effecting the peaceful transfer of the country and the government, from the Hudson's Bay authorities to the . . . Dominion." Canada, *Sessional Papers*, 1870, vol. 5, p. 48.

[23]See Morton, ed., *Alexander Begg's Red River Journal.*

[24]P.A.M., *Red River Papers.*

cannot be considered to have lacked political authority unless it be assumed that such authority springs from the Crown and not the people —a doctrine rejected in all but the formal sense in the seventeenth century.

Riel's government and many of the documents associated with it bear the mark of American influence. McDougall's illegal proclamation of December 1, 1869, was answered by the Declaration of the People of Rupert's Land and the Northwest.[25] The framers of this document used the American Declaration of Independence as their model and probably had the assistance of American friends in drawing it up. Both papers begin by claiming universality for the ideas to follow, or in the words of the Rupert's Land declaration: ". . . it is admitted by all men . . . that a people, when it has no Government, is free to adopt one form of Government, in preference to another, to give or to refuse allegiance to that which is proposed." As in the American Declaration there follows a statement of grievances against Britain which are identified as the opressive nature of the Hudson's Bay Company rule and the abandonment of the settlement to another sovereignty without the consent of the people. The similarity continues down to the final clause which proclaims for the attention of all men that, in accordance with the principles stated and for the reasons given, a new government has been created. However, at this point the similarity between the two documents ends. The American Declaration closes with the statement that all connection with the British Crown is severed. The Rupert's Land counterpart ends on a note of hope that the Crown, as represented by Canada, may see fit to enter into negotiations with the new administration.

The influence of American advisers is also evident in the list of rights appended to the declaration—they must have suggested the clause that the legislature have the right to override the exercise of suspensive powers by the lieutenant governor and the clause demanding that all offices, including magistrates, be elective. The actual structure of the provisional government as it was finally organized provides additional evidence of a substantial flow of ideas from the United States. The structure was decided by a committee which stated its ideas in the form of thirteen resolutions of which the tenth and the last are the most significant. The tenth stated: "The President of the Provisional Government shall not be one of the 24 members," and the thirteenth: "That a two-thirds vote be necessary to override a veto of the President of the Provisional Government."[26]

25For the full text see Appendix C.
26*New Nation*, Feb. 18, 1870.

Obviously the intention of the committee was to adopt the American congressional and presidential form and in the actual operation of the government the members attempted to combine the advice of American friends with the little they knew about British practice. One member, J. H. O'Donohue, argued that because one of the great virtues of the British constitution was its flexibility it could surely accommodate some new ideas without loosing its identity. All members agreed that a lieutenant governor was an essential part of any self-respecting government, but with a splendid disregard for prerogative power proposed to combine the monarchical form with a republican president. Riel, like the American President, was not to be a member of the assembly and was to have a veto over its legislation. In practice he did sit in the house and in fact dominated it completely. Moreover, like a British prime minister, he chose his cabinet from the elected members and made them responsible to the legislature.

The main result of the insurrection was the immediate creation of a new province but the decision was made under very confused circumstances. At Winnipeg the committee of forty citizens who met with Donald A. Smith did not ask for a province and, when Riel suggested that they should, he was overruled. Yet the list of demands that was taken to Ottawa to serve as a basis for negotiation did contain a demand for provincial status apparently put in by Riel on his own responsibility.[27] Why the cabinet at Ottawa agreed to this remains a mystery. Sir John A. Macdonald in introducing the Manitoba bill in the House of Commons pretended that the question of province or territory was not of great significance: "There has been a discussion going on as to whether we should have a Territory or a Province. The answer we made ... was that such a thing as a Territory was not known to the British colonial system, that the expression was not recognized, ... it was not, of course, a matter of any serious importance whether the country was called a

[27]There were four separate lists or bills of rights drawn up during the insurrection: first the one appended to the Declaration of the People of Rupert's Land and the Northwest of December 8, 1869; secondly the list drawn up by the Committee of Forty that met with Donald A. Smith; and thirdly a list found in the papers of Thomas Bunn (Riel's Secretary of State) which, unlike the others, contained a demand for provincial status. Until 1890 it was assumed that Bunn's list was the one taken to Ottawa to serve as a basis for negotiations. When the question of secular schools came up in that year Archbishop Taché, of Saint Boniface, made public a fourth list which he affirmed was the one actually used. Ritchot, the one surviving delegate, verified this statement. This list is identical with the third except for the following additional clause, "that the schools be separate and that the public money for schools be distributed among the different religious denominations in proportion to their respective populations according to the system of the province of Quebec."

Province or a Territory. We have Provinces of all sizes, shapes and constitutions . . . so that there could not be anything determined by the use of the word."[28]

In spite of Macdonald's cavalier attitude the use of the word province did have important consequences. The people within the area were without experience in the art of government—representative, responsible, or any other kind. Hence the province had to be run by federal officers for several years. There was almost no independent source of revenue and for many years Manitoba was little more than a financial ward of the federal government. The area of the province, only slightly more than that of the district of Assiniboia after 1835, was too small and settlement quickly spread beyond. Satisfactory boundaries were not established until 1912. Ottawa retained possession of the public domain and this remained a bone of contention between the capital and its creature for sixty years. In short, the conferring of provincial status on Manitoba in 1870 was unwise and premature—it was not, for many years, a source of satisfaction to those people who lived in the province or to the federation as a whole.

[28]*Report of Debates*, Canadian House of Commons, May 2, 1870, p. 1287.

RESPONSIBLE GOVERNMENT

2

IT IS ASTONISHING that responsible government worked at all in the new province of Manitoba. The experiment appears almost foolhardy if one considers under what conditions the British parliamentary system could be introduced in another society with reasonable hopes for its success. Walter Bagehot gave his answer to this question one year after Manitoba was created.[1] Bagehot found it convenient to divide the essential conditions for cabinet government into two groups: those that could be considered minimum requirements for any elective system and those necessary for the more rarefied form of cabinet government or "prerequisites for the genus and additional ones for the species." For the "genus" the lowest common denominator was said to be first "mutual confidence of the electors." Men must be able to rely on each other, or, at the very least, to tolerate each other's judgments. Secondly, he listed a "calm national mind" which could only come from a sense of security among all groups within the community. He emphasized a high level of general education, for "uneducated men cannot be told to go and choose their rulers, they go wild instead and their imaginations fancy unreal dangers." Finally there must be rationality, which was defined as "the power to form a distinct conception of a distant object." These conditions, said Bagehot, narrowly restrict the use of elective forms of government to a society in which security, education, and rationality are part of everyday experiences. Successful cabinet government requires an even higher stage of development. Concentrating responsibility in the hands of an executive makes essential a competent and experienced legislature from which this important group can be selected.

During the first ten years of responsible government in Manitoba

[1]Walter Bagehot, *The English Constitution* (2nd ed.; London, 1871).

none of Bagehot's prerequisites was present. A less favourable situation for provincial beginnings could scarcely be envisaged, as witness the following description by a local newspaper:

We shall not refer to the events of 1869 and 1870, further than to say that they left behind them memories of the most painful character, and that a portion of the people felt that the time had come to exact a return for the sufferings. The excitement was still further increased by the presence of large bands of roving Indians scattered up and down through the settlement. These savages had been drawn up to the front by the prospects of war, had been appealed to for support and had received promises impossible to fulfill. They were hovering about the settlement in a state of near starvation living by pillage and making hideous noises with their frightful orgies. The antagonism between the English and French races divided the country into two hostile camps—not only arrayed against each other but subject to the danger of collision with the hungry savages who were prowling the settlement.[2]

Perhaps a document as vague and airy as the Manitoba Act was well suited for such conditions. Although no one said so, the authority for the new government was assumed to rest in the person of Adams Archibald, the Lieutenant Governor. He was to carry prerogative powers, which no one could define for certain, across a thousand miles of wilderness to the Red River Settlement and, by use of these powers, summon a council, call an election, and set the machinery of government in motion. During his two years in office Archibald was prime minister and cabinet both and the legislature took orders from him. He was in every sense "dignified and efficient." With certain reservations, the same was true of his successor, Alexander Morris, and between the two of them they literally created the government for Canada's first new province.

Archibald owed his appointment as lieutenant governor directly to Cartier who knew from personal experience that he was a man with a deep understanding of the racial cleavage within the federation. He had shown himself to be a man of faith and conviction when he championed the cause of Confederation in Nova Scotia and had behind him nearly twenty years of experience in public life both as a member and as a cabinet minister in the Legislative Assembly of Nova Scotia. He was a personal friend of many of the leading public men in Ottawa and understood and approved the policies of the Macdonald government. His speeches in Parliament on the Manitoba bill had shown a grasp of conditions at Red River and sympathy with the people's attempt to obtain a constitution. In the debate of May 7, 1870, he had spoken as follows:

This little community which has grown up in the very heart of the continent is unique. . . . Separated by boundless prairies from intercourse with the

<hr />

[2]*Manitoban*, Dec. 1, 1870.

people of the South, barred out from Canada by 800 miles of swamp and wilderness, and mountain and lake, separated from the people on the Pacific shores, by the almost impassable chain of the Rocky Mountains, they have had little intercourse with the outer world. And yet they have among them men, who have had the advantages of the best education which Europe can afford. . . . And yet, these men are brought into immediate contact with the most primitive people in the world. . . . Is it any wonder that a community so secluded from all the rest of the world . . . should be subject to great, to unreasonable alarms, when suddenly the barrier is burst. . . . We must re-establish law and order . . . and the readiest mode of doing so is . . . to show these people that their fears are unfounded . . . and that they shall be secured in all the privileges and advantages which belong to them . . . as freemen.[3]

As a preliminary step towards organizing a government Archibald had to establish the authority of Canada in Manitoba and himself in the confidence of the people. The task was made one of excessive difficulty because of the inability of the federal government to grant at once a general amnesty to all who had taken part in the insurrection. This matter was not settled until 1875 and at times there appeared to be a very real danger that the new Lieutenant Governor would find himself in the position of attempting to organize a government among people the majority of whom were officially fugitives from justice. In complete exasperation he wrote Secretary of State Howe:

Was there ever before a responsible Ministry resting on a House, of whose constituents more than half were liable to be hanged or sent to penitentiary? . . . You allow the electors to choose the members, and to make and unmake Ministries, but electors and members are to exercise their functions with ropes around their necks. To hang all, or to hang a few to whom the rest are blindly devoted, is much the same thing. . . . You can hardly hope to carry on responsible Government by inflicting death penalties on the leaders of a majority of the electors.[4]

Archibald's contributions to the unification of early Manitoba society are of permanent significance to the province. Almost on his own responsibility he assured the local residents that the taking up of arms to obtain a constitution for their country was not a crime which would brand them for the rest of their lives. From the first he treated the French and English as equal partners in the new venture. His success in this was such that he was accused by the Toronto *Globe* of being an Englishman who acted like a Frenchman and a Protestant who behaved like a Catholic.[5]

[3]*Report of Debates*, Canadian House of Commons, May 7, 1870, pp. 1425–6.
[4]Archibald to Howe, Jan. 20, 1872, Canada, *Sessional Papers*, 1874, *Report of the Select Committee on the Causes of the Difficulties in the Northwest Territory in 1869–70*, p. 152.
[5]Editorial from the Toronto *Globe* quoted in the *Manitoban*, Nov. 28, 1870.

The *Globe* went on to suggest that Archbishop Taché was the real ruler of the country. Archibald appears to have realized from the first the wisdom of Macdonald's dictum that " 'If a Lower Canadian British desires to conquer he must "stoop to conquer". He must make friends with the French, without sacrificing the status of his race or language, he must respect their nationality. Treat them as a nation and they will act as a free people generally do—generously. Call them a faction and they become factious. . . . As they become smaller and feebler, so they will be more united; from a sense of self-preservation, they will act as one man and hold the balance of power.' "[6]

Examples of Archibald's policy of treating the French as equal partners are legion. In reporting the organization of the first census he said: "I was anxious that the enumeration should be taken in such a way as to ensure fair play between the two sections of the population. I have therefore divided the Province into five sections and to each section I have appointed two enumerators, one an Englishman and the other a Frenchman. The English enumerator will be a check on the Frenchman in the French Parishes, and the French enumerator on the Englishman in the English Parishes."[7] Two months later in forwarding the results to Ottawa, Archibald commented: "The results show some little difference between the enumerators—enough to prove that they did not act in concert, and not enough to disturb confidence in the result."[8]

The first division of the province into electoral district was done also on a basis of equality between the French and English and the census was used only to reveal the racial and religious composition of each area. Twenty-four electoral divisions were created by proclamation and they were based almost exactly on existing parish lines, with twelve for the English and twelve for the French. The same principle was followed in the selection of the first council; the number of portfolios was fixed at five: two English, two French, and a half-breed, James MacKay, whose presence Archibald said "would in no way disturb the delicate balance since his father was Scotch, his mother French Half-Breed and though he himself a Catholic he has two brothers Presbyterians."[9]

The acid test both of Canada's authority and of Archibald's policy of equal treatment was the Fenian raid of 1871. This raid was the indirect result of the attempt of two former associates of Riel, O'Donoghue and

[6]Donald Creighton, *John A. Macdonald: The Young Politician*, p. 227.
[7]P.A.M., Archibald Letter Book, Sept. 20, 1871.
[8]The census figures are in Canada, *Sessional Papers*, 1871, Paper 20, p. 93: total population 11,960; distribution by race—whites 1,600, English half-breeds 4,080; by creed—Protestants 5,720, Indian householders 560, French half-breeds 5,720, Catholics 6,240.
[9]Archibald Letter Book, Sept. 20, 1871.

Lepine, to secure American intervention. They prepared a petition specifically addressed to "His Excellency" President Grant, and O'Donoghue
personally took it to Washington where, it is said, he was "received
kindly, listened to attentively but not taken seriously." He then attempted
to join forces with the Fenian Brotherhood in New York but was, at
first, repulsed. Six months later he did manage to secure the services of
General O'Neill who had just been released from a federal penitentiary.
Together they organized the raid without the support of the Fenian
Brotherhood who agreed neither to assist nor to denounce the attempt.

The threatened raid was met by a proclamation from the Lieutenant
Governor calling all able-bodied men to arms, and the fact that the
great majority responded indicates that Archibald was firmly in control.
At the time he seems to have been beset by doubts; in October 1871 he
wrote to Macdonald: "You cannot conceive the worry and anxiety I
have had for the last few days. I have already written you that my great
object was to bridge over if possible, the gulf which divides the two large
sections of the population . . . my dread was of a civil war, and that was
what O'Donoghue hoped and tried to bring about."[10]

Later Archibald gave most of the credit to Riel and testified that had
he thrown his influence with the raiders civil war would probably have
been the result. Riel, for his part, summarized his own feelings when he
wrote with masterful understatement: "Your Excellency may rest assured
that without being enthusiastic I have been devoted."[11]

The Organization of a Government

The situation confronting Archibald was so completely unprecedented
that little if any guidance could be offered by Ottawa. The official commission by Letters Patent was a formal document to be filed and for-
gotten. The commission had been supplemented by a personal letter of
instructions from the Secretary of State for the Provinces but it too seems
to have been written more for the record than for use. It purported to
set out "the responsibilities of the Lieutenant-Governor both to his
Province and to Ottawa" and began:

In the Government of Manitoba you will be guided by the Constitutional
principles and precedents which obtain in the older Provinces, and with
which it is assumed you are sufficiently familiar. . . . In dealing with the
Province of Manitoba you will give your advisers the full exercise of the
powers, which in the older Provinces have been so widely claimed and freely
exercised, but you will be expected to maintain a position of dignified impar-

[10]*Report of the Select Committee on the Causes of the Difficulties in the
Northwest Territory in 1869–70*, p. 156.
[11]*Ibid.*, p. 147.

tiality and to guard with independence the general interests of the Dominion and the just authority of the Crown.[12]

Macdonald's informal advice to Archibald's successor Morris was closer to the mark: "Although you have responsible government nominally, nevertheless you must be, for want of men, a paternal despot for some time to come."[13]

The government was actually carried on by proclamation for the first four months. Until an election could be held and a legislature assembled many of the old laws and arrangements of the Council of Assiniboia had to be revived for interim use. In theory Archibald had a council of two to advise him; when he had been in the country two weeks he reported: "Thinking it was now time to organize a Government, and that I had become sufficiently acquainted with the people to form some idea of the material out of which this could be formed, I have chosen a man representing each section of the population here, and appointed them Members of my Executive Council."[14] Alfred Boyd, who was described as "highly esteemed by the English but not obnoxious to the French"[15] was given the title of provincial secretary. Marc A. Girard, who was sent out by Cartier for this purpose, was made provincial treasurer. These men might better have been described as secretaries rather than advisers and the Governor appears to have set them to work at urgent tasks he was unable to find time for himself.

The first election in the new province was held on December 28, 1870. The Lieutenant Governor not only created the entire framework for taking the poll but took an active, if unofficial, interest in the results. Sir John had cautioned and reassured him a few weeks before the election: "Much depends on the successful start of your legislative machine and you will be quite justified in taking a personal interest in the result of the election so as to secure the returns of a respectable body of men representing the various races and interests."[16] Archibald became the behind-the-scenes leader of the "government party," that is, the group who supported his policies. Opposed were the so-called "loyalists" led by John Schultz whose chief demand was for speedy retribution against those who had supported Riel. Under these circumstances it is not surprising that the campaign generated considerable heat which often flared into open violence. Dr. Schultz's newspaper spoke approvingly of a plan

[12]Secretary of State for the Provinces to Lieutenant Governor Archibald, Aug. 4, 1870, Canada, *Sessional Papers*, 1871, Paper 20, pp. 4–5.
[13]P.A.M., Morris Family Papers, Macdonald to Morris, Dec. 9, 1872.
[14]Canada, *Sessional Papers*, 1871, Paper 20, p. 16.
[15]*Ibid.*, p. 17.
[16]P.A.C., Macdonald Papers, vol. 317, p. 325, Macdonald to Archibald.

to tar and feather Alexander Begg and Thomas Bunn, praised Schultz for the "wisdom and courage" he displayed in publicly horsewhipping Thomas Spense, and generally displayed a malignant hatred for the policy of conciliation.

Nominations were carried out at open meetings in each electoral division. The electors frequently tried to give their nominee positive assurance of success by publishing in the newspapers signed declarations to vote for a certain man should he accept the nomination. The enthusiasm in some cases was such that declarations were signed by several hundred more than were qualified to vote. The candidates, in turn, quickly got into the spirit of things and published ambitious platforms of the great things they intended to do once in office—railways to the East at once, reciprocity between Manitoba and the United States, and, as one candidate put it, "free trade the world over." The result was a clear triumph for the "government party," twenty of whom were elected to the twenty-four-member house.

There are no suitable phrases from British parliamentary practice to describe the first "cabinet" selected by the Lieutenant Governor. It was neither a cabinet nor a council; there was no prime minister, no collective responsibility and frequently no unity. In the Lepine trials[17] the Attorney General, H. J. Clarke, acted as prosecutor while his colleague Joseph Royal, the Provincial Secretary, was counsel for the defence, and the two carried on a vendetta in the newspapers with the Attorney General accusing Royal of attempting to incite the French to join the Fenians and suitable countercharges being hurled back by the Provincial Secretary. Archibald described the "ministry" in some detail in a letter to Macdonald: "Before appointing them I discussed with them individually the policy which I had pursued and intended to pursue so as to see if they were prepared to give it hearty support. This they promised to do. . . . I called them together on the 14th and handed them a memo on the work that was to be done before calling the Assembly together . . . in fact I gave the Council a memo of 32 bills which would be absolutely necessary to form the sketch of a Provincial constitution and have set them to work to get their hands in."[18] A few months later he described the results of the deliberations of the council in the following revealing sentence: "If you had seen some of the drafts prepared for my acceptance you would have felt somewhat as I did when a I threw them aside and undertook the labour of drafting them myself."[19]

---

[17]Lepine had been adjutant general in the Provisional Government and had been in charge of the execution of Thomas Scott.
[18]Macdonald Papers, vol. 187, Archibald to Macdonald, Jan. 16, 1871.
[19]Ibid., Nov. 3, 1871.

The main function of the council was not to formulate policy but to give representation to the different religious and racial groups. The changes that Archibald found it necessary to make in the council one year later are a clear indication of this fact. In December 1871 Boyd, the Provincial Treasurer, resigned and stated in his letter of resignation that it had become obvious both to himself and to the Governor that the English half-breeds must be given representation if things were to proceed peacefully. John Norquay was then appointed as spokesman for this group.

The opening of the first session of the first legislature was literally in the British tradition; it might almost be compared to a play with the Lieutenant Governor taking the leading role in the part of the monarch. He drove to the opening ceremonies in a coach and four accompanied by a mounted guard of honour. The setting inside the chamber was as regal as the circumstances permitted: "The Legislative Council," wrote a local paper, "had at one end the Throne of the Lieutenant-Governor. The Throne had a canopy of bright scarlet cloth. In the center of the room at a large oval table sat the council of seven men." The setting was in marked contrast to the personnel of the lower house, many of whom "appeared in rough suits, coats open, no vest, collar or tie, but brightly coloured flannel shirts and around the waist the gay coloured sash worn on the prairies." During the first session one member is said to have sent a note to a colleague suggesting that a motion be made "to go into commity of the hole." Another member, on being called to order while somewhat inebriated, is alleged to have replied, "You may think I am a fool, Mr. Speaker, but I am not such a fool as the people who sent me here."[20]

Goldwin Smith, who out of curiosity was touring the Northwest at the time, was present at the opening and wrote in his reminiscences:

I attended the opening of the new-born Legislature at Winnipeg. The approach of the Lieutenant-Governor was announced by a series of explosions intended to represent the firing of cannon, but made, I understood, by letting off of gunpowder with a hot poker. . . . The Lieutenant-Governor read his speech from the throne in French as well as English. I suspect the effect upon the French ears was like that of the Irish Major's address upon Prince Napoleon, who in reply deplored his ignoraance of 'la belle langue Irelandaise.'[21]

Throughout the first session, the Lieutenant Governor used a strong hand whenever necessary, as in the bill creating the Manitoba Bar. Attorney General Clarke had insisted on including a provision for the

[20]*Manitoban*, Feb. 10, 1871.
[21]Goldwin Smith, *Reminiscences* (London, 1911), p. 416.

benefit of his friends and relatives that membership was to be restricted to the citizens of Manitoba and that all judges were to be chosen from those accepted. Archibald reported the incident to Macdonald: "I told him distinctly that he must either put through bill three which I then handed him or I would be forced to defeat his little game by reserving the Bill."[22] Clarke persisted, however, and Archibald was forced to reserve the bill at the end of the session.[23] In the great majority of cases the council and members accepted the legislation proposed. Only on one occasion did the members show any notable independence and that was with regard to their own salaries. They proposed to give themselves an increase of one hundred dollars (from two hundred to three) and introduced a bill to give their generosity legal standing. The government proposed to quash the bill and Clarke announced that the treasury could not stand the strain, as indeed it could not. When a vote was taken and it was found that the government was defeated, the general feeling was voiced by Mr. Hay when he said: "It is all nonsense to talk about upsetting the government on this little question." The members agreed to reverse their vote and the government agreed to the increase; no one so much as mentioned the fact that the whole procedure was unconstitutional as only the Crown can initiate money bills. At the end of the first session, Archibald found it necessary to reserve four bills:[24] an Act to Authorize the Construction of a Telegraph Line in the Province, an Act to Incorporate the Red River Bridge Company, an Act to Incorporate the Western Railway Company of Manitoba, and an Act to Authorize the Construction of Certain Railways in the Province. All four acts were reserved on the grounds that they were beyond the competence of the legislature to pass and the reservations were upheld by the Minister of Justice at Ottawa.

Archibald was on occasion forced to discipline the public as well as the legislature. In November 1871 delegates from several of the parishes presented resolutions which charged that unsuitable persons had been put on the executive council, that actions of the government had stirred up great dissatisfaction, and that some of the elections had been fraudulent. The resolutions demanded nothing less than a new election and a new ministry, whereupon Archibald delivered a lecture on the principles of responsible government. Later, on recounting the incident to Macdonald, he received the following reply: "You might take the oppor-

---

[22]Macdonald Papers, vol. 187, Archibald to Macdonald, Feb. 28, 1871.
[23]W. E. Hodgins, comp., *Dominion and Provincial Legislation, 1867–1895*, p. 771.
[24]*Ibid.*, p. 1338.

tunity of pointing out the fact that the Dominion Parliament conferred upon them, although an infant province, a Constitution with as large powers as those given to the older and more populous provinces—that they received at once the power of self-government which had been fought for for more than a quarter of a century . . . before it was granted by the Mother Country."[25]

One of the most revealing statements of the early difficulties with responsible government is found in a memorandum prepared for the guidance of a delegation sent to Ottawa in 1873 to seek financial assistance to stave off approaching bankruptcy.[26] The memorandum strikes a plaintive note in describing the the "good old days," when "the manners of the people were eminently gentle, and a ready obedience was at all times yielded to the few and simple laws required for their government. They had never heard of such a thing as a tax. A few hundred pounds covered the whole expenses of government and the administration of Justice in the Colony." Then we read:

Amid this primitive and patriarchal state of things came the revolution . . . thus suddenly called upon to form part of the magnificent system of the Canadian confederation and to enter into the full enjoyment of representative institutions which existed and had been perfected for half a century in the other Provinces . . . on entering the Union Manitoba had to bring into operation a system of government and institutions extremely complicated in their organization and very expensive in operation . . . thence it is the good fortune of the Province of Manitoba to possess the whole detail and mechanism requisite in a large and wealthy province, but unfortunately not the means of putting that mechanism in motion.

The reply of the federal government was to the effect that Manitoba must cut her coat to fit the cloth:

It appears from the financial statement that the total revenue of the province is $77,000 and that over forty thousand of that amount is required to pay the expenses of Legislation, including Printing, Civil Government and care of Government House. The propriety of remedying so abnormal a condition of affairs must be obvious, and a solution to the growing embarrassments can only be arrived at by the people of Manitoba reducing the expenses of government to a sum proportionate to the circumstances and income of that Province.[27]

As a commentary on the nature of responsible government at this time, it is worth noting that one of the claims advanced by the delegates was that the Dominion government should bear the cost of the damages in

[25]Macdonald Papers, vol. 187, Macdonald to Archibald, Dec. 12, 1871.
[26]Legislative Assembly of Manitoba, *Journals (J.L.A.)*, 1873, Appendix, p. 6.
[27]*Ibid.*, p. 25.

the federal election riots of 1872. They were reminded in a tersely worded paragraph that it was their job to see that such things did not happen.

The next year found another delegation in Ottawa to plead again for money and this time they had to deal with the government of Alexander Mackenzie. After lengthy conversations with the delegates Mackenzie wrote to Alexander Morris, then Lieutenant Governor:

I have had several interviews with Messrs. Howard and Royal in regard to the affairs of your Province, and I am much puzzled to know what to do under the circumstances. . . . you are aware that my own conviction always was that the creation of a Provincial Government for Manitoba was a mistake, and that some form of territorial arrangement, with a Governor and small executive council to aid him was really all that would be required in that country for many years to come. . . . I cannot help feeling that some such simple . . . machinery is still what is needed for Manitoba, if that Province would consent to surrender the system now in operation. I have stated this freely to the Manitoba delegates, and they admit that this would be a solution to the difficulty, but express the fear that it could hardly be accomplished.[28]

Alexander Morris agreed with the view that the creation of the province was premature in view of financial arrangements and the inability of the local people to operate the parliamentary system. When the Legislative Council was abolished in 1876 he wrote to the Secretary of State for the Provinces: "We have . . . no men of Parliamentary training and experience . . . the Government has now no Attorney General and . . . there is danger of hasty and crude legislation, being passed rapidly through a single chamber . . . which may lead to embarrassment and difficulty. I am of opinion therefore, that I should reserve . . . all Bills that may involve any change of the Constitution, created by the Manitoba Act. . . ."[29] Morris continued to sit in on cabinet meetings until 1876 and, to judge from correspondence, exercised a powerful influence. In 1873 he reported: "was able to have a three hour council to-day. . . . I have read every bill and play law clerk but they make a sad mess of things with the amendments in the House."[30]

Although doubting the capacities of the local leaders, Morris none the less steadily pushed them to accept the full responsibility. When financial pressures forced the resignation of the first administration in 1874 the Lieutenant Governor called upon R. A. Davis to form a government but

[28]P.A.M., Morris Papers (Ketcheson Collection), No. 110, Alexander Mackenzie to Morris, April 16, 1874.

[29]Ibid., No. 171, Morris to Secretary of State for the Provinces, Feb. 12, 1876.

[30]Macdonald Papers, vol. 252, p. 401, Morris to Macdonald.

forced the new leader to accept the responsibility for choosing his own cabinet. This event was hailed as a milestone and Morris wrote to the Secretary of State: "I would call your attention to the fact that in forming the Government I did so through the intervention of a premier, thus introducing responsible government in its modern form into the Province. The previous ministry was selected personally by my predecessor and none of its members were [sic] recognized as first minister."[31]

By 1876 Morris was ready to insist that all the forms of cabinet government were being observed. This may have been true with strict reference to the form but there were and continued to be many instances of an awkward and odd parliamentary procedure being followed. For example, in the session of 1885 the Public Accounts Committee decided to adopt the minority report written by three members of the opposition censuring the government for financial laxness. The report pointed out that several people had been paid large sums with no indication of the service rendered, that more than $3,000 was completely unaccounted for, that $20,000 was voted for printing and stationery and $40,000 spent, and that the expenses of two cabinet ministers for a trip to Ottawa ($3,628.25) seemed unreasonably high. The report ended with a severe censure on the government in which the government cheerfully acquiesced by passing a resolution that "this house doth concur in said report."[32] The next day when the opposition moved a vote of no confidence Premier Norquay was incensed; he was, he said, "prepared to censure himself when necessary but censure from the opposition he would not stand. He thought he knew as well as most people when he went astray and was not going to submit to the indignity of having it thrown up to him by his opponents when he had already condemned himself."[33] While the debate was raging the clerk announced that the Lieutenant Governor was waiting, with some impatience, to prorogue the house. On this note the first fifteen years of provincial history ended.

[31]Morris Letter Book H, No. 47, Morris to the Secretary of State for the Provinces, July 13, 1874.
[32]J.L.A., 1885, p. 89.
[33]Manitoba Free Press, May 4, 1885.

PROVINCIAL RIGHTS: THE GREAT ISSUES

3

A SUBSTANTIAL PART of the political history of Manitoba concerns the gradual throwing off of the shackles of federal paternalism and development of full provincial autonomy. Manitoba's growth was, in one sense, analagous to the development of Dominion status within the Commonwealth. It took place during a series of incidents and skirmishes on which the local leaders took stands, or at least attempted to do so. Issues of status were all-absorbing because of the province's premature creation— no one was prepared to debate such mundane matters as road-building, municipal administration, experimental farms, or even political corruption in the presence of such questions as federal disallowance of provincial railway charters, separate schools for the Roman Catholics, or the ever-recurring indignity and crowning insult of the retention of the public domain by the central government. The struggle over provincial rights was not, as in other provinces, an attempt to preserve something already in existence but rather an attempt to create a province in reality as well as in form. Provincial political leaders appealed to the electorate, or the members of the legislature, not on the alleged merits of party policies, but on the issue of who could best champion Manitoba against Ottawa, and all groups were really "provincial rights" candidates regardless of the name under which they chose to campaign.

Though admitting the lack of precision common to all generalizations, one can say that political life prior to 1900 revolved around the questions of appropriate provincial status and, for a considerable time after 1900, the grievances and difficulties of the agricultural economy. Public opinion centred on these basic issues. The designations Liberal and Conservative were first used in a provincial election in 1883 and there was a remarkable variety of political affiliation under the umbrellas of these two names. Ten candidates for election to the assembly called themselves Ultra-Conservatives apparently to emphasize that they were the real thing. Seventeen described themselves as Norquay Conservatives,[1] sixteen as Provincial Rights candidates, eight simply as Liberals, two as Liberals but in support of Norquay, and one gave himself the rather cumbersome title of "Liberal but in favour of disallowance." The division lists for the session that followed show that of those elected from the Provincial Rights group, four voted consistently against the government and an equal number supported it. Almost all who called themselves Ultra-Conservatives supported Norquay and only three who were elected as Liberals consistently voted in opposition.

All provinces were aware of the dangers of federal paternalism and excessive centralization but Manitoba was, by the very nature of things, subjected to much closer control than, for example, Ontario or Nova Scotia. For the first ten years federal officers supervised the operation of its government and more than 80 per cent of its revenue came from federal funds. The facts of geography, as well as the newness of the province, made such control inevitable. Manitoba lay squarely across the gateway to the great hinterland then known as the Northwest. The area within the provincial boundaries had been regarded as a strategic one from the earliest times, first in the struggle between rival empires and later between rival trading companies, and the Macdonald government of 1870 had as great a stake in communication to the interior as did the Nor'Westers. The hopes of the federation were centred around the opening and settlement of the West as a frontier for investment and Macdonald made certain that the miniature province could not interfere with or impede federal policy. Safeguards inserted in the Manitoba Act were supplemented by a vigorous and wholesale use of the power of disallowance.

Boundaries

The question of the proper size of the province was a bone of contention between the two governments from 1880 until 1912 (see Figure 1 for extension of 1881 and 1912). Originally enclosing territory less than one-twentieth of the present area, these boundaries were unsatisfactory

[1]John Norquay was premier from 1878 until 1887. A brief interregnum of two months followed with D. H. Harrison as first minister, and in the ensuing elections the Liberals, led by Thomas Greenway, obtained control and remained in power for a decade. For the next seventeen years the régime was Conservative with Hugh John Macdonald as pro-tem leader for the first ten months and then with R. P. Roblin as permanent leader.

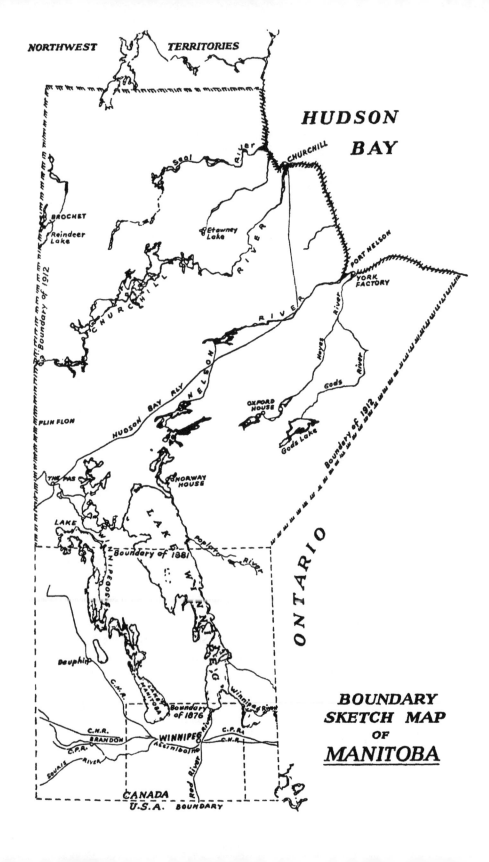

NORTHWEST TERRITORIES

HUDSON BAY

CHURCHILL

Seal River

Boundary of 1912

BROCHET
Reindeer Lake

Etawney Lake

CHURCHILL RIVER

PORT NELSON

YORK FACTORY

Hayes River

Gods River

NELSON RIVER

OXFORD HOUSE

Gods Lake

Boundary of 1912

FLIN FLON

HUDSON BAY RLY.

THE PAS

NORWAY HOUSE

LAKE WINNIPEG

ONTARIO

LAKE WINNIPEGOSIS

Poplar River

Boundary of 1881

Dauphin

C.N.R.

LAKE MANITOBA

Winnipeg River

BOUNDARY SKETCH MAP OF MANITOBA

Boundary of 1876

C.N.R.
BRANDON

WINNIPEG

C.P.R.

C.N.R.

C.P.R. RIVER

Souris River

Assiniboine

Red River

CANADA
U.S.A. BOUNDARY

because settlement extended rapidly beyond them. However, Macdonald was anxious to enlarge the province, not because Premier Norquay desired it, but to thwart the growth of Ontario fostered by his arch-enemy Mowat. A large part of the territory he so readily affixed to Manitoba in 1881, including land almost as far east as Fort William, had already been awarded to Ontario by the boundary commission of 1878.[2] The result was a struggle between Mowat and Norquay with Macdonald holding the coats and shouting words of encouragement to Manitoba's premier.

One aspect of the conflicting claims of jurisdiction is not without a comic note. Both parties established local governments at Rat Portage (now Kenora) but the constables appointed proceeded to arrest each other and the law breakers went free. At one stage Norquay's constables captured two of Mowat's men, carried them to Winnipeg, and put them behind bars. Mowat threatened war: "Manitoba," he wrote, "has treated as criminal offences, acts done by the officers of Ontario in their official capacity and has succeeded by the ingenuity of its officers in carrying off two of our employees. . . . acts such as these would, as between independent states, have been a declaration of war which the aggressor desired to be carried out with rancorous animosity."[3] Instead of a war there was a legal battle with the law lords of the Judicial Committee of the Privy Council as referees. In this form of warfare Mowat was clearly superior and literally overwhelmed his opponent with the weight of his legal learning. Manitoba's case was, by contrast, poorly prepared and the decision went to Ontario.

The "on to the Bay" agitation began about the turn of the century and was combined with persistent claims for a slice of what later became the province of Saskatchewan. Both claims were pressed in Ottawa in 1904 and 1905 and both were rejected by a subcommittee of the cabinet. The proposed extension westward was turned down because a large number of the people within the area concerned "may be said to be unanimously and determinedly opposed to being united with the Province of Manitoba."[4] Laurier was obviously unwilling to put more territory under the

[2]The question of Ontario's western boundary was first considered in 1871 by a commission on which Ontario was represented by William McDougall and Canada by Eugene E. Taché. Ontario withdrew its representative because of alleged unreasonable federal attitudes. In 1878 both sides agreed to submit the dispute to a new commission consisting of Sir Edward Thornton, Sir Francis Hincks, and Chief Justice Harrison of Ontario. The findings upheld Mowat's claims but Sir John A. Macdonald refused to abide by the award and disallowed the provincial statute which gave it legal standing. A full account may be found in Ontario, *Sessional Papers*, 1871, Paper 44, and the Ontario Boundary Papers.

[3]Ontario, *Sessional Papers*, 1884.

[4]Canada, *Sessional Papers*, 1905, Paper 102, p. 6.

control of a province that had refused to allow separate schools for Roman Catholics and the Manitoba cabinet took this as proof that Ottawa was controlled by the Vatican's representative in the capital. The province's desire for an ocean port was met with the rather enigmatic statement that the rights of Ontario must be considered.

These demands for northward and/or westward expansion became perennial and bloomed with each spring session of the legislature. In 1908 Premier Roblin gave the legislature a lurid account of the struggles of his province for recognition and fair treatment. Denying that his motives were narrowly provincial, he maintained that he sought only to strengthen Canada by giving Manitoba her rightful status among her sister provinces and in the Canadian family. The sister who was the cause of the inferiority complex was clearly Ontario and, after reviewing her selfish actions of the past, Roblin concluded that she was as self-centred as ever.

The memorial of 1908 was ignored by Laurier as were subsequent representations over the next two years. In 1910 Roblin wrote a most vigorous letter accusing the Prime Minister of discourtesy and throwing out a challenge: "Possibly you think I do not represent public opinion in this province. . . . Let me go a step further and say that if you will make your proposition and it turns out to be such that I cannot accept, I will submit it direct to the people of this province for their consideration and decision on the principle of the initiative and the referendum.[5] Negotiations were resumed and resulted in a federal offer to extend the boundaries northward with the provision that public lands were to remain under federal control.

In rejecting this proposal as contrary to the principle of equality of treatment the Manitoba cabinet distinguished three grades of provinces within the federation. First were those that had full control of the public domain—Nova Scotia, New Brunswick, Prince Edward Island, Quebec, Ontario, and British Columbia; secondly, those who were denied control but were adequately compensated—Alberta and Saskatchewan; and at the bottom the province of Manitoba which had neither the lands nor adequate compensation for their "alienation." The cabinet suggested that Manitoba would now settle for promotion to a second-class province which could be effected by the simple method of increasing the subsidy in lieu of lands to the same amount received by Alberta and Saskatchewan and extending the boundary north to Hudson Bay. These proposals were incorporated in the settlement reached soon after Borden took office in 1911.

[5]*Ibid.*, 1911, Paper 57, p. 2.

Disallowance of Railway Charters

A second major clash between federal policy and provincial rights occurred in the 1880's over the monopoly clause in the charter of the Canadian Pacific Railway Company.[6] To say that the railway itself was welcome is an understatement. The urgent need for rail connection with eastern Canada had been emphasized by newspapers, politicians, and private citizens individually and collectively since the beginnings of the province. However, the transcontinental railway was only part of the story from the provincial point of view. It was a challenging project for the future but the people wanted and needed immediate rail facilities to get their produce to market.[7] The logical and most economical solution would have been to build branch lines to join the railway systems in the United States, and the Mackenzie government at Ottawa had built one such branch in 1878 from Winnipeg to Pembina where it joined the St. Paul and Pacific road. Manitoba wanted more branches of this kind but they were, of course, precisely what the monopoly clause put in the Canadian Pacific charter by the Macdonald government was designed to prevent.

By 1880 there was a strong public demand for branch lines built or backed by the province but the Manitoba cabinet at that time would not sponsor such a policy for two reasons. First, and this should have been conclusive, the construction of branch lines was beyond the financial capacity of the new province. Secondly, Premier Norquay appears to have made a deal with Macdonald whereby Macdonald agreed to a substantial increase in the provincial subsidy and Norquay agreed not to interfere with federal railway policy. Macdonald relayed Norquay's promise to R. P. Griffith, the president of the syndicate, when he wrote: "Although this cannot be openly stated . . . the Premier of Manitoba made a positive agreement with us at Ottawa that his government would not allow any local legislation to infringe on the agreement with the syndicate."[8]

For a short time Norquay lived up to his agreement and private bills to charter branch lines rarely got beyond the committee stage. But he had to appear before the electors as a champion of provincial rights.

[6]This clause, as given in *Statutes of Canada*, 1881, c. 1, p. 12, was: "for twenty years from the date hereof, no line of railway shall be authorized by the Dominion Parliament to be constructed South of the Canadian Pacific Railway . . . and in establishment of any new Province in the North-West Territories, provision shall be made for continuing such prohibition."

[7]By 1876 there were ten flour mills in operation and the wheat crop was nearly a million bushels. The population by 1881 was 65,954.

[8]P.A.C., Macdonald Papers, Letter Book 21, Macdonald to R. P. Griffith, Feb. 18, 1880.

His opponents, now led by Thomas Greenway, insisted that the administration had sold out to Eastern interests and had been made the dupes of the Ottawa Conservatives. Norquay was between the devil and the deep blue sea; when he weakened and allowed the charters to slip through they were promptly disallowed, causing an even greater outcry. In November 1882 Sir Charles Tupper, the Minister of Justice, called the cabinet's attention to three possible victims for the federal guillotine —an Act to Incorporate the Winnipeg and South Eastern Railway Company, An Act to Incorporate the Manitoba Tramway Company, and An Act to Incorporate the Northwestern Railway Company. All three met an untimely end.

After 1884 Norquay attempted to find a middle ground on the question of provincial railway charters that would satisfy the dignity and economic needs of the province but not offend the federal government. The official policy was expressed in a minute of council: "That the chartering of local railways to connect with the American system . . . would be an exercise of power not conferred upon the province by the constitution; that the right of the province to charter railway lines within its limits . . . can be freely exercised."[9] This policy was based on a promise made in the House of Commons by Sir Charles Tupper that disallowance of the local railway charters would cease as soon as the line north of Lake Superior was finished.[10] This promise was not kept.

By 1886 the province was united in regarding disallowance as an outrage. Lieutenant Governor Aikins reported to Macdonald: "The disallowance feeling is so strong now that should it be your policy to continue it . . . by disallowing the charters passed at this session the government will be forced to undertake the work at once. The Province will be with them as a unit. . . . It seems a pity that seeds of discontent should be sown that may produce an antagonism to your Government in the future, not only in this province but further West."[11] Winnipeg newspapers were unanimous in condemning the federal policy. An editorial in the *Commercial* was typical: "The East has nothing for the West but to keep this country in bondage and under the heel of monopoly, accordingly as its own blind selfishness directs it. Monopoly must be continued in order that the East may continue to extract its pound of flesh from the West."[12] The Winnipeg Board of Trade suggested that secession to the United States might be the outcome and the Manitoba and North West Farmers Union advised immigrants not to settle in the province.

[9]Minutes of the Executive Council of Manitoba, Dec. 22, 1883.
[10]Can., H. of C., *Deb.*, Feb. 5, 1884, p. 109.
[11]Macdonald Papers, vol. 186, Aikins to Macdonald, April 16, 1887.
[12]*Commercial*, May 10, 1887.

Norquay's Conservatives were forced to abandon compromise and espouse defiance in the election campaign of 1886.[13] In the session which followed the rules of the house were waived to permit rapid passage of two bills, the first to permit a private company to build a line to the border and the second to authorize the government to build another as a public work and to raise the money by provincial bonds. The members voted unanimously to call a special session, if necessary, at which they would serve without the usual indemnity and, if all else failed, to carry an appeal right to the foot of the Throne. Everything failed. Provincial defiance was crippled by the fact that no private contractor would undertake the work. Herbert Holt came to Winnipeg and left with the pertinent comment: "You people up here talk entirely too much to get a railway. It will surprise me if you ever succeed in view of the way you must talk, talk, talk, about the matter."[14] Indeed, many of the plans for projected railways were concocted for nuisance value and agitation.

Sir John A. Macdonald was well aware of the hare-brained nature of the schemes and when Norquay attempted to borrow money on the British market he wrote to John Rose in London:

I cabled you yesterday that the Government of Manitoba was destroying the credit of the Province. . . . The members of that Government are all impecunious, and think only of a continuation in office. When you reflect on a legislature of 35 members, with a population of some 110,000, coolly devoting a million of dollars to build a railway from Winnipeg to the frontier, between two lines owned by the C.P.R. running in the same direction, one on the east and the other on the west side of the Red River, when there is not business enough for one of the two existing lines, you can understand the recklessness of that body. . . . All this is of course confidential, but you will do good service both to Canada and Manitoba by discouraging . . . the floating of this indebtedness.[15]

Norquay was unable to borrow in any market—British, American, or Canadian—even in the local Winnipeg market. After he had been turned down everywhere else he offered $300,000 worth of provincial bonds, to be redeemed in one year, for local sale. Less than $5,000 was taken up. In November 1887 the Lieutenant Governor reported to Macdonald: "Norquay is in a dreadful fix. Only a few days ago I had to refuse an order to use trust funds as ordinary revenue. My confidence is all gone."[16] Defiance ended in complete defeat. The Premier resigned and the Liberals led by Thomas Greenway won the next election with the promise that they would succeed where the Conservatives had failed.

[13]The result: Conservatives 19, Liberals 14, Independents 2.
[14]*Morning Call*, Oct. 8, 1887.
[15]Sir Joseph Pope, ed., *Correspondence of Sir John Macdonald*, pp. 403–4.
[16]Macdonald Papers, vol. 186, Aikins to Macdonald, Nov. 12, 1887.

Disallowance did end shortly after but not primarily because of the agitation of Manitoba's politicians. The Canadian Pacific syndicate was also desperately short of money and agreed to relinquish the monopoly clause in its charter in return for additional financial support from the federal government.[17]

Separate Schools

As has already been pointed out Manitoba began its existence with an almost equal and extremely delicate balance between French and English, Protestant and Catholic. The basis of the government formed in 1878 with John Norquay as premier was a dual majority principle similar to that which existed in the Province of Canada after the Act of Union of 1840. The seats in the legislature were almost equally divided between English and French, as were the cabinet portfolios, and to be passed a measure needed the support of a majority of both groups.

The English politicians recognized a partnership with the French at first as absolutely necessary and by 1875 as convenient, but, as their numerical superiority increased, they began to see it as an encumbrance. The French were fighting a losing battle from the beginning. Their Archbishop was a most astute politician but to have won the struggle for his people he would have needed to have been a superlative immigration agent. The English Protestants were receiving daily reinforcements of contingents of immigrants from Ontario. The first real break came in 1878 when Royal, the leader of the French group in the legislature, attempted a kind of palace revolution by which he hoped to seize the post of premier. When this failed completely both French-speaking members of the cabinet were asked to tender their resignations and were replaced by English Protestants. Further blows against the French position followed. In 1878 the house passed a redistribution measure based in part on the principle of representation by population. Twelve years later a majority of members approved a bill establishing English as the official language: "Any statute or law to the contrary notwithstanding, the English language only shall be used in the records and journals of the House of Assembly for the Province of Manitoba, and in any pleading or process or issuing from any court in the Province of Manitoba. The Acts of the Legislature of the Province of Manitoba need only be printed and published in the English language."[18]

[17]For a full account see G. de T. Glazebrook, *A History of Transportation in Canada.*

[18]*Statutes of Manitoba*, 1890, c. 14. This law was never challenged in the courts but had it been it would have been declared *ultra vires*. Section 23 of the Manitoba Act states: "Either the English or the French language may be used by any

The school system was the last bastion of French rights. Prior to 1890 it was controlled by a board of education of which half were Protestant and half were Roman Catholic. Its orders were enforced by two superintendents, one from each faith. Legislative grants were, before 1875, divided equally between the two sections and after that allocated in proportion to the number of children of school age in each group. The School Act of 1890[19] swept away the Church-dominated system and put in its place a system that was public, non-secretarian, and supported by taxes on real property. A provincial department of education was created under the direct responsibility of a minister. The Act stated that all children between certain ages had the right to attend school but it made no provision for compulsion.

What has come to be known as the Manitoba School Question developed from this legislation. Actually, a whole host of questions was raised but three predominate—what rights did the Roman Catholic minority in Manitoba have under the British North America Act and the Manitoba Act; had the province of Manitoba violated these rights, and, if so, what could be done about it? The whole issue became immensely complicated and resulted in a literature of tremendous volume— books, pamphlets, tracts, treatises on the constitution, court decisions, and so on. Anyone who attempts to read all that was written will sympathize with Mr. Jeanotte who said in the House of Commons during the interminable debate of 1896: "If there be a subject that has been discussed to the very limit of human patience it is truly this everlasting question of the Manitoba Separate Schools. . . . it has been said of the learned Origen that to read the works of him alone, would require more than the ordinary life of man. To read everything that has been said and written on what we have agreed to call the school question would require two Methuselahs juxtaposited."[20]

The particular aspects of this complex issue which are relevant to

person in the debates of the Houses of the Legislature, and both these languages shall be used in the respective Records and Journals of those Houses; and either of those languages may be used by any person, or in any Pleading or Process, in or issuing from any Court of Canada established under the British North America Act, 1867, or in or from all or any of the Courts of the Province. The Acts of the Legislature shall be printed and published in both those languages." This section has not been altered and could not have been by Manitoba alone as the right of the province to make changes in the Manitoba Act (which was confirmed by an Imperial Act of 1871, c. 28) was restricted to "The provisions of any law respecting the qualifications of electors and members of the legislative assembly, and . . . elections in the said province."

19*Statutes of Manitoba*, 1890, c. 38.

20Can., H. of C., *Deb.* (Remedial Bill), March 10, 1896, p. 3223.

this study are relatively straightforward. The school question provided the focal point for political life in the province for several years. It also became the basis for what is probably the sharpest clash in Canadian history between a province and the central government, a clash in which Ottawa failed in a determined effort to compel Manitoba to change the legislation.

The decision of the Greenway government to plunge into the issue of separate schools appears to have been taken very suddenly. Indeed, it seems that the Act of 1890 represented a reversal of policy from that prevailing in the cabinet a few months before. Archbishop Taché, in a letter to Greenway, stated:

While forming your government you called at my house . . . and stated that you had been called to form a government and were desirous to strengthen it by taking in one of the French members, who would be agreeable to His Grace, that you were willing, at the same time, to guarantee, under your government, the maintenance of the then existing conditions with regard to Separate Catholic Schools. . . . I expressed my satisfaction and stated that the new Premier could rest assured that I would throw no difficulties in the way of his administration; that I had no objection to Mr. Prendergast being taken into the new cabinet."[21]

The Archbishop's statement was certified as true by two of his clerical associates but denied by Greenway. The circumstances under which the school question was introduced into Manitoba make the denial seem rather less convincing than the affirmation. The issue was brought into focus in Manitoba by D'Alton McCarthy, the leader of the Ontario Equal Rights Association,[22] and taken up by Joseph Martin who was Attorney General in the Greenway cabinet. Martin appeared on a platform with McCarthy in Portage la Prairie in August 1889 and in a belligerent speech stated his conviction that separate schools and official use of the French language must go or he would cease to be Attorney General, thus committing the cabinet to a decision which he had taken largely on emotional grounds. Later it was argued that the Church-dominated system of education was completely unsuited to a developing

[21]P.A.M., Greenway Papers, p. 5066, Archbishop Taché to Greenway, March 23, 1892.
[22]The Equal Rights Association originated as a protest movement against the Jesuits Estates Act of 1888. When the Jesuit Order was suppressed by Pope Clement IV the estates of its members in Quebec were transferred to the government of Lower Canada. Later when the Order was re-established the Jesuit claim to a part of the estates previously forfeited was recognized. D'Alton McCarthy became the leader of a group in the House of Commons who demanded disallowance of the Quebec law and later, as president of the Equal Rights Association, he led an agitation for abolition of all special privileges enjoyed by Roman Catholics anywhere in Canada.

commercial civilization, that a Canadian nationality could not be built on a system under clerical control, and that uniform standards were imperative. Religious bigotry and social intolerance also played a part and electors were often given lurid previews of Manitoba under Vatican control. However, there was never any doubt about the opinion of the majority on the school question; the assembly passed the original bill of 1890 by a vote of twenty-seven to eight and the government won two elections on the issue.

The question became one of constitutional safeguards against a majority decision alleged to be oppressive and the relationship of such safeguards to provincial rights. The question of provincial rights was not brought squarely into the open until after nearly five years of petitions, counter-petitions, and litigation. The Roman Catholic minority first tested the constitutionality of the law setting up secular, free, and non-denominational schools, but, while the action was in progress, also petitioned the federal cabinet for redress, "in the most efficacious and just way."[23] The petition was supported by prominent churchmen and the official hierarchy right across Canada but the cabinet refused to take action because the issue was already before the courts. The case (known as *Barrett* v. *City of Winnipeg*[24]) travelled upwards through the judicial system producing different results at each level. The Manitoba Court of Queen's Bench held the School Act to be *intra vires* of the provincial legislature; the Supreme Court of Canada held exactly the opposite but its decision was, in turn, reversed by the Judicial Committee of the Privy Council. The basis of the last and governing decision was that since no publicly supported schools existed at the time of union the Roman Catholic minority had the same right to maintain private schools, privately supported, as they had always had.

The Roman Catholic minority now turned back to the possibility of a remedy from the federal cabinet directly on the basis of section 22 of the Manitoba Act and/or section 93 of the British North America Act (see Appendix C). The substance of section 93 is that education is exclusively under the jurisdiction of the provinces except that denominational schools existing at the time of union are given a constitutional right to continue to exist and should this be denied the religious group concerned may petition the federal cabinet for remedial action. The essence of section 93, omitting specific reference to Upper Canada, and using a slight change of wording, is repeated in section 22 of the Manitoba Act.

[23]Canada, *Sessional Papers*, 1891, Paper 63.
[24]R. A. Olmsted, *Decisions of the Judicial Committee*, I, 272.

A petition asking for remedial action was heard before a committee of the cabinet in January 1893. The committee, uncertain of what action was possible, sought the advice of the Supreme Court of Canada. Six reference questions were submitted, which, when stripped of legal verbiage, asked: Did section 22 of the Manitoba Act, or section 93 of the British North America Act, or both, apply? Was remedial action under either possible in view of the decision in the *Barrett* case? Did any acts of the province of Manitoba prior to 1890 confer rights or privileges on the Roman Catholic minority and, if so, were these rights prejudicially affected? The Supreme Court of Canada was split on these questions. Justices King and Fournier held that both the Manitoba Act and the British North America Act applied, that rights had been granted after the union and had been prejudicially affected, and that remedial action was legally possible. Justices Ritchie, Gwynne, and Taschereau said that only the Manitoba Act applied, that rights that might have been granted since the union had nothing whatever to do with the case, and, Q.E.D., no remedial action was possible.

The reference questions then went to the Judicial Committee of the Privy Council where the ruling of the Supreme Court was reversed. The Committee decided that section 22 of the Manitoba Act governed. The phrase "at the union" appears in subsection 1 but in subsection 2 is replaced by "any right or privilege of the Protestant or Roman Catholic minority of the Queen's subjects in relation to education." The first phrase was taken as applying to rights existing as of July 15, 1870, and the second to rights granted thereafter. It was then established that the rights granted after Confederation had indeed been prejudicially affected and therefore remedial action proceeding from the federal cabinet would be legal.

The cabinet in Ottawa decided to take action and the cabinet in Winnipeg decided to resist by every possible means. On March 21, 1895, the federal cabinet passed a remedial order-in-council[25] which commanded the Greenway government to amend or supplement its educational legislation to give the Roman Catholic minority the right to maintain their own schools, to share proportionally in any grant made out of public funds for the purposes of education, and to exempt "such Roman Catholics as contribute to Roman Catholic Schools from all payment or contribution to the support of any other schools."[26] The provincial government refused to carry out this order, noting in its reply: "as

[25]Canada, *Sessional Papers*, 1895, Paper 20(c).
[26]*Ibid.*

to the legislative grant we hold that it is entirely within the control of the legislature of the province. . . . it would therefore appear that any action of the Parliament of Canada looking to the restoration of Roman Catholic privileges must be supplemented by the voluntary action of the provincial legislature."[27] Manitoba made it clear that if Ottawa wanted separate schools restored it would have to restore them itself by taking control of matters that were unmistakably provincial.

Nevertheless, the federal government persisted and followed up its order-in-council with an ultimatum: "A session of the present Parliament will be called together, to meet not later than the first Thursday of January next. If by that time the Manitoba Government fails to make a satisfactory arrangement to remedy the grievance of the minority, the Dominion Government will be prepared . . . to introduce and press to a conclusion such legislation as will afford an adequate measure of relief to the said minority, based upon the lines of the judgement of the Privy Council, and the remedial order of the 21st March, 1895."[28] The result was a protracted debate without action of any kind except the dispatch of three emissaries of peace to Winnipeg to talk things over with the insurgents. This solved nothing and the session proceeded to talk itself to death. The five-year life of Parliament expired and Tupper was forced to go to the country.

Laurier, the victor in the ensuing election, had stated in 1895: "The government are very windy. They have blown and raged and threatened and the more they have raged and threatened the more that man Greenway has stuck to his coat. If it were in my power, I would try the sunny way. I would approach this man Greenway with the sunny way of patriotism, asking him to be just and fair, asking him to be generous to the minority. . . ."[29] The sunny approach was tried and resulted in the Laurier-Sifton compromise of 1897. The basis of the compromise was that religious exercises were to take place in any school if authorized by a majority of the members of the school board or if petitioned for by a stated number of parents. A school board was bound to engage a Roman Catholic teacher if one was requested in a town or city where there was an average attendance of forty or more Roman Catholic pupils or in a rural area where the figure was twenty-five or more. Finally the compromise contained the clause which was to prove so troublesome: "Where ten of the pupils in any school speak the French

[27]*Ibid.*
[28]*Ibid.*, 1896, Paper 39.
[29]O. D. Skelton, *Life and Letters of Sir Wilfrid Laurier*, I, 464.

language (or any language other than English) as their native language, the teaching of such pupils shall be conducted in French (or such other language), and English upon the bi-lingual system."[30]

The Natural Resources Question

Boundaries, disallowance, and the school questions are all over-shadowed by the natural resources question which was a continual bone of contention between Manitoba and Ottawa for over fifty years, gathering bitterness and complexity as it aged.

In 1870 in the Committee of Forty Louis Riel had argued that provincial status would be desirable because it carried with it control of the public domain and cited the relevant sections of the British North America Act to prove his point. Although his proposal was rejected, he put it in the demands which the delegates took to Ottawa. Ottawa granted provincial status but withheld control of the public domain, seemingly undisturbed by the hybrid thus created.

Much has been written on the theme that federal control of the public domain in Western Canada was a violation of British constitutional principles. The most emphatic expression of this point of view is found in Chester Martin's *The Natural Resources Question*.[31] Professor Martin was mistaken, however, in attempting to bring in constitutional principles for they have no bearing on the question. It was, and is, just as valid constitutionally for legal title to public land to be vested in the Crown in the right of Canada as to be vested in the Crown in the right of the province.

In a federation one might logically expect a province or state to be in control of Crown lands. However, in the Canadian federation it was more a question of bargaining than of logic. In Nova Scotia, New Brunswick, and Quebec the public lands were, by section 109 of the British North America Act, vested in the provinces. The same practice was followed in 1912 when Ontario was enlarged by nearly one hundred million acres and Quebec by about one hundred and sixty-four million. In British Columbia admission to the union was by an Imperial Order-in-Council which provided that the British North America Act would prevail except as varied by a minute. As nothing was said to the contrary it must be assumed that section 109 also applied to British Columbia. In fact this was tacitly acknowledged by section 11 of the Order-in-Council in which provision was made for a transfer of a "railway belt" from British Columbia to Canada. However, a substantial

[30]Canada, *Sessional Papers*, 1897, Paper 35.
[31]Chester Martin, *The Natural Resources Question*.

element of bargaining had been involved. As part of the terms of union British Columbia had demanded a subsidy of $100,000 more than could be granted even when fictitious population figures were used. Sir George Cartier, the mediator, proposed that the demand be met but asked that the province turn over the railway belt to make the extra amount more readily justifiable before Parliament. When Newfoundland was considering entering the federation in 1867 the local representatives also wanted $100,000 more by way of a subsidy than the formula allowed. It was decided that the request should be granted but that the control of the public domain in Newfoundland should be vested in the Crown in the right of Canada. In Prince Edward Island the public lands had been held by absentee landlords for a century before Confederation. In 1867 the Island refused to join Confederation because no solution was offered for this grievance but joined in 1873 when the Dominion offered $45,000 in lieu of lands. No attempt was made to appraise the income that might have accrued to the province if the lands were in its possession. They were used for bargaining by the province and as a convenient subterfuge by the Dominion to hide the better treatment given the province.

The Canadian federal structure has been built and made to hang together by a whole series of such compromises, most of which are explainable not by the theory of federation but by local circumstances and shrewd bargaining. Manitoba had scant opportunity to bargain beforehand, however. Its delegates to Ottawa in 1870 were, in essence, the representatives of a man who was forced to flee the country, later was denied the seat in the House of Commons to which he had been elected, and eventually was hanged for treason. His bid for local control of the public domain was brushed aside.

There were other reasons why the public domain in the province had to remain in the hands of the central government. In the first place, Macdonald was concerned about the possible obstruction of national policy by the predominantly half-breed population of Manitoba and the subsequent record of this group in the Northwest more than justified his apprehension. The Indian claim on the public domain was recognized in law as an obstacle to a clear title for Canada and only representatives of the federal government could remove it. Western lands were regarded as the real capital behind a transcontinental railway and without the railway the lands themselves were valueless. Finally a uniform and generous homestead policy was needed if Canada were to compete with the United States for settlers. Even Western representatives in the House of Commons at Ottawa were quick to grasp the prime importance of a centrally controlled homestead policy. As minister of the interior in the federal cabinet Sir Clifford Sifton vigorously defended the land reservation policy of the 1905 autonomy bills, in spite of the fact that their educational provisions forced his resignation, and said in part: "if you hand over the land to three separate provincial governments, each with its own ideas of policy, each with its own Minister of Crown Lands . . . every man who knows anything about doing business between governments must know that it would be absolutely impossible that satisfactory results could be achieved."[32] Frank Oliver, the Territorial representative who replaced Sifton as minister of the interior, agreed:

> . . . the settlement of these lands is for the benefit of all Canada. Whatever method of administration will give us the best results in the way of settlement of these lands is the policy that is best not only for the Dominion but for the province. As a representative of the west, I believe the idea of using the lands of the west as a source of provincial revenue would be a very great detriment to these new provinces and to the country at large. . . . So long as we have a land policy the basic idea of which is the land for the settler, it is certainly better for us and for the Dominion that the lands should be administered by the federal authorities.[33]

Dozens of speeches were made in similar vein. The federal policy of reservation of the public domain seems to have been sound; the mistake was in giving subsidies in lieu of lands. Such subsidies gave the Western provinces the impression that the land was really theirs from the beginning but was rented from them for a nominal figure. Also, the subsidy became, as far as Manitoba was concerned, a part of the provincial revenue with which it was loath to part. A settlement was delayed for years because Manitoba demanded both the lands and the subsidies.

The first land subsidy was granted to Manitoba in 1882 by the Macdonald government in a way that has become all too familiar in the Canadian federation. Manitoba was hard pressed financially and had to be rescued. However, a special reason for administering the financial first aid had to be found to ward off immediate demands from all the other provinces as well as a defensible reason to parry questions that might be asked in the House. A land subsidy was the obvious answer and $45,000 was added to the annnual statutory subsidy in 1882 to compensate the province for the want of the public domain.

The federal government made its greatest blunder in 1905 when the new provinces of Alberta and Saskatchewan were created. As originally introduced into the House of Commons the autonomy bills admitted that

[32]Can., H. of C., *Deb.*, 1905, p. 3095.
[33]*Ibid.*, p. 3157.

the provinces were entitled to monetary compensation because Ottawa was to retain title to the public domain. In Saskatchewan it was calculated by pure guesswork that the area reserved would be 25,000,000 acres and that the value per acre was $1.50. The subsidy to be paid Saskatchewan was then calculated by a progressive rise in the rate of interest on this capital sum ($37,500,000) as the population grew. These figures would have been arbitrary with the use of approximate land area and value per acre but when a sliding scale of interest rates and population was added they became simply absurd. Moreover, the concept of paying interest on the capital value of the land clearly assumed a landlord-tenant relationship except that the party who held, and continued to hold, the deed was treated as the tenant. Sifton saw the incongruity of the situation and noted that ". . . within a few days after the Bill was published . . . Mr. Haultain seized upon this [the subsidy] phase of the Bill . . . he took the ground which it must be admitted he could take with some degree of force, that . . . we admitted . . . the right of the Territories to claim that they are the beneficial owners of the land."[34] Sifton's argument prevailed and the bill as passed left out the calculations of land value and put the subsidy on its proper footing—a subsidy designed to meet the needs of new and expanding provinces. However, the damage was done. As soon as the autonomy bills were passed, Manitoba began agitating for equality of financial treatment with Saskatchewan and Alberta but the arch-Conservative Premier Roblin received short shrift with the Ottawa Liberals. Not until after the Borden victory of 1911 was the land subsidy put on a basis of equality with the other Western provinces.

The subsidy became the stumbling block that delayed a transfer of Manitoba lands from federal to provincial control. Borden stated in 1912 that the time was ripe for such action but could not justify giving Manitoba both the lands and the subsidy. Meighen shared Borden's opinions and in 1920 wrote to Premier Norris: "In recent years the difficulty in dealing with the problem has not been any reluctance on the part of the Federal government to transfer the resources in question but the difficulty in arriving at acceptable terms . . . up to now, so far as I am aware, Manitoba has asked not only for such transfer but has insisted as well upon the retention of the extra subsidies."[35] Norris replied that the continuation of the subsidies was looked upon as partial compensation for the alienation from 1870 on and that the only satisfactory basis of settlement was a recognition on the part of the Dominion

[34]*Ibid.*, p. 3097.
[35]P.A.M., Crerar Papers, Meighen to Norris, Dec. 7, 1920.

government that the lands should have been in the hands of the province from the first and a willingness to compensate for the fact that they were withheld. To this Meighen replied:

Manitoba asks in effect, that the Dominion government now admit that at the time of their creation these provinces should have been granted their natural resources . . . the questions as to the merits of the reasons that influenced the Federal government of the time to adopt another course need not now be debated. The fact is another course was taken and public policy especially as regards Federal expenditures has been adjusted through many years to that fact. The Dominion has in relation to western immigration, western railways, western irrigation, mounted police and numerous other subjects carried on through these years, policies involving large expenditures attributable in substantial but unascertainable proportions to the fact that the natural resources were reserved . . . there would be no effective way of following out a long process of accounting. . . . It would be like attempting to unscramble an egg.[36]

Mr. King took up the question soon after the Liberal victory in 1921 but ran into the same difficulties as had Meighen. His statement that "it is desirable and just that such adjustments be made between the Dominion of Canada and the Prairie provinces with respect to their natural resources as will give full recognition to the principle that . . . they are entitled to be placed in a position of equality with the other provinces of Confederation"[37] failed to satisfy Manitoba because it contained no admission that the lands should have belonged to the province from the beginning and that in return the subsidy in lieu of lands should be continued as partial compensation for the mistakes of the past. In 1928 these propositions were admitted and a Royal Commission was created to translate their admission into monetary terms.

The Commissioners appointed to carry out the placing of Manitoba "in a position of equality with the other provinces of Confederation with respect to the administration and control of its natural resources as from the entrance with Confederation in 1870"[38] reported that they found equality a difficult concept to define and an "accounting on a fiduciary basis" virtually impossible to achieve. The federal government had given away nearly 8,000,000 acres of agricultural land for free homesteads and Manitoba claimed compensation despite the obvious fact that the homestead policy had brought many of the settlers to the province. The text of the Commission report evades the question of payment for these lands. Indeed, the Commission arrived at the acreage

[36]Ibid.
[37]Can., H. of C., Deb., 1922, p. 1018.
[38]Order-in-Council, Ottawa, Aug. 15, 1928.

to be paid for (25,000,000) by sheer guesswork. The Dominion, the report concluded, owed the province $18,847,500 of which $11,193,000 had already been paid by subsidies in lieu of land and $3,306,900 by swamp and educational endowment lands already transferred. This left a balance of $4,584,212 which was paid in a lump sum thus ending a dispute that had been going on for over half a century.

Conclusion

Boundaries, disallowance, the school question, natural resources— these were the primary issues prior to 1900 and several conclusions may be drawn from them. The politicians, the press, and the people of the province fought hard over these issues, once they were settled by defeat, victory, or time, provincial rights in the sense that they have continued to be known in Ontario, Quebec, or Nova Scotia almost ceased to exist. Manitobans do not have the sense of history of the original provinces. Once the questions of status were resolved the province was transformed from one of the most truculent to one of the most co-operative. There has in the last thirty years been no fear of centralization—indeed, quite the reverse. But as long as political life revolved around the issues of status genuine political parties did not develop from them for the issues were such that only one stand was possible.

POLITICAL PARTIES: POLICIES AND ORGANIZATION

4

PRIOR TO 1900 political parties barely existed in Manitoba. The group that took office under the premiership of John Norquay in 1878 was called Conservative and the opposition was described as Liberal but the *Manitoba Free Press*, a Liberal paper in federal politics, refused to admit that the Norquay government was Conservative and supported it. Later Norquay did manage a shaky and temporary alliance with the Ottawa Conservatives by agreeing to support federal railway policy in return for a substantial increase in the subsidy, but he does not seem to have been popular with Sir John A. Macdonald who wrote to a correspondent in Winnipeg in 1884: "I have no doubt in my mind that the way to deal with Manitoba is to pay no attention to their grumblings. I should much prefer Greenway [the Liberal leader] at the head of things rather than Norquay who is really a nuisance."[1] Greenway did become the head of things in 1888 and by his school legislation created a racial and religious cleavage that cut across any possible party lines.

Party politics really began about 1900 when a government Conservative in fact as well as in name took office. Other parties developed in the succeeding decade. The period from 1896 to 1910 had been one of remarkable growth[2] in productivity and population[3] in Manitoba, giving

[1]P.A.M., Macdonald Letters, No. 40(a), Macdonald to H. H. Smith, June 17, 1884.

[2]For more details see: J. B. Hedges, *Building the Canadian West*; W. A. Mackintosh, *Prairie Settlement*; A. S. Morton, *A History of Prairie Settlement* and Chester Martin, *"Dominion Lands" Policy*; W. L. Morton, *Manitoba: A History*.

[3]The population of Manitoba rose from 255,211 to 461,630 between 1901 and 1911. During the peak period of growth (1901 to 1906) the rate of increase was

rise to two major problems. In the first place, a relatively simple and uncomplicated society had to adapt to the more complex structure made necessary by a very large and astonishingly rapid growth in population. Secondly, various economic difficulties grew out of the wheat economy. The first problem produced a variety of reform groups that eventually coalesced into a Liberal party and the second produced a farmers' party known as the Progressives. A Manitoba Labour party was formed in May 1910 and contested several Winnipeg seats in the elections of that year advocating direct legislation, the single tax, government inspection of all factories, workshops, and mines, the union label, and "collective ownership of all industries in which competition has ceased to exist." It failed to secure a single seat in 1910 partly because of internecine warfare between it and a Marxist wing of the labour movement and partly because its programme was, except for collective ownership, identical to that of the Liberal party. In the election of 1914 Labour got three seats and in the following election seven, after which its number of members in the legislature fell off sharply.

After the defeat of the Conservatives in 1915, the Liberals held office until they were replaced in 1922 by the Progressives. Since then party nomenclature has been confused by admittance of the Liberals to the Progressive group in 1932 and the subsequent existence of a nameless coalition which was followed by a non-partisan government lasting until 1950. The group that then came to power, the Liberal-Progressives, claimed direct descent from the original Progressives. They were defeated in 1958 and the present government, although more liberal than the Liberals and more progressive than the Progressives, calls itself Conservative.

Conservatives

The Conservative government which took office on January 8, 1900, under the leadership of Hugh John Macdonald for a few months and

---

43.5 per cent over the five-year period. A comparison with Canada as a whole is given in the table below:

Year	Per cent increase in Manitoba	Per cent increase in Canada
1901–6	43.5	13.5
1911	26.0	18.2
1916	20.2	11.0
1921	10.1	9.3
1926	.95	9.8

then under R. P. Roblin, was one of the strongest and most durable in the history of the province. As a party the Conservatives had some of the best characteristics but also many of the worst. The Premier and his cabinet were closely in touch with majority opinion at all times and were able and willing to take decisive action when it was necessary. Party advantage and provincial interest could and did come together on many occasions. On the other hand, Roblin and his lieutenants took too much advantage of the easy political morality of the day and allowed (or encouraged) the growth of a political machine that became scandalously corrupt and eventually made them all its victims.

For many years prior to the turn of the century provincial leaders, newspapers, and business men had complained about the high freight rates particularly on wheat and the slow growth of railway feeder lines in the province. In 1901 Roblin's government took over the lines of the Northern Pacific on a long lease and then transferred them to the Canadian Northern. In return for a provincial guarantee on its bonds the Canadian Northern completed its line to the Lakehead and fixed its rate on grain haulage at a figure considerably below the Canadian Pacific rate which was promptly reduced. On several other occasions the government announced guarantees of up to $10,000 a mile on construction of other badly needed branch lines, one of which passed by a sand-pit in which the Premier was said to have a financial interest. In 1909 the Liberal leader charged that "Mr. Gunn supplied sand, . . . the Canadian Northern the money, and Mr. Roblin political influence."[4] As so often happened in those days the charge was never proved or disproved: a motion in the house for a committee to investigate was defeated overwhelmingly.

The government took equally decisive action in 1905 when the Bell Telephone Company applied to the legislature for incorporation. Its petition was refused and the whole question of future telephone service referred to a committee of the house for study. Surprisingly enough, it recommended public ownership; the cabinet agreed, and one year later a bill was introduced to take over the existing lines of the Bell thus creating the first publicly owned telephone system in North America. Roblin had feared that a private corporation would concentrate its services in the densely populated and hence more profitable urban area but the publicly owned corporation served rural and urban areas alike and in so doing acquired considerable electoral good will for the government that created it. Unfortunately, the government put the operation of the telephone system directly under a cabinet minister instead of an independent commission. For years the opposition tried unsuccessfully to probe the finan-

[4]*Canadian Annual Review*, 1909, p. 500.

cial statements that were handed to the public accounts committee but charges of patronage and mishandling of public funds were proved only after the government went out of office in 1915.

The Conservative party was in theory devoted to the principle of private enterprise but in practice it not only socialized the Bell Telephone Company but also imposed regulations on the privately owned Winnipeg Grain Exchange where fortunes were made and lost daily in grain futures and trading was as active and frantic then as on the Toronto or New York stock exchanges at present. When the Grain Exchange expelled the Grain Growers' Grain Company, organized by the farmers, because it was set up on a co-operative basis, Robert Rodgers, the Attorney General, wrote to the Chairman: "The action of your Council of refusing trading privileges to the Grain Growers Grain Co. cannot be regarded by the government other than as an arbitrary and unjustifiable exercise of the powers conferred upon you through your charter by the Legislative Assembly of Manitoba, and unless remedied by the 15th of this month the Government will call the Legislature together for the purpose of remedying this and other grievances by Legislative amendments."[5] The Exchange reinstated the company forthwith but even so the legislature amended its charter and gave a right of appeal against any of its by-laws to the Court of King's Bench.[6]

As the Liberal opposition began to gather strength the Roblin government was led into actions that now seem unwise. Both parties had to pay the closest attention to the farm vote and one of the farmers' most bitter complaints was that elevator companies to whom they sold their grain consistently overcharged them for handling and storage and frequently assigned unfair grades.[7] In 1909 the Roblin government yielded to pressure and agreed to experiment with a line of publicly owned elevators operated by a commission and financed by public money. Over one hundred elevators were built but the experiment was a total failure as Premier Roblin admitted publicly in 1913, charging that farmers had failed to patronize the elevators that had been built specifically for them.

[5]*Ibid.*, 1907, p. 560.

[6]*Statutes of Manitoba*, 1908, c. 79.

[7]The question of unfair practices of elevator companies has a long history and was discussed in the House of Commons at Ottawa periodically from 1890 to 1910. In 1898 the federal government set up a Royal Commission which in its report (see Canada, *Sessional Papers*, 1900, Paper 81(a)) pointed out that two-thirds of the elevators on the prairies were controlled by three companies, all of whom had headquarters in Ontario. The Manitoba Grain Act of 1900 was based on the Commission's recommendations and made it possible to load grain into railway cars from warehouses built by farmers—a privilege that had hitherto been withheld by the C.P.R. It also provided for stringent government supervision of grading, weighing, and dockage.

A second issue was that of schools. A great many well-informed people in the province felt that the absence of a compulsory clause in the School Act was producing a high level of illiteracy. In addition, with the growing racial complexity of the province the right to teach in a language other than English was getting out of hand. The *Manitoba Free Press*, which carried on a merciless campaign against this right, estimated that in 1913 there were nearly 350 school districts teaching in French, German, Ruthenian, Polish, or Russian.[8] In 1912 the Coldwell Amendments to the School Act were passed.[9] The real intent of these confusing amendments was not clear to commentators of the time but it appears to have been an attempt to placate the Roman Catholics in Winnipeg by allowing class-rooms in primarily Protestant schools to be taught by Roman Catholics if ten or more students of that faith were in attendance. The Coldwell Amendments added little to the government's electoral strength. The Catholic hierarchy wanted, as they always had, the right to separate schools. The militant Protestants were suspicious of any move that suggested such action.

The Roblin government fell in 1915. Its opponents had been charging it with flagrant dishonesty for more than a decade. It is obviously impossible to list all the charges made but those relating to the by-election in the constituency of Gimli in May 1913 will give some idea of their nature. T. H. Johnson, a prominent Liberal, "on his responsibility as a member of the House," stated:

That public moneys were improperly and corruptly employed in influencing electors to vote for E. L. Taylor [the Conservative candidate],—clear evidence of which is to be found in items of the public accounts aggregating to some $93,000 expended by the Government; that bribery was extensively practised and corrupt treating was carried on throughout the constituency to a degree never before known; that liquor was freely dispensed by agents of E. L. Taylor in Local Option territory and elsewhere; that intimidation was largely practised and that employees of the Manitoba Government and officers of the law were personally guilty of acts of intimidation, bribery, corrupt treating and distribution of liquor; that violators of the law in this election were protected by officers of the Government; that prominent among the workers and agents of E. L. Taylor were owners, managers, employees and *habitués* of notorious drinking resorts in Winnipeg . . . that this campaign of corruption, intimidation, bribery and illegal use of liquor was directed and managed by prominent members of the Civil Service of Manitoba.[10]

The government's reply was to charge the Liberals with exactly the same

[8]*Manitoba Free Press*, Jan. 1, 1913.
[9]*Statutes of Manitoba*, 1912, c. 65.
[10]*Canadian Annual Review*, 1914, p. 587.

thing[11] and to offer to refer both sets of charges to the Standing Committee on Privileges and Elections, on which the administration had a majority.

Even a public that had become so used to corruption that it regarded it as a legitimate part of politics was unprepared for the revelations of bribery and dishonesty which emerged from the investigation into the construction of the new legislative buildings. The Lieutenant Governor was forced to intervene and to appoint a Royal Commission which established that there had been systematic and continual violation of contracts and that the treasury had been defrauded of nearly one million dollars.[12] The report also established that the fraudulent practices of the contractors, Thomas Kelly and Sons, had been known to the Minister of Public Works and that part of the graft went into party funds. The Roblin government anticipated the findings of the Commission and resigned some months before the report was presented.

Liberals

The Liberals, who for nearly a decade had been without effective leadership or definite policies, had evolved by 1910 a platform advocating change and presenting a means of adapting to the new circumstances brought about by phenomenal growth. Their platform involved creation as well as adaptation and the party developed the idealism and innovation characteristic of frontier societies. Some of the more important organizations and movements that became associated with the Liberals were the Temperance Movement, a great many of the Protestant churches, the League for the Taxation of Land Values, the Direct Legislation League, and the United Farmers. Others such as the Social Gospel movement and the trade unions were connected by membership with the

[11]In 1915 a prominent Conservative charged that the government had paid the opposition $50,000 to withdraw all protests. An investigating commission found this particular charge to be false but noted in its report: "The whole system which has been followed with regard to disposition of election petitions in Manitoba during many years has defeated the intentions of the Act [i.e. The Controverted Elections Act] . . . we think that these 'saw-off' agreements for the withdrawal of election protests, without bringing them to trial, are very objectionable. . . . The practice of political parties in this regard has been of such long standing that the public have come to regard it as being not illegal, but actually permissible. The evidence given before us by G. H. Walker, Prothonotary of the Court of King's Bench, shows that between the year 1887 and the present time, no fewer than one hundred and twenty (120) election petitions had been filed . . . at most two had been tried." *Report of the Royal Commission Appointed to Investigate the Charges Made in the Statement of C. P. Fullerton, K. C.* (1915), p. 6.

[12]*Report of the Royal Commission Appointed to Inquire into Certain Matters Relating to the New Parliament Buildings* (1915).

Direct Legislation League, and the Liberals eventually provided the highest common denominator for successful political action for all of them.

The Temperance Movement was supported by a large, powerful, and primarily urban group. Its aim was to "banish the bar" which, as it operated in Manitoba until 1915, was essentially a survival of rough and ready frontier days and hence unsuited to a more sophisticated and puritanical society. The Temperance forces united in 1907 to form the Manitoba Social and Moral Reform Council[13] which, though confining itself largely to temperance, described its nature and purpose as "a federation of religious and social reform bodies for consultation and cooperation with respect to legislative reforms growing out of common Christianity."[14] By 1910 the Council was unofficially united with the Liberal party and in 1914 the party put a "banish the bar" plank in its platform. The promise was fulfilled when the Liberals were elected to office in 1915.

A doctrine known as the Social Gospel came into prominence about 1900 under the leadership of J. S. Woodsworth[15] and Salem Bland. The Social Gospel had its origins in the United States and was essentially the American Protestant response to the problems of a new industrial order. In the United States the most vigorous support came from the Unitarians, Congregationalists, and Episcopalians and in Canada from the Methodists. The primary religious assumptions of the movement, which deprecated other-worldliness, were that the Kingdom of Heaven was to be realized in this life, and that progress was not only natural but divinely ordered. Religion became within the movement, both in Canada and in the United States, a tool for reform, and a practical Christianity was applied to specific social questions. The Winnipeg advocates of the Social Gospel focused their attention on the relationships between employers and employees in a city that was beginning to be industrialized. This meant that their support went primarily to Labour but it was the Liberals who fulfilled two of their main demands—compulsory primary education and the eight-hour working day.

The ideas of Henry George had much appeal for the society growing

[13]The supporting groups were the Women's Christian Temperance Union, the Icelandic Lutheran Synod, the Polish National church, the Russian Orthodox church, the Ruthenian Orthodox church, the Unitarian Conference, the United Farmers of Manitoba, and the Scandinavian Anti-Saloon League.

[14]*Statesman* (official publication of the Manitoba Social and Moral Reform Council), Aug. 28, 1913.

[15]See Kenneth McNaught, *A Prophet in Politics: A Biography of J. S. Woodsworth*.

up in Manitoba at the turn of the century.[16] In particular, his analysis of the detrimental effects of speculation in land values seemed applicable to the new province. Shortly after Manitoba's creation speculation had risen to a feverish pitch and then dropped sharply following a serious flood on the Red River. Speculation began again after 1900 and reached gigantic proportions. A great deal of land was held by a few companies who were suspected of making exorbitant profits. In the settlement of 1869 the Hudson's Bay Company had been granted one-twentieth of the land in the fertile belt plus large blocks around each trading post which, all told, amounted to more than a million acres in Manitoba. By 1903 the Canadian Pacific held more than three million acres in the province. Large profits obviously could be made by the simple process of withholding the land from the market until the price rose as J. W. Dafoe demonstrated when he estimated that the average price per acre of land held by the Canadian Northern Railway rose from $6.01 in 1906 to $13.95 in 1913.[17]

T. A. Crerar, an influential farm leader, felt strongly about speculation and wrote in 1916: "Our policy in Western Canada, ever since we started to settle it, has been one largely of exploitation, and the greatest sinners, without question . . . have been those who have made profits out of the advance in realty values. . . . to my mind there is no reform today quite so vital for Canada's development as the adoption of the principles of taxation advocated by Henry George."[18] The *Grain Growers' Guide* complained in 1908: "In practically every school district a great deal of land is held by speculators and railway companies. A heavy tax on this vacant land would provide a vast increase in the funds available for rural schools."[19] Many saw such a tax as the logical alternative to the

[16]The kernel of Henry George's ideas is found in his book *Progress and Poverty* (Appleton, New York, 1879). Briefly his theory may be said to be based on a restatement of the nineteenth-century explanation of the relationships between land, labour, and capital. He accepted the classical position that economic rent was to be defined solely as a return on land but argued that all rent was essentially an unearned increment. The ownership of land, unlike the ownership of other factors of production, meant to George the ability to appropriate part of the product without the expenditure of productive effort; land does not produce but its ownership gives leave to produce. Moreover, rents increase (and wages decrease) as population rises and the arts of production improve, as is particularly evident in new communities and areas being opened up for settlement where speculation in land values is particularly prevalent. The solution, as George saw it, was that "It is not necessary to confiscate land, it is necessary only to confiscate rent. . . . I therefore propose to appropriate rent by taxation . . . to abolish all taxation save that on land values." *Progress and Poverty*, p. 403.

[17]J. W. Dafoe, "Economic History of the Prairie Provinces," p. 316.

[18]P.A.M., Crerar Papers, T. A. Crerar to G. R. Marnock, Dec. 11, 1916.

[19]*Grain Growers' Guide*, May 25, 1908.

customs tariff as a means of producing revenue. Enthusiasts estimated in 1915 that the land tax would produce roughly twice as much revenue as the tariff and be fairer "as the tariff adds 25% to every article purchased."[20] In 1910 the League for the Taxation of Land Values was formed [21] and three years later the League began publishing a magazine called the *Single Taxer*. The leading personalities in the League were T. A. Crerar, president of the Grain Growers' Grain Company, F. L. Dixon, a moderate Winnipeg labour leader, and W. W. Buchanan. The movement linked itself to the Liberal party after 1910 and although the party could not bring itself to endorse the single tax idea unequivocally it promised a commission to investigate its feasibility.

There was intense interest in Manitoba, between 1905 and 1915, in direct legislation in the form of the initiative and referendum.[22] In 1906 the Royal Templars of Temperance, the League for the Taxation of Land Values, and the United Farmers of Manitoba co-operated to form the Direct Legislation League. Organized labour and the Protestant churches, although not represented on the executive, gave the movement their hearty support. Most of these groups would have endorsed Rousseau's statement that: "Any law which the people has not ratified in person is null and void; it is not a law. The English people thinks it is free; but it is very much mistaken. It is free only when it is electing members of parliament; as soon as they are elected, it is enslaved and reduced to nothing. The use it makes of its liberty during these brief moments shows that it well deserves to lose it."[23] In fact, as reams of direct legislation propaganda showed, some members of the federation would have gone Rousseau one better and argued that they were not even free at election

[20]*Single Taxer*, Jan. 1915.

[21]The first proponent of the single tax in Manitoba seems to have been W. W. Buchanan, a Winnipeg journalist, who became interested in the works of Henry George about 1890. The League was given considerable financial support by the Joseph Fels Foundation which had been set up by a wealthy American soap manufacturer to disseminate the ideas of Henry George.

[22]The initiative is a device by which the people may propose laws directly. The referendum when joined to the initiative makes it possible for the people as a whole to approve or reject a measure prevously passed by the legislature. In North America the initiative and referendum were first introduced in South Dakota in 1898, Utah in 1900, Oregon in 1902, and by 1912 the system, with local variations, had been adopted by seventeen other states. In most states the initiative meant that if a certain percentage of the voters (usually five to ten) petitioned the legislature for a particular measure or constitutional change the legislature was bound to pass it or refer it to the voters by a referendum. A second provision usually included was that no law passed by the legislature of its own motion was binding until the voters had a chance to petition against it.

[23]Jean Jacques Rousseau, *The Social Contract*, ed., Frederick Watkins (New York, 1953), p. 104.

time. On the local scene there was the Roblin government which by virtue of its extremely efficient political machine seemed to have a stranglehold on the electorate. In national politics only the Conservatives or Liberals had a chance, and they, it was alleged, were controlled by professional politicians most of whom were the henchmen of the corporate interests and the exploiters of Western resources. The basic assumption of the League was that "the general will" is clearly defined and inherently a force for good, only frustrated or prevented in its expression by the intervention of a representative system of government. True democracy, it was argued, had been side-tracked in Eastern Canada but the West could become a citadel of real liberalism and a shining example of a good society if only popular sovereignty could assert itself.

With strong support from many of the reform groups, the blessing of the United Farmers of Manitoba, and an arrangement whereby Labour contested only certain Winnipeg seats, the Liberals won 21 out of 49 seats in the election of 1914. Six months later the Conservatives resigned. The ensuing five years under the Liberals is the only period when reform and progressive sentiments have dominated in Manitoba. The Norris government excelled itself in meeting the economic demands, specific requests, and ideological predelictions of the groups that had supported it. The Liberals abolished the bilingual school system and made school attendance compulsory, passed a new and greatly improved elections act which gave women the vote, created a comptroller general with real audit powers, made workmen's compensation more generous, enacted a new minimum wage law with a fair wage board to enforce it, and passed a new and better factory law to deal with standards of safety and sanitation. Agriculture benefited by greatly increased credit facilities and a new provincial programme for research.

Some reforms, attractive in opposition, proved impractical in office. The hopes of the Single Taxers were extinguished by the report of the 1919 Assessment and Taxation Commission which, after a careful study, reported against any experimentation in Manitoba with the ideas of Henry George on the grounds that they were not "a method of tax reform but a panacea for human ills."[24] The Direct Legislation statute of 1916 never became operative, being declared *ultra vires* by the Manitoba Court of Appeals in 1917, a decision confirmed when the Attorney General took the case to the Privy Council in 1919.[25] The reason for the invalidation was that section 92 of the British North America Act speci-

[24]Manitoba, *Sessional Papers*, 1919, Report of the Manitoba Assessment and Taxation Commission, p. 16.
[25]*In re The Initiative and Referendum Act*, [1919] A.C. 935.

fically prohibited the provinces from changing any part of their constitutions pertaining to the office of lieutenant governor. The Direct Legislation statute made the royal assent meaningless in that the lieutenant governor might easily find that a bill to which he had assented was subsequently referred to the electorate and nullified by an adverse referendum vote.

Progressives

Soon after the turn of the century, there began to take shape in Manitoba an agrarian protest movement which proved to be the most significant force in the political life and institutions of the province. The farmers' movement was more durable than French-English relations, provincial rights, or Liberal reform and it is easy to see why. For one thing, it arose from certain disadvantages and difficulties imposed by nature and the British North America Act on the region of which Manitoba is a part. Nature erected a barrier of rock and wilderness north of Lake Superior and Confederation forced the produce from the Western plains to pass over it, at very high freight rates. In addition to the difficulties inherent in opening up a new region thus situated, the settlers were faced with the hazards of frost, hail, drought, wind, and grasshoppers. In short, the farmers of Western Canada found themselves the victims of geographical location, terrifying natural phenomena, and economic laws seemingly designed to benefit some one else. If they overcame these difficulties and survived the severe climate the farmers often found that a disproportionate share of the reward for risk-taking went to the elevator owners, the commission agents and the railways, or the implement companies, whose economic power seemed unlimited while that of individual farmers was virtually nil. A farmer was only one among thousands of others and an individual decision to withhold produce from the market had no effect on price. The most likely consequence was starvation for the witholders and their dependents. Three courses of action were open to the farmers—to appeal to the government for regulatory legislation in the interests of agriculture, to organize in an attempt to strengthen their economic power as producers and consumers, or to organize for direct political action. All three were attempted.

It is interesting to note that the agrarian problems in the Canadian West after 1900 were similar to those in the United States after the Civil War and that much the same courses of action were followed and comparable political phenomena were produced. In the 1870's the Grangers had organized a farmers' brotherhood to demand state regulation of monopolies, federal regulation of transportation rates, lower interest

charges, and reduced tariff protection for industry. The Granger movement was short lived but the vacuum left by its demise was filled immediately by the Greenbackers who concentrated on currency reform. The
Greenbackers were even more of a flash in the pan but their grievances
were not, and their place was taken by the Farmers' Alliance which
adopted much the same anti-monopoly, anti-railroad cause as the
Grangers. In 1892 at the Omaha convention the remnants of the Grangers and the Greenbackers and the newly organized Farmers' Alliance
were welded into the Populist party.

It was logical for the farmers in the United States to take direct political action because the federal division of powers there made it possible
for individual states to take action that would have been unconstitutional
in a Canadian province. For example, in 1871 the Illinois legislature
responded to Granger pressure and passed a rate law for railroads and
elevators. The law was declared invalid by the state courts but sustained
by the Supreme Court of the United States in the famous Granger
decision.[26] In Canada the ills of Western agriculture were attributable to
causes that were primarily the responsibility of the national government
and it was logical that the farmers turn first to Ottawa rather than to
Winnipeg, Regina, or Edmonton.

An observer of Manitoba politics in 1918 would have found little
reason to predict the early rise of a provincial farm group to political
power. The United Farmers of Manitoba were suspicious of political
action, bearing in mind the failure of the Patrons of Industry in Canada
and the Populist Movement in the United States.[27] In the election campaign of 1922, the Progressives had no leader and only the barest excuse
for a platform. The central executive, after considerable prodding by
many locals, did put out a short manifesto which began with a reaffirma-
tion of the Christian faith; where it was specific it was very similar to
Liberal proposals. Nevertheless, they won 28 of the 49 seats and formed
the government. The most important reasons for the election results

[26]For a fuller account of this legislation see Russell B. Nye, *Midwestern Progressive Politics*, p. 47.

[27]Farm organization began in Manitoba shortly after the creation of the
province. In 1876 several branches of the American Grange were organized
around Portage la Prairie but this group was superseded by the indigenous Manitoba and North West Farmers Union. The Union agitated for tariff reductions,
government-sponsored grain inspection, and a railway to Hudson Bay, but after
some initial success the organization petered out. The Patrons of Industry entered
Manitoba in 1891 and made an unsuccessful attempt to gain both co-operative
marketing and political power. The Manitoba Grain Growers, which began in
1903, was the first viable farm organization in the province. In 1919 its name
was changed to United Farmers of Manitoba; to avoid confusion this name is
used throughout.

were the breaking up of party ties in the West following the formation of the Union government in Ottawa in 1917, the fact that the Norris administration was too progressive for the Progressives, rural distrust of labour and urban groups, and the wave of anti-party sentiment that swept the prairies.

The provincial Conservative party had been discredited by the scandals of 1915 and with the rise of the national Progressive movement[28] there arose a feeling that the national Liberal party had lived too long in the degrading company of Eastern financial interests and could be regenerated only by a rebirth among the honest folk of the Western plains. At first the Union government of 1917 seemed the answer to political discontent, and T. A. Crerar, president of the Grain Growers' Grain Company, joined the cabinet.[29] He resigned in 1919, however, because of failure of the government to lower the tariff sufficiently on agricultural implements.[30] His resignation accentuated the confusion of party alignments in Manitoba.

The foundation of the Norris government, built as it was on the support of both farm and labour, had always been shaky. The farmers represented a right-wing conservatism that was more in keeping with the traditions of Manitoba than were the radicalism of the trade unions or the reform policies on which the Norris government was based. The desire for reform exhibited between 1905 and 1922 was much more superficial than in Saskatchewan. Manitoba has always been as much an extension of Ontario as a part of the Western frontier society. Even with the wave of central European immigrants after 1900, settlers from Ontario still retained control in Manitoba. The great bulk of American immigrants, many of whom were radical in politics, went to Saskatchewan and Alberta, 20 per cent of whose population by 1911 had come from the United States while the corresponding figure for Manitoba was less than 5 per cent. This preponderance of Ontario influence gave a conservative cast especially to rural Manitoba, in contrast to the more radical nature of farmers' movements in Saskatchewan and Alberta.

There was never any real allegiance or common interest between

[28]For a full discussion of the national Progressive movement see W. L. Morton, *The Progressive Party in Canada.*

[29]J. W. Dafoe wrote with reference to a conversation with Crerar: "Crerar says that he entertained for a time a hope that the Union government could be turned into a Progressive body behind which the progressive elements would unite permanently. . . . he has now abandoned this idea and thinks that the Unionist party will be substantially the old Conservative party." P.A.C., Dafoe Papers, Dafoe to Clifford Sifton, June 21, 1919.

[30]See Can., H. of C., *Deb.*, 1919, p. 3329.

farmer and labourer in Manitoba other than a vague idea that both were fighting Eastern domination and the "big interests." This concept of a common enemy brought the two groups only to the point where it was routine practice for the leader of the moderate trade union movement in Winnipeg to bring fraternal greetings to the annual farmers' convention in Brandon—a conventional pleasantry rather than an indication of any firm bond between them. The farmers were afraid of the labour movement and the Winnipeg General Strike of 1919 convinced many of their leaders that Winnipeg was infested with radicals and bolsheviks. In 1920 labour leaders in Toronto suggested a conference to plan the formation of a national farmer-labour party. Crerar reacted strongly against the idea and wrote to J. J. Morrison: "The Manitoba Branch of the Dominion Labour party here have as the first plank in their platform the socialization of all property through the elimination of capitalism . . . no good can come from any endeavour to co-operate with the Labour people as long as they have this as the main tenet of their political belief."[31] Morrison replied: "The Labour party in Ontario is quite as socialistic as in Manitoba, and I am quite sure that their views are just as objectionable to the farmers here as to the farmers in the West. Personally, I am not afraid of any stable union taking place between the labour and farmer movement. It is quite impossible because we believe in lessening the cost of production. . . . Labour men generally believe in increasing the cost of production by increased wages and shorter hours."[32]

The farmers did find a measure of support among some urban business men. Both groups regarded government finance as they did their own personal bank accounts and the Norris government had been running a deficit. Many of the business men were suspicious of all forms of government activity except the very minimum. When the farmers began to enter candidates in the election of 1922 the business interests organized a group to support them. J. W. Dafoe noted, with some surprise, that the men behind the group, who put up the money for their very lively advertising campaign, included J. H. Ashdown, owner of the city's largest hardware business, Sir Augustus Nanton, a wealthy investment dealer, Mr. Fitzgerald, manager of the Hudson's Bay Company, and Mr. Tucker, manager at Eatons: "This was a curious combination to be behind a political movement which announced that its intention was to co-operate with the farmers. It was, I think, based on the hope

[31]Crerar Papers, Crerar to J. J. Morrison, Sept. 7, 1920.
[32]*Ibid.*, Morrison to Crerar, Sept. 20, 1920.

that there would be a kind of business government and that low taxes would result."[33]

The attitude of the business group was exceptional. Support for the Progressives came primarily from the rural areas as is shown in Table I.

TABLE I

PERCENTAGE OF VOTES CAST FOR PROGRESSIVE
OR LIBERAL-PROGRESSIVE CANDIDATES*

	Winnipeg	Other than Winnipeg
1927	17.4	40.1
1932	19.3	48.5
1936	21.0	42.7

*Figures supplied by the Chief Electoral Officer.

Manitoba is unique among the Canadian provinces in having its urban population concentrated almost entirely in one city. There is no rival centre to balance Winnipeg, as Saskatoon balances Regina, and Calgary, Edmonton. Nevertheless, despite its concentration of power, Winnipeg has not by any means had a proportionate influence in the legislature (see Table II).

TABLE II*

	Population of Manitoba	Population of Winnipeg	Winnipeg as a percentage of Manitoba	Total number of seats in legislature	Number of Winnipeg seats	Winnipeg seats as a percentage of total
1881	62,260	7,985	12.82	30	2	6.6
1891	152,506	25,639	16.81	38	3	7.8
1901	255,211	42,340	16.60	38	3	7.8
1911	461,394	136,035	29.48	49	6	12.24
1921	610,118	1 79,087	29.35	55	10	18.18
1931	700,118	213,785	30.53	55	10	18.18
1941	729,749	221,960	30.42	55	10	18.18
1051	776,541	235,710*	30.35	57	10	17.54

*These figures are for Winnipeg proper. Census records are not convertible to Greater Winnipeg prior to 1911. It is also difficult to equate Greater Winnipeg with electoral seats.

[33]Dafoe Papers, J. W. Dafoe to Clifford Sifton, July 25, 1922. An account of the organization of the group was carried in the *Grain Growers' Guide*, June 7, 1922, p. 14. At the organizational meeting the following resolution was passed: "We accept the political principles enunciated by the United Farmers of Manitoba relating to provincial affairs, and agree to co-operate with their elected representatives in establishing an administration that will meet the needs of both city and country."

On the other hand the rural areas have looked upon themselves as entirely separate and distinct and have often attributed an unsympathetic attitude to city dwellers. T. A. Crerar wrote in 1917:

It seems to me that there is nothing quite so offensive in a supposedly democratic country like Canada as the patronizing attitude of many city people to those who are following the highly honourable profession of agriculture. For example I was disgusted recently to see in one of our Western papers a news item which gave considerable prominence to the fact that some society ladies had shown their patriotism by cultivating their gardens this summer. It is enough to make a person sick. If they did a little real honest labour once in a while it would do them a great deal of good.[34]

There was a tendency within the U.F.M. to attribute a superior wisdom and virtue to those who worked on the land.[35] Many of their pronouncements are reminiscent of the Physiocrats; most agreed with Thomas Jefferson that "Those who labour in the earth are the chosen people of God. . . . Corruption of morals in the mass of cultivators is a phenomenon of which no age or nation has furnished an example. . . . the mobs of great cities add just so much to the support of pure government, as sores do to the strength of the human body"[36] and "cultivators of the earth are the most valuable of citizens. They are the most vigorous, the most independent, the most virtuous. . . . I consider the class of artificers as the panderers of vice and the instruments by which the liberties of a country are generally overturned."[37] Sentiments similar to these are found scattered through the pages of the *Grain Growers' Guide* and the annual reports of the United Farmers in convention. In 1914 the president said: "Agriculture in Canada must be the great national factor which determines and dominates the fortunes of this nation. . . .

[34]Crerar Papers, Crerar to W. L. Smith, March 30, 1917.

[35]The doctrine that agriculture is the most noble of all professions has a long history. "From time immemorial, agriculture has been exalted above all other human occupations. The writings of Aristotle, Zenophon, and Hesiod reflect its prestige among the ancient Greeks, as do those of Cicero, Virgil, Horace, Pliny, Cato, Varro and Columella among the Romans. It was Socrates who contributed to the French Physiocrats of the eighteenth century the motto: 'husbandry is the mother and nurse of all the other arts. For when husbandry flourishes, all the other arts are in good fettle, but whenever the land is compelled to lie waste the other arts well might perish'. Mediaeval and Renaissance writers venerated agriculture, and with the poets and essayists of the eighteenth century the veneration developed into a cult. Cicero spoke for them all, and for a host of writers since their day that has carried on their tradition, when he declared that: 'of all the occupations by which gain is secured none is better than agriculture, none more profitable, none more delightful, none more becoming to a freeman'." A. W. Griswold, *Democracy and Farming*, p. 19.

[36]Jefferson, *Works* (Federal ed.; New York, 1904), IV, 85–6.

[37]Jefferson, *Writings* (Federal ed.; New York, 1904), V, 374.

city life with its army of rich parasites, its hosts of labour slaves ground under the very heel of capitalism is a bad blot on our civilization."[38] J. L. Brown who was president in 1923 saw a direct and naturalistic connection between agriculture and the good life: "Nothing living can blossom into fruitage unless through nourishing stalks deep-rooted in the common soil. Up from that soil, up from the silent bosom of the earth, rise the curents of life and energy. . . . I tell you that the so-called radicalism of our time is simply the effort of nature to release the generous energies of our farm people."[39]

In addition, a strong anti-party feeling grew up in the West and political parties were seen as the agents of Eastern capitalists who exploited the West from behind their tariff wall. The difficulty of achieving an integration of the Western wheat economy with the Canadian economy was at the root of Western feeling against the federal government. Some of the dislike rubbed off on the provincial parties but even without it those who were disposed to condemn parties could find plenty of evidence that corruption was rife. On the other hand, the United Farmers Organization was felt to be wholly pure. It became as significant in many rural communities as the church or the school and the cornerstone of the new rural society that was growing in the West. Many of its organizers approached their work with missionary zeal. A. J. M. Poole, who became president of the United Farmers and a member of the Canadian Council of Agriculture, wrote, for example, "From the time that I joined the United Farmers I entered into its work with whole hearted enthusiasm. . . . The Association became my politics and to a large degree my religion. . . . It was the beginning of an entirely new outlook on life."[40] The essentially moral and idealistic basis of the farmers' movement was reflected in its ideas about politics. "Democracy," said a statement of principles and objects published in 1917,

is a word of honoured and almost sacred significance in the estimation of the Grain Growers of the West. For them it is not merely a theory of government . . . it is the people enlightened and trained, animated by the purest spirit and the noblest principles of our common Christianity, governing themselves not only for the highest good of the greatest number but so that the smallest and humblest individual shall have justice and the common rights of human kind . . . our essential attitude must be forward looking . . . in order that we may move the community with us nearer to the richer life, the fuller democracy, the complete kingdom of right and peace and joy.[41]

[38]*The United Farmers of Manitoba Year Book*, 1914, p. 12.
[39]*Ibid.*, 1923, p. 6.
[40]P.A.M., A. J. M. Poole, Autobiography (unpublished), pp. 13–14.
[41]*The United Farmers of Manitoba Year Book*, 1917, p. 7.

Such principles led the organized farmers of Manitoba to view many orthodox party activities with self-righteous scorn. Many of them regarded the party system itself as inherently immoral, as the president's address at the annual convention of the United Farmers in Brandon in 1914 reveals:

The party system has converted what our fathers contended so nobly for, namely, responsible government . . . by introducing a system of rabid party-ism which has succeeded admirably in removing the government so far from the people that, for the most part, they pay little attention to honest demands. Partyism gone mad, partyism that cannot see any fault in its own party, and cannot see any good in the opposition . . . partyism that puts a premium on dishonesty and . . . condones acts which, if a man or party of men, practised in other business, would mean that they would at once be frowned out of decent society. My candid opinion, reached after somewhat careful observation and mature study, is that such partyism . . . is the great curse of present day politics, inasmuch as it opens the way to all manner of political corruption.[42]

The farmers of Manitoba saw their organization as the beginning of a new, purer, and better civilization. A. E. Partridge, the Manitoban who first suggested the farmers' marketing company, continually referred to the possibility of "a Christian commonwealth ruled by farmers." Norman Lambert, who has since become a Liberal senator, saw the West in the role of St. George: it alone could slay the Eastern dragons of moral turpitude, usury, and patronage and would represent "the bursting into full bloom of those seeds of liberty and freedom which were sown in older Eastern soil by the immigrant settlers nearly one hundred years ago."[43] Their noble sentiments do not seem particularly evident in the record of the farmers in office, however. It is true that they cannot be accused of corruption but also true that they cannot be credited with any positive political virtues or striking achievements. If farmers do possess the superior wisdom which they attribute to themselves and which so many writers have credited to their kind in other times and places, it did not manifest itself in any recognizable way in Manitoba. Two characteristics stand out—economy of administration and dislike of party.

Anti-party feeling led to a fondness for coalition and eventually culminated in a non-partisan administration which was formed in 1940 and lasted nearly a decade. The first move towards coalition, made in 1931 by Premier John Bracken, was supported by the Liberals, who pushed their members into the Progressive camp. In 1929 J. W. Dafoe (whose motives were by no means non-partisan) wrote to Mackenzie

[42]Minutes of the Eleventh Annual Convention, p. 18.
[43]Grain Growers' Guide, June 17, 1920.

King: "It is or ought to be obvious that . . . in a general election in which the Liberals and Progressives fight one another this province will be lost, both in a federal and a provincial sense . . . the province would be handed to the Tories on a platter."[44] Two months later Dafoe reported to Sifton: "Mr. King made it known to a good many Liberals throughout the province that the Dominion government regarded it as of the highest importance that an understanding should be reached between the Liberals and the Progressives. . . ."[45] The Liberals began to support Bracken in the legislature and by 1932 the two groups were almost completely fused.

Prior to the election of 1931 Bracken had proposed the formation of a union government instead of an election and suggested that the Legislative Assembly Act be amended to extend the life of the legislature. He also promised to divide the cabinet posts roughly in the ratio of the current standings in the house. His proposal was rejected but in the ensuing election, he somehow made it appear that the Conservatives had, by refusing to facilitate their own execution, played the province false. His party won 35 out of the 55 seats.

In 1936 the coalition proposals came after the election which was held on July 17 except in two northern constituencies where the voting was deferred until August 22. When the returns of July 17 failed to produce a clear majority for the government Bracken offered to join forces with the Conservatives; he volunteered to split the cabinet posts evenly and suggested that the leader of the Conservative party could take turns with him in being premier. The arrangement was to last for five years during which time members of the cabinet were to refrain from participation of any kind in federal politics. The Conservatives declined the invitation and the seven C.C.F. members refused to give the government any assurance of support in the house. Astonishingly enough, the five Social Credit members stepped into the breach and agreed to give their support. Their decision was promptly repudiated by the Manitoba Social Credit League; however the question was referred to Premier William Aberhart of Alberta who issued a statement saying that he "approved the Manitoba Social Credit members co-operating with the Bracken government especially in measures leading to monetary reform."[46] Negotiations between Bracken and the Social Credit group were allowed to lapse when, through victories in both the deferred elections, the government obtained a majority of one.

[44]Dafoe Papers, J. W. Dafoe to Mackenzie King, Jan. 10, 1929.
[45]Ibid., Dafoe to Clifford Sifton, March 5, 1929.
[46]Tribune, Aug. 19, 1936.

In 1940 the offer of coalition with all parties was repeated, again before an election was due. This time the proposal was based on a united front for the war effort, a square deal for agriculture, and the suggestion that if all parties stood behind the recommendations of the Royal Commission on Dominion-Provincial Relations, they would have a better chance of implementation. The Conservative, Social Credit, and C.C.F. parties accepted although the C.C.F. insisted that it was joining a non-partisan administration, not a coalition, and that its action was based on a desire to combat what was termed the callous ineptitude of the federal government in dealing with the wheat situation. An informal agreement resulted whereby each party agreed not to contest the seat of a sitting member. Acclamations were general throughout the rural areas and such challenges to the arrangement as did occur came from Winnipeg.

The partnership between Liberal-Progressives and Conservatives lasted until 1950. The C.C.F. withdrew in 1942 when Bracken resigned to lead the national Conservative party, and the Social Credit members virtually lost their identity as a group. Elections in 1945 and again in 1949 were formalities with nearly half the members in each case being returned by acclamation.

The attempt to do away with political parties and govern by coalition came long after the moral basis with which the farmers' movement began had disappeared. Those who made the attempt justified it on various new grounds, arguing among other things that the parliamentary system was too complex and expensive for a province and that the municipal system was preferable. Errick Willis, leader of the Conservative group, expressed the general consensus when he described the province in 1945 as a "king-size municipality."[47] He elaborated this theme in 1949, saying, "It is a well-known fact that the matters dealt with by provincial legislatures are almost identical with those of a municipal council, namely, health, schools and roads and it is a well-accepted fact throughout Canada that municipal affairs should be on a strictly non-partisan basis. . . . It therefore seems logical that by using the process of coalition government we should select the best men in provincial affairs from all parties."[48] Premier Douglas Campbell said much the same thing in a speech on October 18, 1949, at Saint Pierre, and similar sentiments have from time to time been expressed by other provincial leaders.

It is not difficult to expose the absurdity of such an argument. In the first place a province and a municipality are not in any way comparable. Municipalities are creatures of the province, existing and having their

[47]*Winnipeg Free Press*, Sept. 8, 1945.
[48]From a speech by Errick Willis over radio station C.B.W., Oct. 11, 1949.

duties assigned to them by provincial statute. Provinces, within the sphere of jurisdiction assigned to them under the British North America Act, are sovereign bodies and have the full range of parliamentary institutions. In municipalities, covering as they do a very small area and usually containing people of similar economic interests, it is quite possible to practise a form of direct democracy, as is commonly done in referendum votes on money by-laws over a certain figure.

Bracken advocated coalition or non-partisan government on grounds of economy as well. When his offer of coalition was spurned in 1931 he pointed out that "Had a union government been possible an election would have been but a formality and would have saved at least $100,000; the length of the sessions of the legislature could have been reduced to three weeks thus saving $75,000 a year."[49]

The various coalition proposals were also justified on the grounds of emergency situations: the depression in 1931 and 1936; the war, wheat marketing difficulties, and the Rowell-Sirois report in 1940; reconstruction and the tax-rental agreement in 1945; and debt reduction in 1949. It would be uncharitable to blame any government for proposing action, however futile, to combat depression. But the other reasons were presented largely to justify a policy regarded as desirable under any circumstances. No other Canadian province found it necessary to form a coalition at the outbreak of war; it was common for oppositions to pass resolutions offering co-operation in any matters relating to the war effort but it devolved primarily on the federal government in any event. Manitoba's point of view on the recommendations of the Rowell-Sirois Commission was made absolutely clear in the hearings and it is difficult to see how the formation of a non-partisan government could have improved in the slightest degree the chances for their acceptance. At the federal-provincial conference on reconstruction in 1945 Premier Garson never once mentioned that he represented all parties and that all parties were in favour of the federal proposals. The same is true of any published negotiations on tax-rental agreements.

One of the primary reasons for the duration of the coalition and non-partisan administration was that it helped to keep a particular group in office. By 1949 the Conservatives had only nine members in the legislature, four of whom were in the cabinet and found their positions much too comfortable to vacate. On occasion they took stands in direct opposition to the party they represented and when the coalition finally broke up in 1950 three of the four became Liberal-Progressives and stayed on in the cabinet. The fourth, Errick Willis, continued to lead the party until he was replaced by Duff Roblin in 1954.

[49]*Winnipeg Free Press*, Oct. 17, 1931.

Political institutions in Manitoba were severely damaged by coalition and non-partisan government—debate in the legislature almost ceased and the cabinet became a kind of regulatory board, a shadow of what such a body ought to be. The theory, held so strongly by Bracken, Garson, Campbell, and Willis, that political parties were unnecessary, shows how little they understood the parliamentary system which, of course, is based on party government. Indeed, they very nearly succeeded in destroying it.

The Conservative party suffered most, for their organizational base was almost gone when the group emerged from coalition. All that was left in most ridings was an old guard which had last seen its party in office in 1915. Dissension and recrimination were rife in the Conservative caucus between 1950 and the leadership convention of 1954. By that time, there were three contestants—Errick Willis, Arthur Ross, and Duff Roblin. Prior to the actual convention all three candidates stumped the province speaking to delegates and the interested public wherever and whenever they could be assembled. Sometimes they all appeared on the platform at once as, for example, at the delegate convention in East Kildonan on June 10, 1954. A Winnipeg paper commented with accuracy but understatement: "Seldom before has a party leadership race in Canada been fought in public with the candidates appearing on the platform in various constituencies."[50]

The successful candidate, Duff Roblin, immediately set about building a new organization. His rule was to find the best possible man to run in each riding, get him nominated, and build the organization around him. The situation in Gimli was fairly typical. The Conservative organization there had been dead for forty years. Roblin simply went and inquired who was best known to the inhabitants of the area and, learning that it was Dr. George Johnson, sought him out and convinced him that he ought to accept nomination. Johnson was nominated, ran, won, and became minister of health in the Conservative government that took office in 1958. In June 1960 the Progressive Conservative party had an organization in every constituency.

Party Organization

Each rural riding in Manitoba is divided into approximately 25 polls, and in the urban areas the figure is 30 to 35. In each poll, the Conservative constituency associations appoint a poll captain who becomes automatically a member of the constituency association and may be on its executive (the size and composition of which varies from riding to riding). The executive is expected to hold an annual meeting as a mini-

[50]*Tribune*, June 11, 1954.

mum function in an off election year. If a provincial election is in progress it must also call a nominating convention. Rules on who is entitled to attend and vote vary; the common one is that anyone can attend but each is invited to sign a declaration of support for the party, receiving in turn a ballot entitling them to vote on the candidate nominated.

The provincial association has two executive bodies, an executive council which has nearly one hundred members[51] and an executive committee, a body of ten members, which is the effective group and meets as often as necessary at the call of the chair. The annual meeting[52] of the association serves as a forum where party affairs can be debated but this annual debate illustrates a basic difficulty of any such organization. A party needs and must have loyal workers to get out the vote at election time but these loyalists are rarely the best people to formulate policy—sometimes their very loyalty makes them uncritical and sometimes their enthusiasm leads them to present poorly thought out and embarrassing resolutions at the annual meeting. Thus the party uses study groups which have been set up on such subjects as highways, public works, and education. Reports of the groups do not necessarily lead to resolutions, but if they do they are likely to be concise and well worded.

The organization of the Liberal-Progressive party in Manitoba is similar in principle to that of the Conservative but different in points of detail. Each poll has a captain but each captain is automatically a member of the constituency executive. Each riding has an annual meeting[53] and each sends seven delegates to the annual meeting of the provincial association. An official who prefers to remain anonymous described the nominating conventions:

In constituencies where the chances of election are regarded as good the "closed" convention is nearly always adopted. The procedure is to fix the number of voting delegates who may attend from each poll on the basis of the number of voters in the poll according to the last enumeration. . . . The poll captain usually calls a meeting of the voters in the poll to elect the required number of delegates. In constituencies where the party strength is low or where the sitting member of the opposite party is a strong candidate the type of nominating convention employed is usually "open." In such cases

[51]It includes all federal and provincial Progressive Conservative members, two members from each of the seventeen federal constituencies, and ten members elected at large by the annual meeting.

[52]Those entitled to attend are the officers and members of the executive council, the president of each provincial constituency plus five regular and five alternate delegates, two regular and two alternate delegates from each Progressive Conservative students' association, and five regular and five alternates from the Conservative Club of Greater Winnipeg.

[53]In a few the meeting is held every two years if there is nothing pressing to be discussed. In 1960 four out of fifty-seven did not hold an annual meeting.

anyone may attend and vote without regard to past political affiliations. Such conventions are usually called by advertisements and posters.

The Liberal-Progressive leaders see the party organization not just as a means of getting out the vote but also as a means of keeping themselves in touch with public opinion. They also attempt to keep all party officials in touch, from the poll captain up, by means of a series of news letters which are sent out through the year.

Patronage has not played a major rôle in Manitoba politics since 1914 when the Conservative government resigned. But patronage of a minor or even petty nature still has a place. Major government works are now invariably let under tender but if the contractor happens to be sympathetic to the party in power he may employ men who are suggested or make a contribution to the election fund—certainly he would be asked to do both. The party in power also controls a considerable number of appointments, for example, solicitors for the Power Commission or the Manitoba Telephone System. Insurance on public buildings is almost always given to a sympathetic company which can be counted on for a contribution. Should the party in power correspond with the one in Ottawa there is a considerable clamour for support in securing positions that range from postmasters to judgeships.

The organization of the C.C.F. party is substantially different from that of the other two. Membership in the C.C.F. is on a much more formal basis, as the Provincial Constitution states: "All applications for membership shall be subject to the approval of the Provincial Constituency association. Membership cards shall be issued by the Provincial Secretary . . . a member to be in good standing must hold an official card." Each member must pay a minimum annual membership due of three dollars with a special family rate of two dollars for each person thereafter in the same household. Only paid-up members who have held a membership card for at least two months are eligible to vote at the constituency nominating conventions.

The Provincial Council of the Manitoba C.C.F. is made up of the usual officers plus one delegate from each of the ridings where a local association exists. The officers of the Provincial Council plus eight elected members constitute the executive which is responsible for the day-to-day affairs of the party including the arrangements for the mandatory annual convention. Authority is much more highly centralized than in the other parties, the constitution providing that the Provincial Council may "Suspend any Association, unit or member if that Association, unit or member does not conform to the principles, policy, constitution and by-laws of the C.C.F., subject to an appeal to the next annual convention" and further, that "all candidates selected at nominating conventions must receive the endorsation of the Provincial Executive in order to be recognized as the official candidates of the C.C.F."

In its ninety years of history Manitoba has accumulated a great variety of political experience. The province has been a testing ground of French, Roman Catholic, and provincial rights within the federation. It has felt the full brunt of the effect of national economic policy on provincial economic life. Its governments have known boom and depression—crop failure and crop surplus. Its political parties have reflected corruption and machine politics, reform and retrenchment. At least one lesson emerges with complete clarity from this experience—it is that political parties are fundamental in the democratic process.

THE LEGISLATURE

5

THE DISCHARGE of the central law-making function of a legislature based on the parliamentary system is made possible by a variety of rules and conventions. There must be a body of internal procedure designed to combine free discussion and scrutiny of proposed legislation with the greatest possible efficiency in the dispatch of public business. Any legislature must have a set of rules and statutes to ensure, or at least make possible, the individual dignity and freedom of its members and the collective authority and independence of the House. Special provisions and procedures are necessary for the raising and spending of public money. Finally and obviously there must be the representative machinery and electoral system by which the laws that the legislature passes are kept in accord with the general will of the people.

All Canadian legislative bodies were formed from a common mould—that of the British Parliament. However, local circumstances have made it inevitable that the replicas are not exact. The Manitoba Act of 1870 gave a provisional outline of legislative organization, providing a bicameral structure with a legislative council of seven members appointed for life and an elective assembly of twenty-four. Six years after the province was created the legislative council was abolished, at Ottawa's demand, for entirely financial reasons. The upper house had been, from the provincial point of view, a useful part of the legislative machinery, for its members had all been prominent both in the community and in the government under the Hudson's Bay Company régime and hence formed a link between the old and the new. The advice its members tendered, individually and collectively, to the first two lieutenant governors had often helped to smooth the way in a most difficult period of transition.

Unfortunately, Manitoba could not afford the council. The proportion of its scanty revenues (69.5 per cent) devoted to legislative organization was excessive. Moreover, nearly 90 per cent of the revenue came from federal subsidies, and in 1874 when an appeal was made for more a subcommittee of the Mackenzie cabinet refused it, writing: "It appears to the sub-committee that the present form of government should be simplified and cheapened by the abolition of the second chamber."[1] Manitoba had no choice but to co-operate and at the next session a bill to abolish the council passed the assembly without debate or dissent. The council, understandably, rejected the bill. A second bill introduced one year later met the same fate. Before the measure was introduced for the third time the Lieutenant Governor took the precaution of guaranteeing several members of the council equally remunerative jobs elsewhere. This time it passed.

The Franchise

For the first eighteen years of provincial history the franchise was extended only to those who were the owners of property or tenants. The Lieutenant Governor drew up rules for the first election, limiting the right to vote to householders.[2] The statute of 1871,[3] which replaced his proclamation, specified that a voter must have owned property to the value of one hundred dollars for one year prior to the election or have been a tenant paying a yearly rental of at least twenty dollars. Property qualifications, although revised in 1886, were retained in some form until 1888.

In 1901 the government made an attempt to impose a literacy test which declared a resident ineligible if he were not "a British subject by birth who has not resided in some portion of . . . Canada for at least seven years preceding the date of registration . . . unless such person is able to read any selected portion of 'The Manitoba Act' in . . . English, French, German, Icelandic or any Scandinavian language."[4] Premier Roblin stated during the debate on the literacy bill that it was aimed at recent immigrants from the Ukraine and Central Europe whom he feared might gain control and destroy British institutions. He argued that denial of the vote to those of this group who were illiterate was justified since

[1]Canada, *Sessional Papers*, 1875, Paper 36, p. 3.
[2]A householder was defined as "Master or chief of a household; one who keeps house with his family. A householder does not mean a lodger, nor a tenant of part of a house, unless he has a separate maintenance and table enjoyed by himself and his dependants, distinct from other householders."
[3]*Statutes of Manitoba*, 1871, c. 5.
[4]*Ibid.*, 1901, c. 11, s. 17(e).

"they take no interest in the affairs of this country and are incapable of learning about them."[5] However, there is ample evidence that all who would agree to vote Conservative were encouraged to do so regardless of race or ability to read. Newspapers of the time are full of charges that the immigrant vote was purchased wholesale, charges substantiated by many Ukrainians who remember the period.

The secret ballot was used for the first time in the provincial election of 1888, voting prior to that year being by a show of hands at an open meeting or by declaration to the returning officer. In Manitoba, as in Britain and in other Canadian provinces, the secret ballot was originally under a cloud of suspicion. John Norquay, the Premier, frustrated attempts in 1878 and in 1885 to have it legalized on the grounds that secrecy sapped the citizens courage, promoted evasion, as a temptation to lie, and generally gave rise to "immorality and duplicity."[6] To prove his point he cited examples from the United States where, because of secrecy, candidates had actually received fewer votes than had been promised. But by 1888 Norquay had apparently reached the conclusion that the immorality and duplicity stimulated by secrecy would be outweighed by its advantages and provision for the ballot was included in a government bill of that year.[7]

Manitoba has the honour of being the first province in Canada to give the vote to women.[8] The first organization to take up the question was the Women's Christian Temperance Union which in 1893 organized a petition for universal suffrage signed by between four and five thousand for presentation to the legislature. The petition was presented by W. McNaught who spoke in support and advanced such arguments as feminine intuition to be used in the assessment of candidates, and the fact that "man was made of dust but women out of a better material —Adam's rib."[9] The petition was rejected as was a similar one a year later. The battle was then taken up by the Equal Suffrage Society of Manitoba which adopted the reassuring motto of "peace on earth and good will toward men." The wave of prosperity and expansion that began about 1900, however, turned public attention to more pressing matters and the movement dropped out of sight for a decade. It was revived in 1911 with the formation of the Political Equality League, this time receiving the active and powerful support of the United Farmers of

[5]*Winnipeg Free Press*, March 31, 1901.
[6]*Ibid.*, April 29, 1885.
[7]*Statutes of Manitoba*, 1888, c. 2.
[8]The Municipal Act of 1886 gave women the same right as men to vote in municipal elections if they could meet the property qualifications.
[9]*Winnipeg Free Press*, March 3, 1893.

Manitoba. In 1914 the Liberal party took up the cause and included the following resolution in its platform: "The Liberal party, believing that there are no just grounds for debarring women from the right to vote, will enact a measure for equal suffrage, upon it being established by petition that this is desired by adult women to a number equivalent to 15 per cent. of the vote cast at the preceding general election in this Province."[10]

The suffragettes, led by an unusually brilliant speaker in the person of Mrs. Nellie McClung, played a large part in the campaign of 1914. When Roblin was re-elected, the political Equality League tried first a direct approach by a representative armed with a signed petition. Mrs. McClung was the representative and in her autobiography recorded Roblin's answer:

"It would never do to let you speak to the Cabinet," he said, in the tone that one uses to a naughty child. "Even if they listened to you, which I doubt, you would upset them and I don't want that to happen. They are good fellows—they do what they are told to do now. Every government has to have a head, and I'm the head of this one; and I don't want dissension and arguments. . . . No, you can't come in here and make trouble for my boys, just when I have them trotting easy and eating out of my hand. Now you forget all this nonsense about women voting. . . . You're a fine, smart young woman, I can see that. And take it from me, nice women don't want the vote."[11]

Orthodox agitation and the usual political processes having proved futile the women turned to the more devastating method of ridicule. A mock parliament with Nellie McClung, who was an accomplished mimic, as premier, was held in the Walker Theatre. According to newspaper reports it was an unqualified success and drew a large crowd, including some of the Conservative politicians. Mrs. McClung, on being presented with a bogus petition from the men asking for the right to vote, is reported to have paraphrased a recent speech by Roblin as follows:

We wish to compliment this delegation on their splendid gentlemanly appearance. If, without exercising the vote, such splendid specimens of manhood can be produced, such a system of affairs should not be interfered with. Any system of civilization that can produce such splendid specimens . . . is good enough for me, and if it is good enough for me it is good enough for anybody. Another trouble is that if men start to vote they will vote too much. Politics unsettles men, and unsettled men mean unsettled bills— broken furniture, broken vows and divorce.
It has been charged that politics is corrupt. I don't know how this report got out, but I do most emphatically deny it. . . . I have been in politics for

[10]*Canadian Annual Review*, 1914, p. 590.
[11]Nellie McClung, *The Stream Runs Fast*, p. 109.

a long time and I never knew of any corruption or division of public money among the members of the house, and you may be sure that if anything of that kind had been going on I should have been in on it.[12]

Nothing could embarrass Roblin to the extent that he would give in and agree to proposals coming from a movement "supported by men who wear long hair and women who wear short hair." He considered Mrs. McClung a "rather conceited young woman who had perhaps some success at Friday afternoon school house entertainments and so was labouring under the delusion that she had the gift of oratory."[13] Only after his defeat in 1916 and the election of the Norris government did the women win the franchise. The *Free Press* described the scene in the legislature: "Amid scenes of unparalleled enthusiasm the Bill to amend the Manitoba Elections Act so as to give the suffrage to women of the province on the same terms as the men was passed in the legislature yesterday. When the third reading had been given the bill, the ladies thronged the galleries, stood up and in the rich soprano of one hundred female voices sang O Canada."[14]

Proportional Representation

The province of Manitoba had more than thirty years of experience with the Hare system of proportional representation in the urban area of Winnipeg and the single transferable vote in the rural areas. There were two main reasons for the introduction of proportional representation. The first was a sincere desire of the reform movement that sponsored it to build a democratic society that would more closely approximate the equalitarian ideal. Secondly, proportional representation was seen as a device which would assist in controlling the political machine and help to break the hold which the Eastern-dominated Liberal and Conservative parties had on the province.

Proportional representation had been one of the planks in the platform of the Canadian Council of Agriculture in 1916. The Hare-Spence system was tried, apparently satisfactorily, in the election of officers at the 1919 convention of the United Farmers of Alberta. The *Winnipeg Free Press* vigorously championed its adoption in the province of Manitoba as numerous editorials on the subject testify. The paper saw proportional representation as a device that would aid in the "widespread rebellion against the old by-partisan system"[15] and argued that, hitherto, "the

---

[12]Catherine Lyle Cleverdon, *The Woman Suffrage Movement in Canada*, p. 59.
[13]Margaret Zieman, "Nellie was a Lady Terror," *Maclean's*, Oct. 1, 1953.
[14]*Winnipeg Free Press*, Feb. 15, 1916.
[15]*Ibid.*, Jan. 6, 1920.

electors have been able to vote only for candidates firmly attached to a party organization . . . because a third candidate of independent views, or sympathies, in one party or the other, without being closely bound, generally drew votes from one side and made the election of the other candidate a virtual certainty."[16] Proportional representation would change this by breaking the hold of party organization and thus eliminate the excitement and bitterness . . . and make old-time strategy useless."[17] Other arguments used by the *Free Press* were that the floating vote often exercised a disproportionate effect on the outcome of an election, that minorities are frequently without representation, that good men often refuse to stand for election if they have to identify themselves with a party, that voters (under the X ballot) are often discouraged by the ineffectiveness of their vote and hence abstain and, finally, that proportional representation is more democratic.

Most of these arguments were repeated and elaborated in the editorials of the *Grain Growers' Guide*; however this paper gave much more attention to the concept that political parties as they had developed in Canada were inherently evil and that democracy would be good only if the art of politics were substantially changed. Arthur Hawkes, a Toronto journalist, wrote to Crerar: "Your people appear to believe that there exists in this country a large body of good men and women who if called together without the detested arts of politics will bring down from heaven happiness in flowing robes of pure white."[18] The *Grain Growers' Guide* saw the adoption of proportional representation as one step in the direction of an ideal democracy.

The amendment to the Manitoba Election Act passed at the 1924 session of the legislature was designed to correct many of the injustices.[19] It provided for the introduction of the Hare system within Greater Winnipeg, which was made one constituency to return ten members.[20] The rural constituencies were left as single-member ridings using the alternative or preferential voting system.

This scheme worked quite differently from the system advocated by such enthusiasts for proportional representation as John Stuart Mill, Thomas Hare, and J. F. S. Ross. The crucial factor in the mechanics of proportional representation is the size of the constituency. If the mathematical concept of electoral justice on which proportional representation rests is to be given full play and if there are one hundred seats to be filled, a vote of one per cent of the total cast should elect

16*Ibid.*
17*Ibid.*, July 5, 1920.
18P.A.M., Crerar Papers, Arthur Hawkes to T. A. Crerar, Sept. 5, 1925.
19*Statutes of Manitoba*, 1924, c. 15.
20Changed in 1949 to three four-member constituencies.

one member. Hence, the larger the constituency the better. However, this principle of full proportionality almost always must be adapted to that of territory. The advocates of proportional representation argue with good logic that where the number of seats in a constituency is less than five there ceases to be any proportionality between votes cast and members elected. Since Winnipeg was divided in 1949 into three four-member constituencies it has been as close to the majority system as to a proper system of proportional representation.

In the rural areas the single transferable vote has been used. It does nothing for proportionality between votes cast and members elected but simply assures that the winning candidate will have a majority rather than a plurality. In fact the results are almost exactly the same as if a straight X were used. In the 1953 election in every rural constituency except one the candidate who received the highest number of first choices was, after the formality of a transfer had been completed, declared elected. In less than ten cases since the system was introduced has the result been different from what would have been obtained under the old system.

Proportional representation of the type advocated by its most prominent apologists in the nineteenth century has never really been tried, except in Winnipeg, and the low density of population in most of the province makes it inconceivable that it should be. The principles of territory, community, and common interests are of more importance in the rural areas than the possibility of being represented proportionally to the nearest whole member. The best that can be said for the hybrid system of proportional representation used in Manitoba is that the worst results forecast by its critics have not occurred. Only in Winnipeg has there been a tendency for splinter parties to spring up. With the strong emphasis on coalition in the province between 1930 and 1950, parties of any kind except the winning combination have been looked upon askance. In 1949 there were 19 acclamations out of a house of 55 seats, thus making elections under any voting system superfluous.

The one concrete result of the system has been to strengthen an already dominant rural electorate at the expense of the urban area of Winnipeg whose voting record stands in marked contrast to that of the rest of the province. Independent and Labour candidates have been successful where they would not have been elected under a simple ballot. The second choices of those voting for Independent candidates often went to the C.C.F. or Labour and vice versa. In the 1936 election, for example, Lewis St. G. Stubbs had a surplus of 17,591 on the first count. The transfer of this surplus was directly responsible for the election of three Labour or C.C.F. candidates on the same ballot.

The secretary of the Proportional Representation Society of Britain analysed the Manitoba system in 1954 and certified that he was completely satisfied with it.[21] He was one of the few who was—at the 1955 session of the legislature a majority of members voted to abolish the entire system.[22] Winnipeg was broken up into single-member constituencies and the ordinary ballot has been used in both rural and urban areas in all provincial elections held since.

Redistribution of Seats in the Legislature

Redistribution of seats in the Legislative Assembly of Manitoba has passed through three broad phases of development and recently entered a fourth. In the first phase the electoral boundaries were drawn in conformity with the racial and religious composition of the electorate. The second phase was characterized by a moderate use of the device of gerrymandering. The third phase (from 1890 to 1956) can be described only as haphazard and based on no apparent principle, good or bad. This is still true for the rest of Canada but Manitoba has been more fortunate: the last redistribution was carried out by an independent commission as subsequent ones will be.

During the first few years of the province's history the twenty-four electoral divisions corresponded roughly with parish boundaries and, as the population was then distributed, this amounted to equality in representation between English and French, Protestant and Catholic. The steady influx of English settlers and the rapid growth of new townships outside the old parish divisions upset the balance very quickly, however, and English members of the legislature began in 1873 to demand representation by population. The Redistribution Bill of 1879 in answer to these demands provided for eight electoral divisions within the French and Roman Catholic parishes, eight for the old English parishes, and eight for newly settled and outlying townships. In 1881 the square survey replaced the parish system and religion and race no longer determined the ratio between French and English.

In 1886 Premier Norquay tried his hand at gerrymandering. The real masters of the art in Ottawa and parts of the United States would have considered his efforts modest. Territory considered to be solidly Conservative was transferred to doubtful constituencies only when the two areas were adjacent; hence the constituencies retained a plausible shape in contrast to the surrealistic outlines given by Sir John A. Macdonald to Ontario in 1882. The Greenway redistribution measure of

[21]*Voting in Democracies* (London, 1954), p. 212 (quoting report of John Fitzgerald to the Proportional Representation Society of Britain).
[22]*Statutes of Manitoba*, 1955, c. 17.

1892 was another attempt to protect the government against defeat by rearranging the constituencies more advantageously. The riding of Dufferin, which in the previous election had returned R. P. Roblin, the foremost critic of the administration, was completely abolished. Roblin was forced to run in Morden where, to Greenway's entire satisfaction, he was defeated. The ridings known as Morris and Cartier whose representatives had deserted the Liberals for the Conservatives in the previous session were combined. Some areas thought to be permanently Liberal were encouraged to send out sprouts from which the same stock might grow, for example the new riding of Avondale which was formed by decreasing the size of several other constituencies. Unfortunately the sprout was a "sport" and much to the chagrin of the gardeners it flourished Conservative.

Since the turn of the century four redistribution bills have been framed by committees of the legislature, each seeming to add to the illogicality of its predecessors. It would be tedious and unenlightening to examine them in detail but the situation prevailing immediately before the independent commission took over in 1957 is of interest, if only to underline the magnitude of the commission's task. In June 1952 there were 228,280 registered voters living in urban areas returning 17 members and 224,083 in rural areas returning 40 members. There were many examples of a wide discrepancy between comparable rural and urban constituencies. St. Clements, for example, had nearly double the number of electors of any other rural riding and the urban district of Kildonan-Transcona had nearly twenty thousand electors on the roll, while Winnipeg North had just over eleven thousand. The constituency of Kildonan-Transcona consisted of the entire municipalities of East and West Kildonan and the town of Transcona despite the fact that no geographic or economic bonds exist among any of the three parts. East and West Kildonan are separated by the Red River and there are no connecting bridges. No road or highway leads directly from East Kildonan to Transcona. Economically there is no connection between Transcona and the two Kildonans and the latter are more competitive with than complementary to each other, in that each desires more industry. In short the constituency as it was could not be represented.

These inconsistencies have now been corrected. For the first time in Canadian history the redistribution of 1957 was carried out by an independent commission operating under terms of reference set by the legislature and not by a legislative committee dominated by a government majority. A select committee of the legislature was struck during the 1953 session to consider the best means of drawing electoral boundaries. It sat intermittently for two years and after hearing briefs from interested parties and making a careful study of the British and Australian systems recommended a commission. The Act which gave effect to this recommendation was passed at the 1955 session of the legislature.[23]

The Electoral Divisions Boundaries Commission consists of three men: "the person who, from time to time, is Chief Justice of Manitoba, the person who, from time to time, is President of the University of Manitoba and the person who, from time to time, is Chief Electoral Officer."[24] The Commission is given two sets of instructions in the Act creating it, the first specific, the second general. The fifty-seven seats in the legislature must be divided between urban and rural in the ratio of seven to four. The Act sets out the boundaries of the urban areas and all else is considered rural. The Commission must establish a quota— the population divided by the number of seats assigned—for both; the number of people in any constituency may not vary from the quota by more than 5 per cent. The number of rural seats is 36 and this figure divided into the rural population produces a quota of 11,516. The quota for urban[25] seats, established in the same way, is 20,197. The second injunction is that in fixing the boundaries of any electoral division the Commission is required to take into account the community or diversity of interests of the population, the means of communication between the various parts, the physical features, and "all other similar and relevant factors."

The Commission handed its first report to the Premier in February 1957 and its recommendations were accepted without change by the legislature. The report suggests that, before the next decennial redistribution, consideration be given to allowing a maximum variation of more than 5 per cent, a figure which did not allow sufficient weight to be given to community of interest, communications, and topography.

Personnel

The legal qualifications of a candidate for a seat in the Manitoba Legislative Assembly are simply that he or she be twenty-one years of age or over, a British subject by birth or naturalization, resident in the province for at least one year preceding the date of the election writ, and not, by reason of corrupt practices, ineligible for any other Canadian

[23]*Ibid.*
[24]*Ibid.*, s. 2. An amendment passed in 1957 makes the following provision for alternatives if any of the three are unable to serve or because of vacancy in the office: for the chief justice of Manitoba, the chief justice of the Court of Queen's Bench; for the president of the University of Manitoba, the dean of the Faculty of Arts and Science; and for the chief electoral officer, the comptroller general.
[25]This actually means Greater Winnipeg, as the city of Brandon, the only other urban area, is assigned one seat by subsection 6D(4) of the Act.

legislative body. A person otherwise qualified is not eligible if a member of the Senate or House of Commons of Canada or any other provincial legislature or legislative council.[26]

Any elected member is disqualified if he accepts an office of profit or emolument under the Crown or if he holds a contract with the government, either by himself or through a trustee or third party. A legislator may, however, be a shareholder or director of a company having contracts with the government provided that the contracts do not call for the building of public works. Any member may also buy and hold provincial securities on the same terms as any other citizen. All members are solemnly assured by the appropriate statute that they may avail themselves of the facilities of the government-owned telephone system or the power commission without resigning their seats.[27]

The general rule prohibiting any elected member from holding an office of profit or emolument under the Crown would, if strictly interpreted and enforced, make the formation of a cabinet illegal because a cabinet minister is a salaried official. This situation was first covered by a statute in 1872 which provided that a member on being sworn to cabinet office for the first time had to return to his constituents for re-election but not if returned while holding cabinet office. This situation was further clarified in 1875 by a statute specifying that the holder of a particular office might resign and take another within one month without the necessity of re-election. These rules had to be waived for Winnipeg when, with the introduction of proportional representation in 1924, the city became one large ten-member constituency. The rule was retained for rural seats but changed in 1927 so that any member could be appointed to the cabinet without re-election if the appointment took place within one year of the last general election. And in 1937 electoral re-confirmation for members accepting cabinet office was abandoned completely.

It is often said that elections are not won by prayers. In Manitoba the monetary supplement to any prayers that are offered is regulated. An individual member is allowed only personal expenses which are defined in the Act as rent for halls, reasonable travelling expenses, and advertising. Each elected member must, within thirty days after election, file with the chief electoral officer a sworn and itemized account of his

[26]This disqualification did not exist for the first four years of provincial history but was first enacted in the *Statutes of Manitoba*, 1874, c. 16. There are several examples between 1870 and 1874 of simultaneous membership in the House of Commons at Ottawa and the Legislative Assembly of Manitoba.

[27]This is specifically stated in the Manitoba Telephone Act, s. 27, and the Manitoba Power Commission Act, s. 48.

expenses for publication in the *Manitoba Gazette*. Should a member fail to do this his seat could be forfeited. The general or central committee of any political party is allowed a maximum expenditure of $15,000 for any one election and the purposes for which this money may be spent are specified by law. The parties must also file a detailed return but this is not published. Any voter may inspect the statements on file for a fee of twenty-five cents but few do or know that they can. A cynic might write off the formal statements of election expenses as window dressing but, at the risk of seeming naïve, it can be said that Manitoba political life is exceptionally honest.

A tabulation of the occupations of members of the legislature is interesting in several ways. As can be seen from Table III, it follows closely basic changes in the economic structure of the province. Two groups

TABLE III
OCCUPATIONAL GROUPS IN THE MANITOBA LEGISLATURE

	Percentage 1870–90	Percentage 1890–1920	Percentage 1920–61
Merchants	10	23	5
Farmers	18	33	42
Physicians	8	6	6
Lawyers	18	17	20
Traders	15	—	—
Land surveyors	8	—	—
Business	5	5	13
Teachers	—	—	6
Publishers	8	4	—
Real estate	5	2	—
Agents	—	—	1
Implement agents	—	2	1
Miscellaneous	4	8	6

that were of major importance before 1900, the traders and the land surveyors, have completely disappeared. The decline in the number of merchants and grain dealers in the legislature after 1920 is explained partly by centralized marketing under the Pools and partly by the rise of compulsory marketing under the Wheat Board. Farmers, as might be expected, have grown steadily in importance and the administrations since 1920 have been "farmers'" governments in fact as well as in name.

The occupational background of the members of the legislature is perhaps of less significance than its racial composition.[28] One index of

28The racial composition of Manitoba as recorded in the 1951 census was: British: 46.7; Ukrainian: 12.7; French: 8.5; German: 7.0; Netherland: 5.4; Polish: 4.9; Scandinavian: 4.2; and Jewish: 2.4.

degree of integration into the provincial melting pot of the main non-British groups is their participation in the provincial assembly and the institutions of local government.

The Ukrainians, who form the largest single group apart from the Anglo-Saxons, first came to Manitoba in small numbers in 1892 but successive waves of immigration since then have raised their numbers to nearly ninety thousand.[29] Ukrainian participation in business, professional, and political life began to be significant only after 1920. In earlier years the typical Ukrainian was either struggling with a newly acquired homestead or, because of the language difficulty, employed as an unskilled labourer. J. S. Woodsworth wrote in 1908:

> Much of the rough work of nation-building in Western Canada is being done by the despised Galician [Ukrainian]. The unskilled labor for which contractors and railway builders have been loudly calling is supplied principally by the Galician. In the cities and the towns, where new works are being pushed to rapid completion, or out on the farthest stretches of the prairie, where the steel is being laid for the coming settler, can be found the the grimy, stolid Galician, puffing his ever-present cigarette and working with a physical endurance bred of centuries of peasant life and an indifference to hardships that seems characteristic of the Slav.[30]

Municipal government was the first area in which Ukrainians participated in the political life of Manitoba. Because of an early tendency to settle in groups they came to have a numerical majority in at least half a dozen municipalities and it was inevitable that candidates of their race would eventually take over the municipal offices in such districts. The first occurred in 1908 when Ivan Storosczuk became reeve of the rural municipality of Stuartburn. Since then more than seventy men of Ukrainian origin have been reeves or mayors of Manitoba municipalities. In several instances a predominantly Anglo-Saxon community has elected a Ukrainian to its highest civil office—Mayor Juba of Winnipeg is, perhaps, the best-known example. Participation in the legislature began with the election of T. D. Ferley as an Independent in the constituency of Gimli in 1915. Since then twenty-one Ukrainians have been members and since 1940 the average number in a fifty-seven member house has been seven. Members of Ukrainian origin are also beginning to hold prominent positions. N. V. Backynsky was elected speaker in 1950, John R. Solomon became deputy speaker in 1953, and in 1954 H. N. Hryhurczuk became, on his appointment to the office of attorney general, the first Ukrainian to hold cabinet rank.

[29]For a full account see Paul Yuzyk, *The Ukrainians in Manitoba.*
[30]J. S. Woodsworth, *Strangers within Our Gates*, p. 135.

The Polish group in Manitoba,[31] on the other hand, has taken little part in the public affairs of the province and has yet to elect a representative in the legislature or a reeve in a municipality from among its members. The Polish immigrants did not bring with them any experience in the art of self-government and their numbers have not been large enough to make possible the formation of a majority in any town or village. They have tended to be absorbed into the Ukrainian communities and more than 20 per cent of them use Ukrainian as their language.

Mennonites first came to Manitoba in 1874 and there are now nearly forty thousand in the province. They brought with them a church-dominated communal organization and for more than ten years governed themselves quite apart from provincial laws. Justices of the peace, commissioners for taking affidavits, and coroners were not appointed in Mennonite settlements until the late 1880's—these functions were carried out by officers of the church. Even after the organization of municipalities within the Mennonite settlements the officers of the church automatically became municipal officials and carried on according to their own customs until after 1900. The church was the government for these communities and political participation was forbidden. As E. K. Francis, who has made a thorough study of the Mennonite settlements, wrote: "Any appeal to the courts or other authorities of the country was declared a grave sin. If a Mennonite was perchance summoned before a judge or magistrate, he had to submit to indictment and fine without the slightest attempt to defend himself. . . . The church ban was an almost omnipotent means of social control, a sanction whose impact was more painful than jail or fine."[32] Among the second-generation Mennonites there is an increasing tendency towards participation in public life and the old church laws against it are no longer strictly enforced. Most Mennonites now vote and some have held municipal office.

---

[31]Polish settlement in Manitoba can be traced as far back as 1817 when a Polish regiment of De Meuron soldiers employed by Lord Selkirk was sent to Red River and a few became settlers. Growth of Polish population is shown in the table below:

	1901	1911	1921	1931	1941	1951
Numbers	1,674	12,321	16,594	36,550	40,243	57,933
Per cent of provincial population	.66	2.70	2.70	5.70	3.00	4.90

(Manitoba in 1951 had 17.2 per cent of the total Polish population in Canada.)
[32]E. K. Francis, *In Search of Utopia: The Mennonites in Manitoba*, p. 85.

The Icelandic group in Manitoba[33] has participated fully in public affairs and in fact has made notable contributions to the political life of the province. The Icelanders brought with them a long tradition of parliamentary government and quickly became a source of strength for the institutions of local government in the areas in which they settled. They have had periodic representation on the Winnipeg city council since 1892. An Icelander was first elected to the legislature in 1896 and since then twenty have been members.

Numerous writers on political science have stressed the importance of municipal institutions both as a means of education in the art of self-government and as a training ground for future politicians. Lord Durham suggested in his report that the partial failure of representative government in Lower Canada was due largely to the lack of municipal organization and De Tocqueville credited the success of democracy in New England to the strength of units of local administration. In Manitoba over the years, about 40 per cent of the total membership of the legislature has had previous experience in local government, and the institutions of local government have undoubtedly contributed to the political education of the immigrants. There is, however, some doubt if the quality of a legislator who is not a newcomer to the country is improved by previous experience in municipal government in which there is very little room for policy making because of the narrow range of its autonomy. The work of a municipal officer is mainly administration of the most routine character. Acclamations are common and a candidate may easily attain municipal office without ever having fought an election. A man who comes to the legislature after twenty years as secretary-treasurer of a rural municipality may easily bring with him a set of rather narrow, petty, but firm attitudes. It is quite possible that he will peer at provincial affairs through the end of a municipal drain-pipe.

Privilege

The phrase parliamentary privilege refers, in its broadest sense, to the power of a parliament or an assembly to maintain its authority, safeguard its independence and dignity, regulate its own proceedings, and protect its members from interference with the performance of their

[33]The Icelanders established their first colony in Manitoba in 1875 in the Interlake region which until 1882 was a part of the district of Keewatin. The census does not show Icelandic as a racial origin but it estimates that there are approximately 25,000 in Manitoba. For a full discussion see S. J. Sommerville, "Early Icelandic Settlements in Canada," *Proceedings of the Manitoba Historical and Scientific Society, 1944–45.*

duties. The history of privilege in Britain is a long one, springing as it does from the rights of Parliament as a court, and developing rapidly in the Tudor and Stuart periods when Parliament was attempting to assert its independence from the monarch. In the older Canadian provinces where the local assemblies struggled to win a full measure of authority and complete protection for their members parliamentary privilege is as cherished a possession as it is in Britain.[34] But in Manitoba there is, of course, no such tradition. Privilege has always had a purely utilitarian function, being essential for the efficient and dignified conduct of public business. There was, however, a brief struggle with the federal government before the Manitoba legislature won the right to confer privilege on its members. The first statute on this subject was disallowed[35]—in keeping with the policy of Sir John A. Macdonald established in 1869 when he nullified similar acts passed by Quebec and Ontario. The ground in each case was that a provincial legislature had no inherent right to confer privileges on itself or its members. The federal Parliament, Macdonald argued, had such a right with the limitation that privileges conferred were not to exceed those of the Imperial Parliament. The provincial legislatures were subject to no such limitation and might, if unchecked, confer privileges and immunities indiscriminately.

The whole question of the rights and powers of provincial legislatures was aired before the Judicial Committee of the Privy Council in 1896. The Mayor of Truro had been sentenced by the Nova Scotia assembly following his refusal to appear and answer for an alleged libel on one of its members. He appealed on the grounds that the Legislative Assembly Act of 1876 was *ultra vires*. The result was a confirmation of the validity of the Act as coming within the meaning of section 92 of the British North America Act as well as being consistent with the Colonial Laws Validity Act.[36] The specific mention of section 92 made the Legislative Assembly Acts of the new province of Manitoba valid.[37]

[34]For an account of the early history of the assembly in Nova Scotia see J. M. Beck, "Privileges and Powers of the Nova Scotia House of Assembly," *Dalhousie Review*, Winter (1956).

[35]*Statutes of Manitoba*, 1873, c. 2.

[36]Olmsted, *Decisions of the Judicial Committee*, I, 373.

[37]Arthur Beauchesne, a recognized authority on procedure and privilege, refuses to admit that provincial legislatures are parliaments. In an article in the *Canadian Bar Review* he wrote: "The judgement in the Fielding-Thomas case does not increase the function of the Nova Scotia legislature any more than the condemnation of Galileo by the Privy Council at the time prevented the earth from turning." *Canadian Bar Review*, XXII (1944), p. 146. For an illuminating discussion of the question in an earlier period, see Alpheus Todd, *Parliamentary Government in the British Colonies* (London, 1880), Part II.

At present the privileges of the individual members and the rights of the assembly and its committees are governed by a statute of 1937 which for the most part repeats the customary privileges of the British Parliament. Complete freedom of speech is obviously necessary in any legislature and the legal basis for this freedom is provided in Manitoba law by guaranteeing its members legal immunity in any actions that might arise from anything said in the assembly or in its committees. The same immunity extends to members in regard to any act done under authority of the legislature whether or not it is in session. No member is liable for civil action for debt or other cause while the assembly is in session. All these protections apply in the standing committees (and are usually extended to special committees) both to members and to any witnesses who are summoned or who appear of their own volition.

The members are protected in another way in that certain acts that might be committed by people outside the house could be tried in the assembly as breaches of privilege or contempt of court. Ten possible offences are listed in the Act, the most important of which are assaults, insults to or libels on a member during a session, any attempt to intimidate or bribe a member, and, in general, any deliberate obstruction of the business of the house. If such powers were used (and they never have been in Manitoba) the procedure would be a warrant for arrest issued by the speaker, a trial before the bar of the house, and a final sentence which cannot be appealed.

The legislature as a body has the power to compel the attendance of witnesses before it and can also compel the production of information relevant to the decisions it may be in the process of making. In any hearing conducted before it, the assembly has all the rights, powers, and privileges of a court of record. By statute, all the standing committees have a similar power with respect to the presentation and hearing of evidence and this power is always extended to special committees where it is necessary.

The assembly also imposes certain prohibitions on its members, the most important of which forbids a member to accept compensation for anything he might do in respect to any legislation, claim, or controversy. It may also discipline its own members "to the end that all debates may be grave and orderly."[38] A mild form of discipline, being called to order by the speaker, is, of course, a daily and routine occurrence during a session. Should a member wilfully violate the rules of the house he

[38]*Rules, Orders and Forms of Proceeding of the Legislative Assembly of Manitoba* (1954), p. 75.

may be censured by the speaker. He must then make amends and desist and should he fail to do so the speaker has full authority to have him ejected to await the pleasure of the house.

Procedure

The opening of a session of the legislature in Manitoba is one of the great events of the winter social season. An impressive ceremony is staged for a distinguished gathering, with the lieutenant governor playing the main part. When he enters the grounds the lieutenant governor is greeted by a salute of fifteen guns after which he inspects a guard of honour. He is then conducted to a reception room where a procession consisting of the cabinet and premier and senior officers of the armed forces is formed up to enter the chamber. On the occasion of the opening of a new house there are certain formalities which are not repeated in subsequent sessions. The first is to elect a speaker. The clerk informs the members that the lieutenant governor does not choose to reveal his reasons for summoning the assembly until a speaker has been chosen and directs them to proceed at once. When this has been accomplished the lieutenant governor enters the chamber and reads the speech from the throne. The first business after the speech is always the introduction of a fictitious bill (an act respecting the administration of oaths of office) to indicate that the peoples' business is to be attended to before the "royal instructions" are carried out. Following this an address in reply is moved by the premier and seconded by two members who are followed by the leader of the opposition.

There are three different procedures by which a bill becomes law and the one used depends on whether the bill is a public bill, a private bill, or a financial bill.[39] Public bills are introduced into the house on a motion for leave which is debatable. The debate, if there is one, must centre around the objects and principles of the bill. After leave is granted the bill is read (meaning simply that its number and title are cited) for the first time. It is then automatically given a place on the order paper which fixes a day for second reading. In the interval the bill is printed and distributed. When the order of the day is called for second reading the speaker asks if it is the pleasure of the house that

[39]Public bills deal with matters of general public concern and may be introduced either by a member of the cabinet, in which case they are known as government bills, or by a private member, who may or may not be a government supporter, in which case they are known as private member bills. Private bills are narrower in scope and usually deal with an individual, a corporation, or a special locality. Bills dealing with the raising or spending of public money are always "government bills" but are referred to as financial bills.

the bill be read a second time. If, after debate, the bill is accepted for second reading, the house is committed to accept it in principle but not necessarily in detail.

Unless specifically referred to a standing or select committee, a public bill after a second reading goes directly to the committee of the whole house. If it is referred it must, on being reported back, be considered by the committee of the whole which is simply the house sitting as a body, with the deputy speaker as chairman. The rules of debate are relaxed to permit direct questions across the floor and the bill is considered section by section. In Manitoba the committee of the whole has wide powers and may make amendments including those that change the character of the bill and require an alteration in title. When the bill is reported back to the house and proposed changes have been accepted or rejected it is ready for third reading. It is rare to have a debate on third reading because it has become the mechanism for final passage. The only other step necessary to make the "bill" an "act" is the assent of the lieutenant governor.

The procedure on private bills is quite different. Before a private bill can be brought before the house several procedural requirements must be met. The house must be satisfied that no other interests would be prejudicially affected if the favour asked for is granted. The sponsoring party is therefore required to publish advance notice of the proposed bill setting out its nature and objects. He must then pay a fee to the provincial treasurer in accordance with an established schedule of charges. The introduction of the bill takes the form of a petition praying for leave. If it is granted (and it is rarely refused) the petition and other papers are referred, without motion, to the committee on private bills. If this committee finds that all is in order it so reports and the bill is read for the first time. When it comes up for second reading it is again referred to the committee on private bills for detailed consideration which may take the form of a public hearing at which all parties interested in opposing or supporting the bill may be heard. If this committee reports unfavourably the bill is to all intents and purposes dead; if the report is favourable the bill goes on the order paper for reference to the committee of the whole and third reading, and the procedure from there is formally the same as in public bills.

The procedure in financial legislation is again different. Financial legislation is not in the first instance presented to the house in the form of a bill but rather in the form of resolutions that do not become bills until an elaborate procedure has been fulfilled. In supply bills by which the legislature votes money for government services for the coming fiscal year the elaborate procedure inside the house is preceded by a great deal of work outside. Some months before the beginning of a session the provincial treasurer asks each department to prepare estimates of the amount of money required for the next year. The preparation of the estimates begins at the branch level of the department. Any request for money in excess of that spent the last year or any new request must conquer several hurdles before it achieves a place in estimates as printed for the legislature. The branch director must first convince his deputy that the money is needed, the deputy must convince his minister, the minister must convince the provincial treasurer and treasury board, and the treasurer must persuade the cabinet that he can raise the money to cover new expenditures being contemplated.

When the estimates are tabled in the house, the provincial treasurer moves that the committee of supply be called. All members of the house are members of this committee whose function is to carry out a detailed consideration of the estimates during which any member of the house can question the responsible minister. The committee reports back to the house in resolutions recommending the expenditures of each department. After the report, the provincial treasurer moves that the house go into committee of ways and means which in Manitoba is the signal for the budget speech to be delivered before the motion is put. The budget speech is a report on both the financial and the economic position of the province. The treasurer dwells at length on available revenues, departmental requirements, the tax structure, and provincial indebtedness and also discusses the general conditions prevailing in agriculture and industry. This speech is, or should be, the occasion for a general debate on government policy after which the house goes into committee of ways and means.

The function of this committee is twofold. It must, by resolution, authorize the withdrawal of money from the consolidated revenue fund to provide for the expenditures authorized by the committee of supply and it must adjust revenues to expenditure which may mean a change in the levels of taxation. After this committee has finished, a bill embodying the resolutions and schedules of both committees is presented by the provincial treasurer. After the usual three readings and royal assent it becomes law.

The Standing Committees of the House

One of the first items of business of any new session is the nomination from the floor of the house of a group of seven members to strike the standing committees. Membership on these committees is not necessarily in ratio to party standing in the legislature; the government does, however, show a strong and understandable desire to retain a comfortable majority on each. The large number of cabinet ministers is a notable feature of committee personnel—not less than 5 out of an average membership of 25, and, on law amendments in the 1953 session, it was 9 out of 41.

The basic purpose of the committee system is to provide a means of detailed consideration of legislation before the house, to allow interested parties to appear and present briefs on contemplated legislation, to serve as a fact-finding body for the legislature through the examination of witnesses, and to investigate special subjects that come up and report. There are at present nine standing committees of the house: privileges and elections; public accounts; public utilities and natural resources; agriculture and immigration; municipal affairs; law amendments; private bills, standing orders, printing and the library; and industrial development.

The committee on privileges and elections though listed first is actually of least importance because bills are rarely referred to it. It meets infrequently, and questions or bills referred to it are not usually of great consequence, an example being clarification of expenses that a member may claim. Two matters which should logically fall within its jurisdiction, amendments to the Election Act and redistribution, are always handled by special select committees.

The committee on public accounts is a means of satisfying the collective conscience of the house that all has been honest and above-board during the preceding year. Each main heading in the printed report of the comptroller general is read, discussed, and voted on and any member of the committee can inquire about any item or ask that vouchers and other relevant documents be produced. The committee is also often asked to report on charges of dishonesty. For example, in 1947 the committee inquired into the location of the Winnipeg-Emerson highway and reported to the house that charges that the highway had been located for the special benefit of a few were without foundation.

The main responsibility of the committee on public utilities and natural resources is an annual review of the affairs of the Manitoba Liquor Commission, the Manitoba Telephone Company, and the Manitoba Power Commission. For the past twenty years the committee has invariably reported that all was well. The committee confines itself to two inquiries on "natural resources": one into the adequacy of the province's game laws and their administration, and the other into the state of the fishing industry. Curiously enough, bills whose subject matter clearly brings them within the scope of the committee are not referred to it. In 1948 for example, a bill dealing with taxation of minerals and mineral produce went to the committee on law amendments as did a bill to amend the Telephone Act.

The title of the committee on agriculture and immigration is something of a misnomer; it should be only the committee on agriculture for all its activities in the past decade have related to that subject. Unlike the three committees already discussed, it does examine a considerable number of bills each session and report them back to the house. It has also, on orders of the house, conducted several investigations; for example in 1948 it inquired into the cost of distribution of milk in Greater Winnipeg.

The municipal affairs committee is, next to law amendments, the most active in the house. Its work arises largely from bills referred respecting changes in municipal boundaries, incorporation of towns, changes in city charters, or amendments to the Municipal Act. Over the past ten years it has considered an average of twenty such bills per session.

The committee on law amendments has handled more than 90 per cent of the bills referred by the house in the past decade. It does not, as its name indicates, handle only bills that contemplate a change in existing law. Indeed, many bills that are not amendments and might more logically go to another committee are often sent to it by the house. Law amendments is the largest of the committees, having a membership of 40, and is therefore more like a committee of the whole than a standing committee. It is in continuous session and cabinet ministers frequently send bills to it rather than call the committee which the subject matter of the bill would suggest, particularly in the last week of a legislative session.

The committee on private bills, standing orders, printing and the library deals almost entirely with legislation for private groups, the most common form of which is the incorporation of a particular society or company.

The industrial development committee began operations in 1956. In 1957 it considered the amendments to the Workmen's Compensation Act and in the following year a new maximum hours and minimum wages bill, but during 1958 and 1960 it was inactive.

In addition to these standing committees there have been many special select committees to report on specific subjects on which legislation exists but is regarded as unsatisfactory or incomplete, or where legislation is contemplated. There were over twenty of these in the decade 1950–60, for instance, the Select Committee to Inquire into and Report on the Adequacy of the Labour Relations Act and Its Administration (1953), the Select Committee on Liquor Laws (1951) which recommended a Royal Commission, and others on health services, Hutterites, redistribution, teachers' pensions, and so forth.

An exceptional feature of the committee system is the opportunity for representation of the public. It has long been the practice in Manitoba to allow any interested person to come before a standing committee and make representation for or against a bill whether it be a government bill or any other public bill or a private bill. In some cases, of course, the government seeks these representations and the press is advised that the bill be considered at a certain time. However, whether or not representations are sought they are almost invariably allowed. Before beginning to consider any bill, the committee chairman always inquires if there are any representations. As the committee rooms are open to the public there frequently are and the greatest latitude is always allowed.

Ontario is the only other province that allows and encourages representations on bills before standing committees. In Newfoundland there is only one standing committee and it is on private bills. Other committees are appointed by the speaker as needed but open sessions are rarely held. In Nova Scotia all bills (except supply) are normally sent to the committee on law amendments, which usually sits *in camera*, or the committee on private and local bills. In New Brunswick it is not the practice to refer public bills to any special standing committee although in rare instances they do go to the committee on law, practice and procedure. Anyone wishing to make representations is therefore forced to do so through a member of the legislature. In Prince Edward Island all government bills go first to caucus and then directly to the committee of the whole house. In Alberta public bills go to the appropriate committee only on reference by the minister introducing the bill, usually only where the bill is controversial from the public point of view, when public representations are sought.

Legislative Control over Finance

The power of a legislature, whether provincial or federal, rests primarily on its maintenance of control over the granting of supply. The basic principles governing control are that the executive must take responsibility for all financial legislation introduced into the House, that not a cent may be spent until the legislature votes it, and that the legislature, having voted the money, has an opportunity to make sure that it was actually spent for the purpose named in the vote.

In Manitoba, as in other provinces, the lieutenant governor's recommendation of any resolution involving a payment out of the public treasury must be given formally by a minister at the initiation of the proceedings in words which have been incorporated into the rules of the house: "His Honour the Lieutenant-Governor, having been informed of the subject matter of this motion recommends it to the consideration of the House."[40] Furthermore, a minister must accept responsibility for any change in the estimates when they are discussed in committee of supply.

In theory the legislature keeps control because it alone can vote the money although the discussions in committee are designed to give the ordinary member a chance to inquire closely into government business. Unfortunately, during the days of non-partisan administration, and to a considerable extent during coalition also, they became a mere formality.

The right and duty of the legislature to check on whether or not the money voted was spent for the purposes intended has a chequered history in the province. In 1888 when the Norquay government was defeated at the polls its successors found that the only available records of receipts and expenditures were the cheque stubs that littered the floor of the provincial treasurer's office. Although some improvements were made no systematic accounting was instituted until 1915 when the scandal connected with the construction of the new parliament buildings so shocked the public conscience that the legislature found it necessary to guard against any future occurrences of a similar nature. An officer known as the comptroller general was appointed and given, subject to an appeal to the treasury board, complete control over the auditing of all receipts and expenditures of the province. The comptroller has security of tenure and can be removed from office only on address of the assembly carried by a two-thirds vote, though he can be suspended to await the pleasure of the assembly "on the written advice of the majority of a committee consisting of the Premier and the recognized leaders of . . . political parties in opposition."[41]

At present the comptroller general is required by statute to pre-audit all accounts submitted by the departments for payment, including securities being purchased by the treasury. His pre-audit consists in making sure that money for the proposed expenditure has in fact been voted by the legislature, that it is being spent for the purpose intended, that it has been authorized by the proper officials, and that any special conditions

[40]*Rules, Orders and Forms of Proceeding of the Legislative Assembly of Manitoba* (1954), p. 61.
[41]The Treasury Act, *Revised Statutes of Manitoba* (R.S.M.), 1954, c. 272, s. 9(3).

(such as calling of tenders) that may have been attached by statute are fulfilled. He must also see that appropriations are not exceeded and maintain the proper ledgers and books associated with the general budget funds.

The comptroller general in Manitoba is in part an auditor and in part an administrative officer. In making the pre-audit he becomes a partner to an executive decision to spend; in making a report to the legislature he is, in effect, auditing his own accounting entries and, to an extent, his own administrative decisions. Moreover, the office of the comptroller general is a branch of the treasury. Thus there is a certain anomaly about his position. There have been occasions in the past when the comptroller general himself was drawn into basic policy decisions, his usefulness as an independent official thus being seriously restricted. (This difficulty has now been solved by an informal arrangement.)

The solution to the whole problem is, as A. E. Buck points out:

for the provinces to adopt a simplification of the system now being followed by the Dominion government. This would require the central accounts for each province to be kept in the Treasury or Finance Department under the direct supervision of a permanent officer—a comptroller—reporting to the provincial treasurer or minister of finance. The audit of the central and departmental accounts and the checking of all provincial revenues and expenditures would then be performed by the provincial auditor, who would have no powers of administrative control but simply those of post audit. The provincial auditor should, in all cases, be an officer of the legislature, reporting his findings directly to the public accounts Committee of that body and keeping no accounts of any kind.[42]

The history of the legislature and the analysis of its machinery presented in this chapter reveal, of course, only the bare bones of the institution. The most satisfactory and equitable machinery that man can devise cannot ensure that a legislature will discharge adequately the functions entrusted to it by the parliamentary system. The representative machinery and the electoral system have as their purpose the harmonizing of public will and governmental action which can take place only if accompanied by two other activities—criticism and education. Where necessary the legislature must criticize the administration and in so doing contribute to the education and formulation of public opinion. Over its history the Manitoba legislature has fulfilled the critical and educational functions of the executive with varying success. The sudden creation of the province and the lack of a parliamentary tradition made an early awkwardness inevitable. But the debates, as reported in the press, made up in vigour what they lacked in finesse, particularly during the 1880's

[42]A. E. Buck, *Financing Canadian Government*, p. 269.

when disallowance was the major topic. The low point in the history of the legislature was undoubtedly the period from 1922 to 1950 when the institution was dominated by farmers who seemed to feel that reticence was a virtue in the assembly and who eliminated potential discussion by coalition and non-partisan government. During most of the 1940's only 3 members out of 57 were in opposition, making critical debate obviously impossible. The last decade has been the most successful, for the parties have not only been revitalized but no one of them has secured an overwhelming majority.

THE CABINET | 6

FEW PHRASES CONVEY fully and aptly the true importance of the cabinet under the British parliamentary system. Some of the better attempts at neat characterization have been, "a combining committee—a hyphen which joins, a buckle which fastens, the legislative part of the state to the executive part," "the centre of gravity of the system," and the "mainspring of government." Phrases such as these describe the British executive or the Canadian cabinet but not necessarily a provincial executive. In some cases local ground rules and customs have altered the nature of the institution to such a degree that even the word cabinet is barely applicable. In Manitoba lack of experience and primitive frontier conditions led to constitutional novelty and variation from the model, and, after the turn of the century, to a zeal for reform. The election of the Progressives in 1922 marked the end of intellectual ferment and speculation about a cure for cabinet domination but the institution was not allowed to settle into its traditional role. The farmers, whose views on government were a mixture of idealism and ignorance, destroyed the party system and in effect the foundation on which cabinet government rests.

The functions which a government must discharge determine the organization, activities, and even powers of the executive. Adam Smith once stated that the essential functions of government were administration of justice, provision of essential public works, and national defence. In Manitoba until 1900 the functions were justice, public works, and agriculture. The first report of the Department of Agriculture was actually a summary of some of the more important interests of the department at that time.[1] It included the vital statistics collected on births,

[1]Manitoba, *Sessional Papers*, 1882, Report to the Department of Agriculture.

death, and marriages, information on communicable diseases both human and animal and what, if anything, was done about them, details of provincial imports and exports, municipal assessment, and a summary of recent weather conditions. The Ministry of Agriculture remained until 1900 very much like a bureau of statistics. Indeed, not until comparatively recently has the provincial government been called upon to perform promotional, research, and regulatory activities on behalf of agriculture.

The administration of justice, which from the first necessitated a minister, involved primarily the delineation of property relationships and the preservation of law and order. Both functions grew steadily with the passage of statutes dealing with such things as bankruptcy, debts, bills of sale, chattel mortgages, registration of deeds, incorporation of companies, estates of deceased persons, landlord-tenant relationships, partnership, and so on. The Department of the Attorney General has always administered and enforced these statutes as well as carrying out the administrative work ancillary to their interpretation by the judiciary.

Because Manitoba began as a primitive society and grew very rapidly, thus intensifying the demand for roads, public buildings, and so on, public works have always been important. Indeed, the activities of this department have been and still are limited only by available revenue. Education, although one of the original departments created in 1870, did not have any great significance until after the passage of the School Act of 1890. The discharge of even the minimal functions before 1900 necessitated a provincial secretary to publish the proclamations and a treasurer to handle the accounts.

Executive organization was dictated by these essential functions and any new activities were, until 1916, added to one of the original portfolios. By 1888 municipal affairs had become important. In addition, the federal government had transferred a large amount of swamp lands to the jurisdiction of the province and Manitoba was, or wanted to be, in the railway construction business. These new functions were included without increasing the personnel of the cabinet by a single member. Thomas Greenway as premier[2] held the post of minister of agriculture and simply added railways to it; municipal affairs were tacked on to the office of the provincial secretary, and the administration of lands to

[2]The private papers of Thomas Greenway in the Provincial Archives of Manitoba provide a revealing account of the nature of the office of premier during this period. Greenway seems to have attended to the most minute details of party organization and patronage for, out of 17,000 papers, a good two-thirds relate to matters that should have been attended to by a secretary or, in the case of considerable number, not attended to at all.

public works. The Roblin government which came to power in 1897 retained the original six portfolios and adopted the same practice of adding any new functions to existing departments. In 1909, for example, the government created a publicly-owned telephone system which was made responsible to the legislature through the provincial secretary. In every ministry from 1910 to 1916 the premier held one major port-folio, the most usual one being agriculture and immigration. In 1916 the size of the cabinet was increased to seven when the new head of the government, T. C. Norris, became simply premier. In 1927 the cabinet was increased by the creation of a Ministry of Mines and Resources, and in the following year a Department of Health and Welfare was created. In 1934 a Ministry of Labour brought the cabinet to ten mem-bers;[3] its present size is eleven.

A second aspect of the organization of Manitoba's cabinet concerns its representative character with regard to religious groups and geographical regions. As has been mentioned, the French and English were, in 1870, almost equal in numbers. Until 1878 the cabinet was composed of four English Protestants and two French Catholics but in that year the French representation in the cabinet was dropped to one. In the interests of re-election as well as equity the subsequent governments consistently main-tained one French Catholic on the executive until 1890 when the crisis over separate schools forced the resignation of the French member. Cabinets were entirely Protestant until 1913 when Premier Roblin, in a desperate bid for French support, appointed Joseph Bernier, a French Catholic, to the post of provincial secretary. Premier Norris reverted to a solidly Protestant ministry in 1914. The Bracken ministry of 1922 included a representative of the French as has been the practice in every ministry formed since that date except the one currently holding office.

There has not been, at any time in the history of Manitoba, any sys-tematic attempt to represent particular geographical regions, except Win-nipeg, in the cabinet. The present practice, as stated in 1954 by the then premier, D. L. Campbell, is true for any period:

In the province of Manitoba the necessity for geographical representation, which is almost imperative as far as the federal Parliament is concerned, is not of similar importance. . . . I have always acted on the assumption that a Cabinet Minister when appointed does not represent any particular con-stituency or geographical region and therefore the matter of where his con-stituency is located geographically is not one of vital importance. On the other hand, if all other qualifications were thought to be equal, in making a

[3]Provision for a Department of Labour was made in 1931 by the Department of Labour Act (*Statutes of Manitoba*, 1931, c.28). The Act was proclaimed on July 6, 1934, by Order-in-Council 869.

choice between two members for advancement to the cabinet, I would give consideration to geographical representation . . . such occasions would be rare.[4]

The small size of the cabinet and, until recently, the narrow scope of its responsibilities have made a large measure of informality in its proceedings possible but this has been gradually breaking down. In 1945 R. E. Moffat was appointed executive assistant to the premier and secretary to the cabinet but the position was discontinued when D. L. Campbell became premier in 1949. When Duff Roblin took office in 1958 he revived the notion of a cabinet secretariat by appointing Derek Bedson as secretary. Since that time the secretariat has been conducted on the same principles as those followed in Ottawa and Westminster, if on a smaller scale.[5] Roblin has also given the treasury board a much larger role; by statute the board is the financial committee of the cabinet but it has actually been so only since 1959. Previously, activities that might have been carried out by it were dealt with by the whole cabinet and the board was left with the relatively minor duties of certifying public accounts for presentation to the legislature and serving as a court of appeal on certain decisions of the comptroller general. Now the board reviews the annual current and capital budgets of the government and makes recommendations to the full cabinet, overseas expenditures, and directs research into matters having financial implications.

Naturally the cabinet system of government in Manitoba did not evolve in a vacuum of public indifference. Soon after the turn of the century a strong current of opinion that favoured far-reaching reform in the system developed. As O. D. Skelton wrote in 1920:

In the provincial legislature the most persistent and significant development has been the growth of the power of the Cabinet at the expense of the back-benchers. The legislature in many cases has seemd to be merely a panel from which the real governors of the province are drawn. The Cabinet has become all powerful in the making of laws as well as in their execution. Probably the election of independent members, and particularly the ten-

[4]D. L. Campbell to M. S. Donnelly, April 19, 1954.
[5]In *Cabinet Government* (Cambridge, 1936), Ivor Jennings gives the functions of the British secretariat as follows (p. 189):
"(a) to circulate the memoranda and other documents required . . .
(b) to compile under the direction of the Prime Minister the agenda of the Cabinet and, under the direction of the chairman, the agenda of a Cabinet Committee;
(c) to issue summons of meetings of the Cabinet and its Committees;
(d) to take down and circulate the Conclusions of the Cabinet and its committees and prepare reports . . .
(e) to keep, subject to the instructions of the Cabinet, the Cabinet papers and conclusions."

dency toward group instead of the two party system, will do much to shake the power of the Cabinet by undermining party solidarity and cohesiveness upon which the Ministers have built their power.[6]

Each of the provinces had its own distinctive ideas on how to reform the cabinet.[7] Manitoba, as represented by the United Farmers and the Winnipeg Labour movement, showed a distinct preference for direct legislation and also toyed with the idea of having the cabinet elected by the members of the legislature rather than chosen by the leader of the majority party. The Direct Legislation Statute of 1916, had it been capable of implementation, would seriously have restricted the individual and collective responsibility of the cabinet. When direct legislation proved impossible the reformers turned to the notion of a cabinet elected from the legislature. In the last days of the Norris government, A. E. Smith, the Labour member for Brandon, moved: "Be it resolved that in the opinion of this legislature the time has arrived when the executive council for the administration of affairs of this province shall be selected by the present representation in this legislature."[8] The motion brought a tie vote and was only defeated by the deciding vote of the Speaker. The question of an elected cabinet was discussed by a large number of U.F.M. locals in 1920 and 1921 and in the latter year came before the central executive who decided against it on the grounds that it was likely to cause dissension among the membership.[9]

The U.F.M. did, however, include in its platform of 1922 a plank which read: "In order that all measures coming before the legislature may be considered on their merits only the refusal of supply or specific vote of want of confidence shall necessitate the resignation of a government."[10] The reason behind this, as stated in numerous articles and editorials in the *Grain Growers' Guide*, was a conviction on the part of the Manitoba Progressives that the traditional and desirable relationship between the legislature and the cabinet had been inverted. The legislature had become responsible to the cabinet. The measures which the cabinet decided were necessary were simply pushed through by a majority controlled by the whips or threatened with dissolution. It was argued that members of the majority party were often compelled to support the executive even if it meant going contrary to the dictates of constituency

[6]O. D. Skelton, *Grain Growers' Guide*, July 7, 1920.
[7]For a summary of them see W. L. Morton, "The Western Progressive Movement and Cabinet Domination," *C.J.E.P.S.*, XII (May, 1946), pp. 136–47.
[8]*J.L.A.*, 1920, p. 99.
[9]P.A.M., Executive Minutes, United Farmers of Manitoba, April 21, 1921, p. 7.
[10]P.A.M., Platform of the United Farmers of Manitoba, 1922. (A similar motion was introduced by Irving of Alberta in the House of Commons at Ottawa and defeated on division. See Can., H. of C., *Deb.*, Feb. 12, 1923, p. 208.)

or conscience. The Manitoba Progressives wanted to correct these alleged shortcomings of cabinet government by allowing free votes. It is, then, rather surprising that they never implemented the idea when in power. On one occasion the cabinet itself split and voted differently on a matter of policy but there appears to have been more confusion than conviction on the particular issue. In 1922 the federal government passed an act creating a wheat board to market the crop of that year but stipulated that the act was to come into force within a province only after the passage of enabling legislation. In April 1923 Premier Bracken introduced such legislation as a government measure. It was defeated in the house and the Attorney General, Provincial Treasurer, and Minister of Agriculture were among those who voted against it.

The naïveté of the newly elected farmers should not obscure a substantial element of validity behind the criticisms of the cabinet system. The objections raised regarding cabinet domination and controlled majorities were fundamental issues in no way peculiar to Western Canada. What is peculiar to Manitoba was her handling of them.

The situation in Australia and New Zealand in an earlier period provides an interesting parallel with and contrast to Manitoba. In some Australian states about 1890 a strong movement began to eliminate the traditional cabinet system and replace it by an administrative body elected from among the members of the legislature. In Victoria in 1891 Edward Jenks, in his book, *The Government of Victoria*, looked forward with some eagerness to the "euthanasia" of the traditional cabinet system and the formation of a permanent executive made up of experts in administrative matters. Throughout the 1890's the legislature of New South Wales was confronted with resolutions condemning party government and recommending that executive functions be carried on by a permanent committee of the House.[11] In New Zealand in 1891 a parliamentary committee studied the whole question of cabinet practice and theory, decided that the principle of cabinet responsibility was "an old constitutional fungus," and recommended that adoption of the Swiss system. No action was taken and though the demand became "a hardy quinquennial of New Zealand politics" it "bore no fruit."[12] In the final analysis, the movement for elective ministries in both countries probably had its basis in the unstable nature of earlier régimes and typical frontier concepts of the nature of the general will.

[11]The force of the movement for an elective cabinet seems to have been spent by 1900 but the idea has been revived periodically in the Australian House of Representatives (see *Journals of the Parliaments of the British Commonwealth*, 1926 and 1941).

[12]J. D. B. Miller, *Historical Studies of Australia and New Zealand*, VI (1953).

Reactions against cabinet domination were not confined to frontier areas like Western Canada or Australia, however. The criticisms made in Manitoba were remarkably similar to those voiced by the Independent Labour party in Britain.[13] The chief spokesman for this group was F. W. Jowett, the Labour member of Parliament for West Bradford. Largely as a result of his efforts two select committees on procedure were appointed, one in 1914 and one in 1931, both of which were to consider ways and means of improving the cabinet system. On both occasions Jowett argued that the real mind of the Commons was rarely brought to bear on a public question because of cabinet domination. He proposed that the principles of municipal administration be applied to the national government which would mean that committees representing the numerical strength of the parties in the House would be set up to administer each department of state. Each member would then know exactly what the government was doing and the power of the cabinet would be largely nullified as the minister would be only chairman of the committee in charge of his department. The cabinet as a collective body would exist only as a general purposes committee. Finally Jowett proposed that the duration of Parliament be fixed for five years with no dissolution allowed except at the end of that period. Though neither select committee was able to reach a conclusion of any kind and Jowett's proposals were not accepted, they did become official doctrine of the Independent Labour party which approved them at its 1914 convention.[14] They were reaffirmed in 1925 over the loud protests of Harold Laski and again in 1929.

The Manitoba Progressives never conducted any systematic rational inquiry into the type of government considered desirable for the province though they did seem to be guided by two basic concepts. Both Bracken and Garson wanted a more or less permanent executive composed of men of superior administrative talent and both wanted the executive thus formed to be similar in structure to a municipal council. In 1940 a cabinet in which the main parties were represented was created but it was really only a coalition and the result was the perennial difficulty of coalition—compromise and inaction. Almost no new legislation was introduced in the five ensuing years. The session of 1941–42 dealt with some forty amendments to existing statutes. The speech from the throne stated

[13]One of the earliest and most vigorous attacks on the British cabinet system is found in David Syme, *Representative Government in England* (London, 1881). The book attracted little attention in Britain, appearing as it did at the height of the Empire, but it did have a substantial impact in Australia.

[14]For the text of the resolution see Herbert Morrison, *Government and Parliament* (London, 1955), p. 156.

that "for the most part these amendments do not provide for changes in principle but rather for clarification and more effective administration of existing policy."[15] In 1943 the situation was the same and in 1944 out of 86 bills, 80 were amendments and the majority of the remainder were private bills. Again in 1945, 90 per cent of the legislation consisted of minor changes and no bills of any consequence were introduced.

After the election of 1945 the word "coalition" was dropped and the cabinet was officially described as non-partisan. It was made up of four Conservatives and six Liberal-Progressives who by this time had developed into a kind of family compact, each group refraining from opposing the other at election time. A moratorium was also declared on participation in federal politics, Premier Garson announcing in 1945: "When I became leader of the government I recommended to Cabinet council that as long as the non-partisan provincial government continued each and every one of its members should refrain from taking part in partisan federal politics in a manner which would bring members of the Manitoba cabinet into partisan conflict with one another. My colleagues unanimously concurred in this recommendation, and since the time that I became Premier that rule has been strictly followed by all members of the Cabinet."[16]

The fundamental question about non-partisan government is whether or not it produced good government. The question raises a second: what are the criteria for good government within the democratic tradition and what are the traditional techniques by which men have attempted to achieve it? In the first place the criteria for good government must obviously be related to the period of history and to the circumstances. It is inevitable and desirable that the system of government should adapt itself to local conditions and there is therefore little point in attempting to judge Manitoba by the standards of Erskine May, A. B. Keith, or Ivor Jennings. Nor can it be asserted that a government following the British parliamentary system is open to censure because it neglects certain British precedents. It can if it wishes, and indeed as Bentham recommended, deny the wisdom of its model although any departures from precedent must pass the acid test of success.

Certain criteria are, of course, applicable to any government purporting to be democratic: its policies must be broadly in accordance with the public will; it must show a sense of responsibility and merit public trust; it should be reasonably efficient in the performance of its functions and

[15]*J.L.A.*, 1941–42, p. 14.
[16]Quoted from the script of a speech by Stuart Garson over radio station C.K.Y., March 14, 1945.

the dispatch of public business; and finally the cabinet or executive should provide leadership in the policies it recommends.

Under the traditional system of parliamentary government various devices, apart from elections themselves, help to ensure that cabinet policy is kept broadly in accordance with the public will. The opposition have a chance to review the whole course of cabinet policy in the debate on the speech from the throne; they may use the device of questions addressed to ministers to seek information or point up government weakness or failure; they may use the motion of adjournment to debate a matter of public importance in order to challenge government policy; they may voice grievances before supply; and finally they have recourse to a motion of want of confidence. These devices were weakened by the non-partisan régime in Manitoba, on the theory that the cabinet instead of listening to the representatives of the people listened through various organizations and pressure groups, the most prominent of which were the Union of Rural Municipalities and the Manitoba Federation of Agriculture. Government policy, so it was said, could be debated within these organizations and would result in the formation of a real grass roots opinion. But no really meaningful debate on government policy did in fact take place within these organizations. Indeed, for the past decade the Federation of Agriculture has been engaged in internecine warfare with the Farmers Union. Members of the cabinet listened closely to certain individuals in the Union of Rural Municipalities simply because these people, apart from the fact that they were officers of the group, had something worthwhile to say. This is something any sensible premier would do and is in no sense a substitute for the parliamentary process.

It is ironic that the coalition and non-partisan cabinets produced exactly the situation which the Progressives had decried in 1921—complete cabinet domination. The basic non-partisan idea was that a board of directors (the cabinet) made decisions behind closed doors and, where legislation was necessary, it went through the assembly without being challenged, questioned, or debated. When it had been decided that certain actions were necessary, why waste time in useless talk which was neither business-like[17] nor efficient? Efficiency is only one of the values or tests of good government, however. Like honesty, it is not enough in itself. Debate, even about a law that is sure to pass, is part and parcel of the democratic process and valuable for the very reasons that make it

[17]This undefined concept of a business-like government goes back to the Patrons of Industry who put the following plank in their 1896 platform: "It is especially necessary that we get rid of all out of date party methods and procedures. . . . the cost of legislation and administration can be largely reduced by the application of business methods to public matters." *Patrons' Advocate*, Jan. 8, 1896.

repugnant to cabinets: it compels the ministers to formulate reasons for their acts and lays bare the motives behind legislation.

All the evidence indicates that the non-partisan administration was a failure. Cabinet government simply will not work without a vital party system and very few policies are right in the sense that only one clearly defined course of action is possible. All too often the farmer legislators were guilty of oversimplification and of a rigid self-righteous approach to the policies they were to carry out. Economy was their creed and they applied the most rigid economy measures during most of the post-war decade.

The educational policy in the ten years from 1945 to 1955 illustrates both the overemphasis on economy and the effect of the absence of party struggle and competition. In 1959 a Royal Commission reported on education and found the situation roughly comparable to that of the farmer who complained that, after he had taught his horse to go without eating, the ungrateful beast went and died. Figures cited in the report show that in spite of a financial capacity which compared favourably with every province except Ontario and British Columbia, Manitoba consistently spent less per capita than any other province except Prince Edward Island. When expenditure on education (or any other government service) is taken as a percentage of personal income Manitoba has been at the bottom by a very substantial margin. Moreover, the Commission found that

In Manitoba, the province bears a far smaller share of the cost of education than in most other provinces. The consequent burden on municipal finances, whose tax capacity varies so widely, has reached or even passed the point of diminishing return in many communities with low assessments. If these are to provide anything approaching equal educational opportunity for their children, the present cost and more particularly the steadily rising cost thereof cannot be borne by them without much greater grants from the province.[18]

The question of a larger school unit for secondary education is a good example of the failure of the non-partisan system and its "philosophy" of democratic government. Educational leaders and the conscious public at large had long realized that the school board of the local community was, in rural areas, incapable of meeting the demands of a diversified secondary educational programme. Indeed, this was recognized by members of the non-partisan group itself. In 1945 a committee of the legislature reported: "The Committee, having considered the arguments, accepts the general principle of the larger unit of school administration.

[18]*Report of the [Manitoba] Royal Commission on Education* (1939), p. 18.

It considers that such units could provide a greater degree of equality of educational opportunity, particularly at the secondary level. It further considers that administrative areas should be sufficiently large to provide a complete educational programme. . . ."[19] Yet during the decade that followed almost nothing happened. The position of the non-partisan government and of the Liberal-Progressives who came into office in 1950 was that if a community or district gave a clear indication that it wanted a referendum on the larger unit, the government would make arrangements to hold one. The demand must come from the grass roots—this was "democracy." The cabinet offered no leadership and took no positive stand for or against, and the result was that the larger unit was organized in one area only. In contrast, the revitalization of the party system made a great difference.[20] The Conservative party made the question of the larger unit and educational policy generally a campaign issue. Following its election it set up a boundary commission to outline the proposed districts, announced a date on which a provincial referendum vote would be held, campaigned on behalf of the plan in each district, and offered financial support for those that voted to accept it. The result was that 33 districts voted in favour and only 3 against.

The beneficial effects of a revival of the party system in Manitoba have not been confined to educational matters; a whole range of propositions previously regarded as axiomatic have been challenged and the whole philosophy of the cabinet system has changed in the last few years. The cabinet no longer regards itself primarily as an administrative agency. It has accepted the political responsibility of developing imaginative policies and stimulating public opinion. This is all to the good. A cabinet must be forced to take a stand on public issues and survive or fall on the basis of its decisions. Only the existence and healthy functioning of a party system can force such stands without which public opinion stagnates.

[19]*Report of the Special Select Committee on Education of the Manitoba Legislative Assembly* (1945), p. 56.

[20]The Progressive Conservatives won the election in 1958 but failed to secure an over-all majority. A second election held in June 1959 resulted in the following party standings: Progressive Conservatives, 35; Liberal-Progressives, 11; C.C.F., 10; and Social Credit, 1.

THE LIEUTENANT
GOVERNOR

7

THE FUNCTION OF THE LIEUTENANT GOVERNOR in any province is and always has been a dual one. On the one hand he is a federal officer appointed by the cabinet and paid out of money voted by the federal Parliament. Should he find it necessary to reserve a bill he does so in the name of the governor general. On the other hand he is, for purposes of the provincial government, a representative of the sovereign and acts as such when he assents to a bill, opens or prorogues the legislature, or holds his New Year's levee.[1]

The character of the office of lieutenant governor in Manitoba has been shaped largely by the two variables of the personality of the man himself and local circumstances. No institution of provincial government has undergone more marked changes since 1870. The status of the incumbent has changed from that of a paternal despot to that of a vir-

[1]The question of whether the lieutenant-governor could be a representative of the sovereign was, until 1892, a controversial issue. Manitoba contributed to the controversy when Lieutenant Governor Archibald accepted the help of Louis Riel in 1871 in combating a Fenian raid. The question was, had he by this action bound the Crown to pardon Riel? The answer as given by Lord Carnarvon, the Colonial Secretary, was: "The Lieutenant Governors of the Provinces of the Dominion, however important their functions may be, are a part of the Colonial Administrative Staff. . . . they do not hold Commissions from the Crown, and neither in power nor privilege resemble those Governors or even Lieutenant Governors of Colonies to whom . . . the Queen . . . delegates portions of Her prerogative and issues Her own instructions." (Canada, *Sessional Papers*, 1875, Paper 11, p. 38.) His answer was largely nullified by the Judicial Committee of the Privy Council in *Liquidators of the Maritime Bank of Canada* v. *the Receiver General of New Brunswick*, [1892] A.C. 437, whose decision read in part: "a Lieutenant-Governor . . . is as much the representative of Her Majesty for all purposes of provincial government as the Governor-General himself is for all purposes of Dominion Government." For a full discussion of this question see J. T. Saywell, *The Office of Lieutenant-Governor*.

tually powerless figurehead—from a governor with power to make and unmake ministries to one whose power is often very much less than "the right to warn, to encourage and be consulted." Until 1900 the lieutenant governor was functionally as well as legally a Dominion officer and was usually sent to Manitoba from Eastern Canada. Since the turn of the century the office has been filled by local citizens whose contributions to provincial society justified, or at least made plausible, their elevation to government house and whose political pasts rendered them *persona grata* with the party in power at Ottawa. Since 1900 the duties as a federal officer have almost vanished while those as a social leader have materially increased.

The exceptional character of the office of lieutenant governor due to the premature creation of the province has already been mentioned. Adams Archibald and Alexander Morris organized and ran the provincial government for the first six years of its existence and in addition performed a number of other exceptional duties, for they were not only the senior officers in the province but for a time they were the only officers. The list of chores that they were called upon to perform is a long one and includes the organization of postal facilities, the organization of a system to collect customs duties (and for a time the actual collection), the administration of Crown lands, the issuing of liquor permits and marriage licences, and the negotiation of Indian treaties. Moreover, the two lieutenant governors were not only governors of Manitoba in fact as well as in name but they were, quite literally, rulers over the entire Northwest. The statutory basis for the largely personal rule they exercised over the interior as far west as the Rocky Mountains was the Act for the Temporary Government of Rupert's Land of 1869. On the creation of Manitoba in 1870 this Act was, of course, replaced by the Manitoba Act as far as the province was concerned but it continued until 1875 to be the basis for government in what is now the northern part of Manitoba and all of Saskatchewan, Alberta, and the Northwest Territories. During this time Archibald and Morris provided, with the nominal support of a council, such government as there was. Both lieutenant governors exercised a major influence on the development of federal policy towards the Northwest and the establishment of a territorial administration from which the rudiments of law and order later developed. The North-West Council was reconstructed in 1875 on Morris' specific recommendation and the creation of the district of Keewatin in the same year was also his idea.[2]

[2]In 1875 Morris wrote to the Secretary of State for the Provinces: "In the course of my recent tour in the northerly Lake Winnipeg region, I was forcibly impressed with what I had for some time thought to be a necessity, viz. the making

A more conventional power of the lieutenant governor was the reservation of provincial bills.[3] There were three main grounds for reservation. The first might be called subjective for it involved a personal judgment on the wisdom of the legislation or the accuracy of the drafting. Secondly, several bills were reserved because they interfered or seemed likely to interfere with federal policy. The last ground was unconstitutionality. Between 1870 and 1900 twenty-one bills were reserved for the consent of the governor general of which four were assented to and became law. Of the seventeen which failed, four appear to have had no reaction from the governor general, either refusal or assent.

In April 1871 the Lieutenant Governor reported to the Secretary of State for the Provinces that he had reserved a bill to incorporate the Law Society of Manitoba because "This bill, even if the policy were sound, under any circumstances, seemed to me premature. In a country like this, obstacles should not be thrown in the way of any person in good standing at the bar of any other province, to be admitted to the practice of law here. . . . it would not be desirable so to restrict the government at Ottawa, in their selection of judges to such persons as the existing members of the bar here might think fit to admit."[4] A bill respecting land surveys was reserved for similar reasons, the Lieutenant Governor arguing that it created a monopoly where none had existed and would keep out those amateur surveyors who "can run a line with the compass, and in whose judgment their neighbours have confidence and yet who could not pass such an examination as the bill contemplates. . . . I see no reason why this class of men should not be allowed to continue their services, or why others who may come here similarly qualified should not be permitted to do the kind of rough work which a new country requires."[5]

---

of better provision for government of that region than can be accomplished by entrusting the administration thereof to the proposed new North-West Council. . . . the people inhabiting the country hold no intercourse with the western portions of the territories, their only communications are with Fort Garry or in the case of Great Britain through Moose Factory." (P.A.M., Morris Letter Book 5, p. 208.) After the first meeting of the council of the new district of Keewatin Morris wrote: "There was a special fitness in my being called upon to take the necessary steps to organize this new government, inasmuch as the Privy Council acted on my advice in constituting the district." (*Ibid.*, p. 310.)

[3]The power of reservation is derived from sections 55, 56, 57, and 90 of the British North America Act which provide in essence that the governor general may assent to a bill in the sovereign's name, withhold his assent, or reserve the bill for the sovereign's pleasure. If he reserves the bill it does not become law unless the governor general proclaims the royal assent within two years. By section 90 these provisions are extended to lieutenant governors *vis-à-vis* the provincial legislatures except that a period of one year is substituted for two. A clear case of withholding assent has never arisen in Manitoba.

[4]W. E. Hodgins, comp., *Dominion and Provincial Legislation, 1867–1895*, p. 771.   [5]*Ibid.*, p. 772.

Several reservations indicate the inexperience of early Manitoba legislators and attempts by the lieutenant governor to save them from themselves. In 1872 the bill to incorporate the Manitoba Central Railway was reserved because it was "wretchedly drawn."[6] Among other things the Lieutenant Governor pointed out that parts of the bill appeared to be copied from the Intercolonial Railway Act and hence dealt with matters not only beyond the jurisdiction of the province but also totally inapplicable to a private company. Several more bills from the 1870's and 1880's whose aim was the incorporation of private companies were reserved because the shareholders were, by the language, made partners to the company and hence liable to be sued in their individual capacity. The Lieutenant Governor reserved a bill relating to prairie fires in 1873 because of "clauses which make surveyors, railway companies and contractors liable for the result of fires caused by any of their men, irrespective of the fact of whether there was negligence, or whether the men were at the time under the control of the employers, provisions which I would fear would seriously interfere with the survey of the public lands."[7] As late as 1890 Lieutenant Governor Schultz reserved a bill affecting tax arrears in the city of Winnipeg partly on the ground that assessments for the year had already been completed and hence the bill would cause "confusion in municipal accounts and hence injustice to individuals."[8]

A second ground for reservation as has been noted was that proposed legislation might interfere with federal policy. At the first session of the first assembly the Lieutenant Governor reserved a bill to incorporate a railway from Fort Garry to Pembina and one from Portage to St. Joseph because he suspected that though "the language confines them to Manitoba territory . . . they are really intended to connect with foreign lines"[9] and hence might embarrass or thwart plans for a transcontinental railway. Two years later a similar bill to incorporate the Eastern Railway Company was reserved even though it too was to run only within provincial boundaries. This time the Governor General, on the recommendation of the Minister of Justice, gave his assent. In the same year, foreseeing possible interference with Canadian Pacific land grants and homestead policies, the Lieutenant Governor reserved a bill to impose a tax on wild lands but assented to it within a year when it was found that sufficient protection was in fact offered.

Three bills have been reserved on the grounds that they exceeded the legislative jurisdiction of the province. In 1871 a bill to authorize the construction of telegraph lines was held to be *ultra vires* because it was

[6]*Ibid.*, p. 771.   [7]*Ibid.*, p. 775.
[8]*Ibid.*, p. 915.   [9]*Ibid.*, p. 767.

to connect with a line in the United States. In the same year a bill to authorize the construction of a bridge over the Red River met a similar fate because it was likely to interfere with navigation and shipping. In 1876 a bill to incorporate the Manitoba Investment Association was reserved because it was worded in such a way as to entrench on federal authority in banking.

Finally, bills have been reserved for reasons that are officially unknown. In 1879 Lieutenant Governor Cauchon reserved a bill to eliminate printing in the French language.[10] His reservation does not form part of the official record of the Department of Justice in Ottawa although he reported the circumstances directly to the Governor General:

Inadvertently the Bill had been carried through the Assembly before it was shown to me or had I seen it all, otherwise the difficulty might probably have been averted; but as the case then stood no other alternative was left to me, but to veto it and run the risk of producing a possible graver result, or reserve it for the signification of your Excellency's pleasure . . . and thus obtain, for all time, a guiding precedent and permanent rule for all the legislatures of the Dominion similarly situated.[11]

Cauchon also reserved a bill to incorporate the Loyal Orange Lodge in 1882; at least the *Journals* of the assembly describe the action as a reservation and in so doing form the only record of the bill.[12] Milligan suggested that Cauchon's action may have been a veto "which has been overlooked by Canadian constitutional historians."[13] A more probable explanation is that the Minister of Justice did not report on the bill; the procedure followed is still the same:

When a bill is reserved it is the duty of the Minister of Justice to deal with it by virtue of section 4 of the Department of Justice Act. . . . in dealing with such bills, however, the Minister usually reports to the Governor-General recommending that assent be given or refused, and a copy of the Report is transmitted to the Lieutenant-Governor. But this practice has not been invariable; a number of reserved bills do not appear to have been reported upon by the Minister. The bill in such a case never becomes law for, according to Section 57 of the British North America Act, assent must be given to it by the Governor-General-in-Council before it can have validity.[14]

A second function of the lieutenant governor of Manitoba before 1900 in his capacity as a federal officer was that of securing amend-

[10]*J.L.A.*, 1879, p. 83.
[11]P.A.M., Cauchon Letter Book M, pp. 686–7, Cauchon to Lord Lorne, Sept. 20, 1879.
[12]*J.L.A.*, 1882, p. 74.
[13]Frank Milligan, "Reservation of Manitoba Bills and Refusal of Assent by Lieutenant-Governor Cauchon 1877–1882," *C.J.E.P.S.*, XIV (1948), p. 247.
[14]G. V. La Forest, *Disallowance and Reservation of Provincial Legislation*, p. 27.

ments to bills to which the federal government objected. There were 120 of these, all before 1900, and they all fall in the general class of legislation that was acceptable in principle but open to objection on specific points of detail. Such a bill could not, with justice, be disallowed, at least not until the provincial legislature was given a chance to remove or amend the objectionable sections. Objections were sent to the lieutenant governor who was expected to press for the required amendments. In 1877, for example, a bill to incorporate the Mutual fire insurance companies in Manitoba was objected to on the grounds that certain sections dealing with insolvency were beyond the legislative competence of the provincial government. On this occasion the acting Minister of Justice wrote in his report to the Governor General, "Relying on the assurance of the Lieutenant Governor, I recommend that the power of disallowance be not exercised but that the Act be left to its operation."[15]

Some of the objections were rather petty: in 1875 and again in 1877, the Minister of Justice objected to the word "Parliament" appearing with reference to the provincial legislature. However, most of the objections were well taken. In two statutes, the province legislated on weights and measures, a subject clearly federal.[16] On ten occasions the legislators forgot or ignored the fact that Crown lands were under the control of the central government. Thirty different statutes had phrases or sections impinging on criminal law, at least three more constituted a limitation on the right of the cabinet to appoint judges, and one provided that county court judges would automatically forfeit their offices if they failed in certain matters.

In addition to his power of reservation and attempts to secure amendment to unsatisfactory bills, if the lieutenant governor were in favour at Ottawa and trusted by the prime minister he was frequently called upon to report on subjects ranging from the prospects for wheat to those for the Conservative party in Manitoba. J. C. Aikins, lieutenant governor from 1882 to 1888, is a good example. Secretary of state in the first Macdonald ministry, he had gone into exile with the Conservatives at the time of the Pacific scandal and had been reappointed to the cabinet when the party was returned to power in 1878. Aikins' position as lieutenant governor was, in part, that of a confidential adviser to Macdonald on Western affairs, keeping the Prime Minister informed on the state of feeling on disallowance and giving advice on financial relations between the province and Ottawa. In a letter of November 1883 he urged the appointment of more and better judges, reported on the damage to wheat by frost, and discussed at length the reasons for reduc-

[15]Hodgins, comp., *Dominion and Provincial Legislation*, p. 813.
[16]*Statutes of Manitoba*, 1873, c. 7, and 1877, c. 6.

ing the tax on agricultural implements from the United States. The letter ended: "Perhaps I ought not to write about grievances. . . . I know you will do me the credit that what is said is from an honest desire to serve you in saying what I think and in representing matters as they are here viewed."[17] Aikins also received letters of candid but friendly advice from Macdonald. For example: "By the way, I hope you will press Norquay to accept the new terms [i.e. financial] . . . remember you hold the same position as a Dominion officer as the Governor General does under the Imperial Parliament—for the time being he does what he can, without infringing on the principle of self government to urge the carrying out of Imperial policy. Go thou and do likewise."[18]

Sir John Schultz, who was appointed lieutenant governor in 1888, carried on the same tradition as Aikins.[19] Schultz had been elected to the House of Commons in 1871 as a Conservative and made a senator in 1882, but he viewed the governorship as the crowning achievement of his career. His relationship with Macdonald was largely that of a close political adviser; for example, he wrote in 1889:

Norquay is earning a precarious livelihood as life insurance agent for an American company. . . . he is said to be very anxious for a reconciliation. . . . I don't think he can be trusted with the best interests of the Conservative cause. He can be disposed of a year before the general election if you can devise department employment investigating something or other up North. He wants a senatorship badly but in my opinion . . . the matter might well rest till the next election when it may be found useful.[20]

Joseph Cauchon, who became lieutenant governor in 1876, was also sent to Manitoba to serve the purposes of the Dominion, in his case to get rid of an unwelcome colleague. Cauchon had been forced to resign his seat in the Legislative Assembly of Quebec in 1872 when he was charged with renting, under an assumed name, a building to the government of which he was a member. There was apparently "some surprise" when he was made a member of the Mackenzie cabinet in 1875 but presumably Mackenzie soon discovered that Cauchon was useless, "and in October, 1877, he was appointed lieutenant governor of Manitoba."[21] Cauchon's entry into the province was most inauspicious. On his way he had read in the American newspapers that, like McDougall, he might

[17]P.A.C., Macdonald Papers, vol. 186, Aikins to Macdonald, Nov. 30, 1883.

[18]Macdonald to Aikins, July 28, 1884, Sir Joseph Pope, ed., *Correspondence of Sir John Macdonald*, p. 314.

[19]Schultz had come to Winnipeg in 1860 and practised medicine there. He was a staunch loyalist during the Riel Rebellion, was captured by Riel and sentenced to death, but escaped by climbing down a rope made out of bed-clothes.

[20]Macdonald Papers, vol. 264, Schultz to Macdonald, May 6, 1889.

[21]W. Stewart Wallace, *The Dictionary of Canadian Biography* (Toronto, 1945), p. 108.

be refused admission. Apparently unnerved, when he arrived at the border he mistook the scroll of welcome for a notice to stay out and refused to accept it but continued on to Winnipeg in a state of panic.

Many people thought that Cauchon would use his office to protect the French. However, the only interest he guarded was his own. He purchased real estate leading to the approaches of an important bridge to be constructed and demanded an exorbitant sum for it. Winnipeg finally wrested it from him but only after a prolonged struggle. In the affairs of the province, however, he maintained an attitude not of impartiality but of complete indifference.

The nature of the office of lieutenant governor changed abruptly about 1900 as a result of two events. First, the functions of the official as a Dominion officer ceased to be important. No Manitoba acts have been reserved, disallowed, or objected to since 1900. Even the duty of sending certified copies of the acts to the secretary of state was taken over by the clerk of the house. Secondly, in 1900 the policy of sending men from Eastern Canada to fill the position was discontinued. Daniel Hunter McMillan was the first Manitoban to fill the position and no one has been appointed since who has not lived the greater part of his life in the province. There has been no attempt to secure men who might be expected to have a knowledge of constitutional practice. The main qualifications for office have been a major contribution to provincial society, strong ties with the party in power in Ottawa at the time of the appointment, and a private income sufficient to maintain a high standard of hospitality at government house. Until recently there was a distinct tendency to favour successful pioneers for the office. McMillan had come West with Colonel Wolsley's troops in 1870, built a sod hut, become a successful farmer, and had eventually erected the first steam flour mill in the country. When he died the *Tribune* commented: "Sir Daniel's ten years of incumbency of government house . . . might be described as a long reign of warm and genial hospitality. Understanding the pioneers of the earlier days, as well as the newer people whose influx followed the railways, closely associated with military and business life, the church and social life . . . he was the ideal Lieutenant Governor."[22]

Theodore Arthur Burrows and J. D. McGregor are both examples of the pioneer rewarded. Burrows came to Winnipeg in 1875 and was admitted to the Manitoba Bar. He later went into the lumber business and acquired extensive properties in the Swan River valley and was partly responsible for opening up that area for settlement. As lieutenant governor he was a great social success, one of his assets being "a magnificent baritone voice" in which he "sang the old songs to the delight of

[22]*Tribune*, May 6, 1930.

everybody."[23] J. D. McGregor went to Brandon as a homesteader in 1877 where he built his own log cabin. Some years after, he was employed in Alberta as a cowboy and in 1904 he joined the Klondike gold rush where he became affectionately known as "Big Jim." He later became a stock breeder of international reputation and when he was appointed lieutenant governor said, "I feel that the honour was not so much to me as to agriculture. . . . I take this as a compliment to the whole farming industry."[24]

All three men were very strong Liberals. McMillan had become a Liberal M.L.A. in 1879 and later provincial treasurer in the Greenway government. He retained the closest connection with Clifford Sifton after the latter entered the Laurier administration and seems to have performed any and every party service required. For example, Sifton wrote to him in 1900: "There is a man named J. J. Matthews who went to Winnipeg about the 17th of September to take the Gold Cure. . . . I am satisfied that Tupper offered to pay his expenses if he would talk against me and I would like you to get a declaration to this effect. . . . it would be extremely valuable in the case of any Tupperite appearing here."[25] Burrows, like McMillan, served as a political errand boy for Sifton and owed his appointment in 1926 in part to services rendered. Both he and Norris, the leader of the provincial Liberals, had wanted the position. J. W. Dafoe had discussed their respective merits in letters to Sifton: "Norris is about through politically and financially and the Winnipeg Liberals are trying to make him believe that by running the governorship on the cheap he could get a living and something more out of it. . . . this would mean closing out the governorship as a social institution as Norris has no means of his own."[26] Burrows was endorsed: "I would like you to write King . . . with regard to the governorship of Manitoba and intimate to him that in your judgment Burrows is the only suitable candidate with claims that make it imperative that the government should recognize him. . . . for 35 years Burrows has been a Liberal member either of the local legislature or of the Dominion Parliament, or a candidate, until the last few elections, and when he was not in the field himself he has been effective in supporting the Liberal party."[27]

The appointment of lieutenant governors on the basis of party service and distinction in the community because of successful operation of a saw-mill or a livestock farm raises the whole question of the importance

[23]*Winnipeg Free Press*, Jan. 19, 1929.
[24]*Tribune*, Jan. 31, 1929.
[25]P.A.C., Sifton Papers, File K 353, Clifford Sifton to D. H. McMillan, Oct. 5, 1900.
[26]P.A.C., Dafoe Papers, J. W. Dafoe to Clifford Sifton, June 1, 1926.
[27]*Ibid.*, Sept. 27, 1926.

of the office. It must be admitted that for long periods of time the general public often forgets entirely that the office exists for it is called to their attention only when the legislature opens once a year. Only a select few participate in the hospitality offered at the annual New Year's levee or are privileged to meet representatives of the British royal family. Indeed, it may be doubted if the cabinet itself is particularly conscious of the office except when a new appointment is to be made. Policy is never discussed with the lieutenant governor and his only means of knowing what is going on is the legal requirement that his signature must appear on orders-in-council, a process which usually involves nothing more than having a clerk take them to His Honour's office at the proper time.

Nevertheless, the office is one of potential significance and importance. Since 1900 there have been two instances in which the lieutenant governor of Manitoba has had to take exceptional action or exercise a degree of personal initiative. In 1914 the members of the opposition began to suspect that there was widespread corruption and dishonesty in the construction of the new legislative building. Their efforts both on the floor of the assembly and in the committee on public accounts to discuss the matter were successfully blocked by the government. They were, therefore, forced to take the one course still open, that of petitioning the Lieutenant Governor, Sir Douglas Cameron, to create a Royal Commission to investigate and to refuse to prorogue the house until it had reported. Cameron, who obviously had been watching the situation for some time, wrote:

The suspicion that something might be wrong in connection with the contract for the Capital building first came to my mind in September 1914, on reading newspaper reports of the statement by the Minister of Public Works, Honourable Dr. Montague, during the special war session of the Legislature, that the original contract price would be greatly exceeded. I was particularly struck by his statement that the cost of foundations would exceed the estimate by $700,000.00. From that time I took an increased interest in the progress of the work, but nothing developed until the Session of the Legislature which opened on February 9, 1915. The reading of newspaper reports of evidence before the Public Accounts Committee from day to day strengthened my suspicion that there was something wrong and this was still further strengthened by the fact that the efforts of the Opposition Members of the Public Accounts Committee were led and directed by Mr. A. B. Hudson, who represents possibly the most important constituency in Manitoba, Winnipeg South, and whose standing in his profession was such that I felt I had to recognize the gravity of the alleged irregularities, which it was plain to me he was making every effort to have proven. My alarm was still further aroused by the speech made by Mr. Hudson in the Legislature on March 30th, 1915, in which he charged that there had been total overpayments of some $827,000 to Thomas Kelly & Sons, contractors, and in connection with which he moved for an investigation by Royal Commission.

On March 31st, 1915, I noted that speeches in the Legislature by Government supporters indicated that it was the intention to refuse a Royal Commission. On the evening of March 31st, 1915, Mr. T. C. Norris, Leader of the Opposition, came personally to Government House and presented a petition signed by twenty-one members of the Opposition.[28]

Once the petition had been presented Premier Roblin's strategy was to attempt to get his own nominees on the Commission and to delay its appointment as long as possible but the vigorous action of the Lieutenant Governor protected the public interest. In April 1915 he wrote to the Premier:

Yesterday you stated to me from an independent investigation which had been instigated that you were satisfied that a sum approximately $250,000 had been paid out for concrete that was never put in. The money was paid on application of Mr. Kelly. . . . Notwithstanding this, I can see from where I sit that Kelly is now proceeding actively with the work. . . . I would suggest that you consider the propriety of permitting a contractor who has been guilty, acording to your own statement of defrauding the province of a large sum of money to continue under his contract pending an investigation. . . . It is now over two weeks since it was announced that a commission be appointed. Delay in such a matter is not in the public interest and I therefore have to ask that you take action putting into effect my views at the earliest possible moment. Kindly let me hear from you during the day.[29]

All the evidence indicates that the Lieutenant Governor had lost confidence in his ministers and refused to accept their advice on the personnel of the investigating body or the terms of reference under which it should operate and the date on which it should begin. The upshot was that the charges of the opposition were sustained and the Roblin government was forced to resign.

A second but rather less important instance in which the lieutenant governor was called upon to exercise personal discretion occurred at the dissolution of the legislature in 1922. One year after it had been elected, the Liberal Norris government had had a motion of censure passed against it. This motion was introduced by P. A. Talbot, an Independent, and charged the government with arbitrary and autocratic behaviour in that it had failed to abolish the Public Utilities Commission as instructed by a majority vote at the previous session. Premier Norris immediately tendered his resignation to Lieutenant Governor Aikins and sent with it his recommendations for dissolution. Aikins refused to accept the resignation, writing by way of explanation: "I am satisfied

28P.A.C., Hudson Papers.
29P.A.M., Roblin Papers, Lieutenant Governor Cameron to R. P. Roblin, April 7, 1915.

from the disputes and conflicting views of the several groups in the Assembly that it is not only improbable but practically impossible for them to work in harmony or to form an administration strong and durable which would efficiently and beneficially carry on His Majesty's government in Manitoba. . . . I have the gravest doubt whether the legislature as at present composed correctly represents the wishes, the opinions or the views of the people. Indeed I believe it does not as a whole."[30] Instead Aikins instructed Norris to carry on with the session until supply had been voted and routine business discharged, but warned, "I need hardly add that where the resignation of a ministry is not accepted and while they continue to possess their official authority and functions, they are not expected pending an appeal to the electors, to perform more than routine duties."[31] Aikins' assessment of the situation proved correct. Without his firm lead, however, a confusion bordering on anarchy would probably have resulted.

Decisions of the lieutenant governor requiring personal initiative or discretion are rare and, considering most of the appointments since 1900, one is thankful. But that is no reason why the office should have developed into little more than a sinecure as R. F. McWilliams, who ended fourteen years in office on August 1, 1953, proved. McWilliams watched closely formal procedure and in particular the use of orders-in-council which now number more than 2,000 a year in Manitoba. In the past many lieutenant governors had regarded their signatures on these documents as a mere matter of routine,[32] but McWilliams took the view that his signature would be affixed only if the order came to him in proper form. His firm stand on this question did much to regularize procedure. Furthermore, McWilliams felt that Manitoba with its diverse racial composition was in need of some unifying symbol and he made his office just that. During his term of office he visited every sizable community in the province and kept in close contact with religious and lay organizations of all different racial groups, actions which have had a marked effect on the development of a closer sense of unity within Manitoba.

[30]P.A.M., Norris Papers, Lieutenant Governor Aikins to T. C. Norris, March 21, 1922.

[31]Ibid.

[32]Sir James Aikins, who was appointed in 1916, is an exception. In June 1923 the newspapers carried reports that he had objected to the purchase of securities by the provincial savings office before an order-in-council authorizing it had been presented to him for his signature. The government argued that the offence was not serious because the Act setting up the savings office also stipulated the kind of securities that might be purchased. Aikins took the view that it was, nevertheless, a reflection on the dignity of his office.

THE CIVIL
SERVICE

8

DISCUSSION OF ANY CIVIL SERVICE, provincial or federal, inevitably centres on two main questions. By what methods does the government recruit its personnel and how is the personnel organized to discharge its functions? The answers to either or both of these questions vary with the period of history under consideration. The most striking fact about the early civil service in Manitoba was its small size. A complete list of the civil service staff for 1880 was one deputy for each department plus one full or part-time clerk, a private secretary to the lieutenant governor, an auditor, a printer, a caretaker, and three jailers. In 1881 the total number of civil servants was five, of whom four were deputies; the provincial secretary and the attorney general ran their departments single-handed with no clerical assistance and no deputies. Agriculture and Immigration was the only department to rate a clerk.

Obviously, in such a situation neither the recruitment of personnel nor its organization would require any particular attention. All it received is found in the Civil Service Act of 1885 which remained on the statute books virtually unchanged except for minor amendments until replaced by a completely new statute in 1918. The Act of 1885 began by dividing the service into two parts, the inside service who were attached to departmental headquarters in Winnipeg and who numbered twenty at that time, and the outside service. The responsibility for recruiting and organization was placed on the deputies who were given a certain security of tenure. "The deputy head shall be appointed by the Lieutenant-Gouvernor[sic]-in-Council, and shall hold office during pleasure; but when such pleasure is exercised in the direction of removing a deputy head from his office a statement of the reasons for so doing shall be laid on the table of the Legislative Assembly within fifteen days of the open-ing of the next following session thereof."[1]

Any three of the deputies were, on appointment by the cabinet, to form a civil service board and were charged with the duty of "framing and publishing regulations to be observed by candidates for employment in the civil service," examining candidates by whatever means they saw fit, and granting certificates of qualification.[2] Individual competency had to be certified by the board. Classification was extremely simple, how-ever, for only five categories (deputies, chief clerks, senior clerks, ordi-nary clerks, and messengers) were provided. Salaries were firmly fixed; indeed, "Any application for increase of salary made by any member of the civil service, or by any other person on his behalf, with such per-son's consent or knowledge, shall be considered as a tendering of a resignation of such member." Furthermore, no appointee had any secu-rity of tenure. The Act stated that the board of deputies could act as a council of discipline to prescribe suitable punishments for recalcitrant servants but "nothing herein contained shall prevent the Lieutenant-Governor-in-Council from dismissing any employee when he sees fit to do so." Until 1918 almost all appointments to the Manitoba civil service were by patronage. Dismissals for party reasons following a change in government were common. After the elections of 1888, 1897, and 1915 there was virtually a 100 per cent turnover in the outside service. Dis-missals in the inside service do not appear to have been as sweeping, possibly because the number of positions was small and a certain con-tinuity in office administration was desirable.

The Manitoba Civil Service Act of 1885 was quite in keeping with the general practices prevailing in the federal government and in the other provinces. The idea of a civil service examining board composed of deputy ministers had been incorporated in the Canada Civil Service Act of 1868 which was modelled after legislation that had been in force in the united province of Canada before Confederation. Patronage and dismissals after a change of government were common in all provincial capitals as well as in Ottawa. However, in Ottawa gestures towards reform began as early as 1875 and before the service was finally re-formed in 1918 it had been probed and investigated by a select com-mittee and four royal commissions.

Each investigating body condemned the patronage system though their recommendations were powerless to alter it, but in Manitoba no one

[1]*Statutes of Manitoba*, 1885, c. 8, s. 9.
[2]For a full account see R. MacG. Dawson, *The Civil Service of Canada*, chaps. 4, 5, and 6.

bothered to condemn it. However, patronage was in fact a reasonably satisfactory basis for choosing the type of personnel then required in the province. The Public Works and the Attorney General's departments were the largest and both were decentralized. In the Department of Public Works in 1900 there were only ten employees of the inside service and seventy-seven, among whom only the medical doctors required any professional skill, were employees of the asylum for the insane at Selkirk. In the Attorney General's Department more than two-thirds of the employees worked in various land-titles offices throughout the province and, except for the senior clerks, needed little more than an ability to read and write.

Reform of the Manitoba civil service and abolition of the patronage system began to be an issue about 1910 and was vigorously championed by the reform movement that developed in Winnipeg and by the United Farmers of Manitoba. Even the most docile public conscience could scarcely overlook the notorious corruption of the Roblin régime when it was, for example, rather common practice to issue pay cheques to fictitious persons which, endorsed by the party bosses, found their way into the election fund. In road work the Department of Public Works sometimes paid both the duplicate and the original pay sheets—one for the road gang and one for the party.[3]

By 1918 the Manitoba civil service was approaching the point where it required considerable numbers of trained and competent personnel. A real audit of public funds did not begin until after the scandal of 1915 but by 1918 the office of the comptroller general had a staff of twenty-two people, most of whom were professionally qualified and the progressive legislation of the Norris government necessitated the creation of special branches in many departments.

Both the Ottawa civil service and the civil service of British Columbia were reformed in 1918 and the Manitoba Act of that year was drafted

---

[3]There is documented evidence of this in the *Report of the Commission Constituted to Enquire into and Report on all Expenditures for Road Work during the Year 1914.* The following is a good example of much of the testimony (evidence of Paul Fedohuk, p. 6):

Q. I believe you were a road foreman.
A. Yes.
Q. What [were you told] to do when appointed foreman?
A. I was told to be a good foreman . . . to work for the Conservative Party.
Q. What else?
A. I can't tell you all of it.
Q. Were you told to work?
A. He didn't say work.
Q. Were you told to attend political meetings?
A. I have to go to every meeting so I have no time for road work.

by Professor Adam Shortt, a member of the Ottawa Civil Service Commission, who had also framed the British Columbia statute. The two were almost identical. The new Act[4] provided first for a one-man civil service commission, the commissioner to have security of tenure in that he could be removed only on an address of the legislature carried by a two-thirds vote. He was not, however, given financial independence, for the Act stated that "the salary of the commissioner shall be fixed by order of the Lieutenant-Governor-in-Council." The major weakness of the Act was that it did not give the commission control over job classification.[5] In addition, the cabinet retained control over the requirements of experience and training necessary for particular positions. The overall effect was that no systematic attempt was made to work out detailed qualifications commanding specific rates of pay. The commissioner's position became virtually that of an interviewer though he was in fact given two other jobs as chairman of the censorship board and clerk of the house. The commissioner had no say whatever in promotions, which were left entirely to the discretion of the deputies. The Act did provide that all new positions were to be advertised, that lists of qualified candidates be published in the *Manitoba Gazette*, and that appointments should be made only from those certified by the commissioner. Because there were no prescribed examinations, the effect of this system on patronage appointments depended entirely on the character and integrity of the commissioner.

In 1922 the civil service entered a relatively static period. Because of the rigid economy practised by the Progressives the number of civil servants fell immediately after their election and establishments on the whole remained fixed until 1930 when further reductions were made. Numbers did not begin to increase until 1935. The work of the commissioner was, therefore, largely that of finding replacements for those who retired or resigned. The inevitable conclusion is that the Act of 1918 was not an effective measure of reform and was quite inadequate in its scope.

The Act of 1918 continued to be the basis for the civil service organization in Manitoba until 1947 when a new act was passed. In 1940 the civil service commissioner had been instructed by the cabinet to prepare a new job classification scheme for the service, to which were to be attached rates of pay regarded by the cabinet as suitable. In 1944 the scheme was put into effect and resulted in dissatisfaction so widespread that the government was forced to create a joint board of cabinet ministers and employee representatives to devise something more palatable.

[4]*Statutes of Manitoba*, 1918, c. 13.

In October 1945 the board recommended that "the government arrange for an overall survey of the Provincial civil service to be undertaken, either by an independent person or firm qualified in modern professional technique, or under the direction and guidance of such an independent person or firm—in order to obtain (a) a complete analysis of all salaried positions in the civil service, (b) a grouping of the respective positions into grades and classes, (c) an evaluation in terms of salary range of the respective positions and classes of grades."[6]

In 1946 J. S. Anderson and M. B. Newton were appointed to make a classification survey of the civil service and some of the Crown agencies. When this survey was completed the Civil Service Assembly of Canada was invited to carry out a wage survey to determine the rates to be attached to the various classes. The new system was introduced in February 1947 when employees were notified of their classification and given ten days in which to file appeals with a special board set up for this purpose. There are at present some 480 specific job classifications with appropriate prescriptions of training and experience, statement of duties, minimum and maximum salaries, and rates of annual increment. The number of civil servants by department is shown in Table IV.

TABLE IV
NUMBERS OF PERMANENT AND TEMPORARY EMPLOYEES
IN THE MANITOBA CIVIL SERVICE
(as of June 1)

Department	1949	1952	1954	1960
Agriculture	130	164	168	328
Attorney General	353	425	458	591
Education	233	240	245	340
Executive Council	17	18	22	21
Health	1,065	1,281	1,451	2,076
Industry and Commerce	—	—	32	106
Labour	58	67	68	92
Legislative	52	63	64	75
Mines and Municipal Affairs	358	569	526	464
Provincial Secretary	30	39	40	69
Provincial Treasurer	69	80	90	66
Public Utilities	32	32	37	174
Public Works	472	564	572	687
Total	2,869	3,542	3,773	5,089

The new Act produced several major changes. The commission was enlarged to three members with a permanent chairman as chief commis-

[5]By section 4 six classes were created: deputies, technical officers (those with professional training), administrative and executive officers, clerks to perform work of a routine nature, guards, messengers, and janitors, and a special class whose work required skill but not professional training, mechanics, for example.

[6]Quoted from the files of the provincial secretary.

sioner and given full control over job classification: "The commission may by an order . . . prescribe or change the specifications or the duties and responsibilities appertaining to any position."[7] Commission control over promotions is equally full and complete.[8] Rates of pay, however, are fixed by the lieutenant governor-in-council. The statute, of course, provides for appointment on merit which, except where productivity can be measured (as in typing), is decided almost entirely on the basis of an oral examination. For appointments to the technical officer class, the general practice is to have a board consisting of the civil service commissioner, a representative of the department concerned, and an outside examiner from the appropriate trade or profession. The full commission usually sits to hear contentious cases or appeals.

The general structure of the commission is now satisfactory except in two respects. There are no provisions in the Act covering the commissioner's salary though ordinarily his rate of pay moves consistently with that of other deputy ministers. The cabinet thus has a lever for controlling the commissioner but there is no evidence that it is used and nothing to suggest that it would be successful if it were. Secondly, one of the members of the commission is, at present, the Deputy Provincial Treasurer. It is, of course, bad practice to have a regular employee of the government as a member of a commission no matter how great his integrity and competence. The commission must not only be independent; it must also appear to be so.

The internal organization of the government departments (as in other governments) is based upon function and order, as is illustrated in the organization of the Department of Agriculture. The work of this department is at present divided into eight functions each of which is distinct enough to warrant the creation of a branch with a director and staff. The livestock branch takes a census of animal population and keeps statistics on monetary returns from the sale of livestock and its products. It also administers the schemes of government assistance for the purchase of purebred stock and financial assistance offered to students of veterinary science, and has general charge of government measures for the control of animal pests and diseases. A complete diagnostic service for animal diseases is provided by the veterinary laboratory branch. The dairy branch has four main duties: maintenance of statistics on production and sale of dairy products, inspection of butterfat content tests used by

[7]R.S.M., 1954, c. 39, s. 9(1).

[8]Section 24 of the Civil Service Act reads: "Except where the Commission finds that competition is impractical, it shall make promotions on a competitive basis with appropriate considerations beng given to the applicant's qualifications, record of performance, seniority and conduct."

creameries, promotion of exhibitions and displays, and research, particularly on the subject of costs of production. The main responsibility of the extension service branch is a specialized programme of education in agricultural communities carried on largely through agricultural representatives. Special attention is also given to regional fairs, ploughing matches, and garden competitions. Government regulation of co-operative societies and credit unions justified the creation of a branch for this purpose and part VII of the Companies Act, administered by the branch, lays down the general conditions under which such organizations may operate. The work of the farm help service branch is the placement of farm labour in co-operation with the National Employment Service. A publications branch makes available articles, reprints, and other relevant literature to individuals and associations. Finally, there is an audit and accounting branch. At the head of the department is the minister who is responsible to the legislature for the entire department, and immediately below him is the deputy. Within each branch there is a director and an assistant director and various clerical and professional members of staff whose order of importance is indicated by civil service classifications.

Many other departments follow the same principles of organization: Public Works divides itself into six branches comprising highway building, highway maintenance, highway equipment, surveys, inspections, and public buildings; Mines and Resources divides into forestry, game and fish, land, mines, water resources, and surveys. In the Attorney General's Department a territorial principle is added and the central office has only two branches, administration and accounting. The major part of law enforcement is decentralized through judicial districts.

Attempts to work out a satisfactory basis for relationships between civil servants as employees and the government as employer have a long history of ups and downs in Manitoba. A civil servants' association, organized in 1919, after some initial success became defunct in 1923. In 1934 a provincial club was created but it confined itself to the innocuous activity of "promoting social, sporting and dramatic activities and . . . good fellowship in the Civil Service."[9] In 1942 the Manitoba Civil Service Association was created and since then it has grown steadily in importance and effectiveness. Its most important single achievement was the creation of a joint council in July 1951 consisting of three nominees from the association and three members of the cabinet. The provincial secretary is a permanent member; the other two cabinet representatives vary from meeting to meeting depending on

[9]*Bison* (publication of the Manitoba Government Employees' Association), Dec. 1952, p. 5.

what is to be discussed, who is free at the time, and who is interested. The civil service commissioner almost always attends in an advisory capacity. The council has been an unqualified success and has obtained concrete results in the five-day week, a better pension plan, and moderate salary increases.

The salaries of employees in the public service is, of course, a crucial question in the relationship between employees and the government. One major accomplishment of the employees' association was in 1948 when the government agreed to base rates of pay on what is called prevailing rates, that is, rates comparable to those paid equivalent employees outside the service. The Department of Labour makes an annual wage and salary survey in thirteen different occupational groups and civil service salaries are kept roughly in line with its findings. Unfortunately there is a time lag of approximately one year between publication of the findings of the Department of Labour and adjustment of salaries. Also, comparison between the rates of wages in commercial enterprises and those in the public service is possible only in a limited way. The comparisons used relate largely to employees engaged in routine work such as filing clerks, typists, stenographers, caretakers, mechanics, and operators of mechanical equipment, and do not take into account a large number of positions in the public service which have no counterpart in private business. In general, the system of basing civil service salaries on this survey is successful only for those earning less than $350 a month.

Boards and Commissions

During the past decade a fairly wide use has been made of boards and commissions in the provincial administration. At present there is statutory provision for 91 boards of which 77 are active. The great bulk are either advisory or regulatory. Advisory boards most commonly facilitate the regulation of an activity or provision of a service by organized consulation with a representative group most familiar with the particular service or activity. Though the majority are restricted to the right to warn, to encourage, and be consulted, some of the advisory boards, the Health Services Advisory Commission, for example, have real power.[10] The board was set up in 1945 when a new Health Services Act was passed to provide for a complete revamping of provincial medical serv-

[10]There are advisory boards for health services, civil defence, education, frozen food lockers, game, public welfare, highway safety, historic sites, horned cattle, horticultural societies, industrial development, municipal affairs, weeds, practical nursing, libraries, women's institutes, livestock protection, fertilizer, and protection of fur bearing animals.

ices. There had been a danger that its new activities would bring the Department of Health into conflict with the medical profession, the hospitals, and the municipalities, and as a consequence all these groups were given representation on the board. It was given the task of advising the minister, "at his request, or of its own motion, in all matters relating to this Act and the administration and operation thereof, and to discharge such other duties relative to this Act as the Minister may request it to perform."[11] The board is also given a real if negative power in that no departmental regulation has any force unless the board has previously given its approval. In the formative years of the health services programme it met at least once a month; more recently it has met three or four times a year.

None of the other advisory boards has a veto power over the regulations issued by a department. Much more common is the function of the Frozen Food Locker Advisory Board which was created in 1950 when the government found it necessary as a public protection to license frozen food locker plants. In the great majority of cases the standards applied were as much in the interests of the trade as the public and the advice of the trade was considered valuable. The board suggests standards to the government which, if accepted, are made into regulations having the force of law.

Advisory boards are also used as an additional method of keeping certain activities of the government broadly in accordance with the public will and at the same time giving certain members of the public some insight into the problems of government. The Business Advisory Council is one example. It consists of "not more than thirty members, actively identified with private enterprise in the field of industry and commerce, chosen to be broadly representative of the province from a geographical point of view."[12] This council meets, on the average, about four times a year and has considered and reported on such questions as the development of industry in small towns, the probable effect of the St. Lawrence Seaway on Manitoba, and credit facilities for small business.

The Advisory Board on Education is also designed to give influential citizens a sense of participation in one aspect of the government's work. Its membership includes eight citizens appointed by the cabinet, nominees of the school inspectors, teachers, and trustees, the deputy minister of education, the chief inspector of schools, and the president of the University of Manitoba. The board once had real powers including a large measure of control over the curriculum but in 1945 the Minister

[11]R.S.M., 1954, c. 111, s. 15(a).
[12]Minutes of the Executive Council of Manitoba, 1954. Order-in-Council 73.

of Education became impatient with it and limited its activities to prescription of content, time, and duration of religious and patriotic exercises plus whatever might result from the clause in the Education Act stating that "All regulations respecting the examination, training, licensing, and grading of teachers, courses of study, text books and reference books shall, before being adopted or amended, be referred to the board for its discussion and report; and the board shall report thereon to the Minister within three months after the date on which a proposed regulation is submitted to it."[13]

Boards and commissions with the power to issue regulations are becoming increasingly common, largely because the responsibilities of modern governments are steadily growing. It has become necessary to guarantee minimum safety conditions for employees in certain trades found in the construction and manufacturing industries and also to protect the public against carelessness or fraud. A wide variety of activities is subject to direct or indirect regulation. Under direct regulation are barbers, electricians, electrical contractors, chiropractors and osteopaths, garage keepers, nurses, fish dealers, bee keepers, well borers, and so on. A number of professions, on the other hand, are left to regulate themselves according to provisions set out by a statute. There is, for example, an Act Respecting the Manitoba Dental Association[14] on the statute books, an act which is an interesting example of giving a group the power to regulate itself, imposing certain conditions upon it, and, to an extent, lending it the authority of the province. Under the Act a dental association is created and definitions are given as to who may be members. The association is required, following a legislative prescription as to procedure, to choose a board of directors which is given wide powers but its by-laws, to have effect, must be published in the *Manitoba Gazette*.

Regulatory functions have been delegated to a board or commission in thirty-seven instances. The Municipal and Public Utility Board, which began in 1921, has always been by far the most significant of the regulatory boards. Indeed, it became so significant that in 1959 it was split into two boards, one to deal with municipal matters and the other with public utilities. The Minister of Public Utilities explained the reason for the division as follows: "The Board is burdened with so many decisions and must make so many investigations with respect to such a wide variety of activities that it is almost impossible for them to give the individual time and attention to each case which they really should. We

[13]The Education Act, *R.S.M.*, 1954, c. 67, s. 22(2).
[14]*Ibid.*, c. 62.

feel that they will now be able to specialize."[15] The Municipal Board has a wide variety of functions with respect to local government. Local authorities must have its permission to issue debentures over a certain amount or to enter into certain agreements. If the minister so requests the board will inquire into the financial affairs of a local authority and may even take the municipality under its direct control.[16] It also serves as an appeal body for the Winnipeg Zoning Board, has a general supervisory power over the subdividing of land and building restrictions, and, in addition, administers the Real Estate Agents Act and the Securities Act. The Public Utility Board has regulatory jurisdiction over the rates charged for telephones, public service vehicles, and natural gas, and prices paid the brewers of beer by the Liquor Control Commission. Both the Municipal and Public Utility Boards have the power of a superior court in examining witnesses, producing papers, and enforcing orders and payment of costs. In cases involving a jurisdictional dispute an appeal lies with the Court of Appeal. Points of law may be appealed to the Court of Queen's Bench if leave to appeal is granted by the court.

None of the other thirty-seven regulatory boards operating in Manitoba has as wide powers as the Public Utility Board. On the whole their activities are confined to regulating a specific phase of some economic activity such as the price of milk, the conditions of apprenticeship, or minimum wage rates.

The central problem is how to combine this necessary delegation of authority with sufficient protection against arbitrary behaviour and bureaucracy. The authority delegated is almost always both specific and general. A board is usually given a list of enumerated subjects on which it may, in effect, legislate. Any gap in the enumerated powers is almost always covered by such phrases as ". . . the board may make regulations . . . generally for the better carrying out of this Act"[17] or "for the purpose of carrying out . . . this Act [the board] may make such regulations and orders as are ancillary thereto and not inconsistent therewith."[18] The main protection against the arbitrary use of such powers as these is that in most instances a regulation is not binding until it has been approved by the cabinet, and cabinet approval of regulations is by no means a formality in Manitoba. It is common for senior officials to

[15]Manitoba, Legislative Assembly, *Debates*, 1959, p. 1098.

[16]The following municipal corporations are under the supervision of the Municipal Board (as of June 1960): rural—Assiniboia, St. Vital, West Kildonan; towns and villages—Transcona, Brooklands; cities—Portage la Prairie, St. James, St. Boniface.

[17]The Apprenticeship Act, *R.S.M.*, 1954, c. 8, s. 19(1)(t).

[18]The Factories Act, *R.S.M.*, 1954, c. 79, s. 35.

be required to appear before their minister or even the whole cabinet to explain in detail why proposed regulations are necessary. In dubious cases an *ad hoc* committee of the cabinet is sometimes struck to investigate. A second but somewhat less effective protection against bureaucracy is found in the method by which regulations are published. In 1945 the Manitoba government accepted a recommendation of the Conference on the Uniformity of Laws in Canada and passed An Act to Provide for the Central Filing and Publication of Regulations,[19] a statute which provides that no regulation has any force unless filed with a registrar of regulations who must, within one month, publish it in the *Manitoba Gazette*. In addition, the regulations for each year are published in bound volumes.[20]

Boards and commissions are, of course, not alone in being delegated power. A cabinet is often the recipient of a very wide and sometimes loosely defined legislative competence. There are at least ten statutes giving the Manitoba cabinet almost unlimited power to issue regulations and almost as many more confer an equally broad power on individual ministers. For example, by sections 6 and 7 of the Education Act[21] the minister may prescribe regulations setting out the required qualifications of inspectors and teachers, discipline of students, establishment of model, normal, and technical schools including "the groups, kinds, classes or types of persons to be admitted," textbooks to be used, the "dimensions, equipment, style plan, furnishing, decoration, heating and ventilation of school buildings,"[22] and generally respecting all matters having to do with education.

[19]*Statutes of Manitoba*, 1945 (1st sess.), c. 56.
[20]An important development occurred when this study was being prepared for the press. At the 1961 session of the legislature a standing committee on statutory orders and regulations was created and given the task of examining all regulations. Should the committee report unfavourably on any particular regulation and should the house confirm the report then the minister or authority responsible for the regulation must revoke it or amend it in accordance with the instructions of the House. The Premier suggested the following guiding principles:
"(a) The regulations should not contain substantive legislation that should be enacted by the legislature, but should be confined to administrative matters. (b) The regulations should be in strict accord with the statute conferring the power, and unless so authorized by the statute should not contain a retroactive effect. (c) A regulation should not exclude the jurisdiction of the courts. (d) A regulations [sic] should not impose a fine, imprisonment, or other penalty, or shift the onus of proof of innocence onto a person accused of an offence. (e) The regulation in respect of personal liberties should be strictly confined to the authorization of the statute. (f) The regulation should not impose anything in way of a tax, as distinct from the fixing of an amount of a licence, fee or the like. (g) The regulation should be precise and unambiguous in all its parts." Man. L.A., *Deb.*, March 10, 1961, p. 700.
[21]R.S.M., 1954, c. 67.   [22]*Ibid.*, s. 49.

There are fifty statutes currently in force in Manitoba which contain clauses shifting the onus of proof of innocence to the accused. In 75 per cent of the laws the reversal of the time-honoured precept of innocent until proven guilty might be considered minor and inconsequential —they concern proof of holding a licence, proof of age, payment of dues in certain cases, proof that a return called for was actually made, that a stallion was enrolled as required, and so on. Other statutes go well beyond minor regulations, however. The Game and Fisheries Act[23] makes it an offence to ship the skins of fur-bearing animals out of Manitoba without a permit and section 46(3) of the Act states that "All such skins or pelts shall be deemed to have had their place of origin in Manitoba unless the contrary is proven to the satisfaction of the Director of Game." Section 46(4) states that proof of "the origin of such skins and pelts alleged to have been imported from outside of Manitoba shall be upon the person found in possession thereof." In all game and fish that are under protection proof of legal possession always rests with the holder and the finding of any device prohibited in the Act in the possession of any person is considered as *prima facie* evidence of guilt. Where a violation of the Game and Fisheries Act is suspected an officer of the department may search any private dwelling or building without a search warrant if the building is more than ten miles from the nearest justice of the peace.

Several sections of the Liquor Control Act are based on the same principle of guilty until proven innocent.[24] Section 212, for example, reads: "where, on the prosecution of a person charged with committing an offence against this Act, in selling or keeping for sale or giving or keeping or having or purchasing or receiving liquor, *prima facie* proof is given that that person had in his possession or charge or control any liquor in respect of, or concerning, which he is being prosecuted, then, unless that person proves that he did not commit the offence with which he is so charged, he may be convicted of the offence."

One final example comes from the Natural Products Marketing Act,[25] section 11 of which provides that "In any prosecution for an offence under this Act or the regulations it is not necessary for the informant or person prosecuting to prove that the natural product in respect of which the prosecution is instituted was produced in the area to which any scheme for the regulation of the natural product relates; and if the accused person pleads or alleges that the natural product was not pro-

[23]*R.S.M.*, 1954, c. 94.
[24]*Statutes of Manitoba*, 1956, c. 40.
[25]*R.S.M.*, 1954, c. 179, s. 11.

duced in the area to which the scheme relates, the burden of proof thereof shall be upon the accused person."

All of these sections owe their origin to the insistence of enforcement officers who have come to take their work too seriously. Undoubtedly they have seen people escape through technicalities when the officers bringing the charge felt sure of guilt or when they have been unable to prosecute because of lack of evidence. Far better surely to have the few bootleggers or poachers go free rather than continue this breach which well-meaning but excessive bureaucratic zeal has made in a basic legal principle.

LOCAL GOVERNMENT | 9

A CIVIL SERVICE ORGANIZED on a departmental basis and responsible to the legislature through appropriate ministers is only one of two systems through which the province of Manitoba discharges its administrative responsibilities. The second is through the institutions of local government organized as rural municipalities, towns, villages, or cities. In June 1960 there were 112 rural municipalities, 35 incorporated towns, 37 villages, and 6 cities. Fourteen districts under resident administrators have been organized in areas where the population is too sparse for municipalization. Finally, there are 1,800 school districts for primary education and some 41 larger units for secondary education with 5 more projected.

All these institutions are creatures of the province and exist by virtue of provincial statutes. Section 92 of the British North America Act confers certain enumerated powers on the provinces, one of which is "municipal institutions in the province." Under this section Manitoba has created municipal institutions and conferred on them parts of the general power it has by virtue of the British North America Act. Like other provinces, Manitoba constitutes the inhabitants of a certain area as a corporation and gives it defined powers and responsibilities to be exercised through a council elected by the inhabitants.

Although the idea of delegating power to a local corporation is found everywhere in Canada, circumstances have produced a pattern in Manitoba that is, in some ways, distinctive. The new province, of course, inherited few institutions of local government from the pre-Confederation period. Indeed, the only such institution in existence in 1870 was the church parish. In the absence of other institutions, therefore, the legislature at its first meeting organized local works in the Winnipeg area on a parochial basis. The Parish Assessment Act of 1871 clarified boundaries and provided that if the heads of families of a particular area met in a public place and presented the clerk of the peace with a formal resolution demanding a certain local work, officials could assess each family proportionally and carry out the work.

To provide for local works in the rest of the province, the County Assessment Act, drafted by Lieutenant Governor Archibald, was passed. Four counties, corresponding to the four electoral districts of Selkirk, Provencher, Lisgar, and Marquette, were created. The Act provided that at the first meeting of the Court of Sessions in each year the Grand Jury was to present to the presiding judge two lists of nine names. The judge was required to select one from the first list to be county treasurer and three from the second to be assessors. The jury also presented a statement of local works that were necessary which when approved by the judge became the basis of a levy.

The first attempt to organize municipalities was made in 1873 when an act was passed authorizing the cabinet to create a municipality whenever two-thirds of the male householders petitioned, provided that there were more than thirty in the area. Each municipality so created was authorized to pass by-laws dealing with roads and bridges, poor relief, drainage, fire protection, dykes, public health, and pounds but such by-laws were not to be valid unless approved by the cabinet. The act was permissive, not mandatory, and in the first year of its operation only one municipality, Sunnyside-Springfield, was created. By 1881, when an attempt was made to create a full-fledged municipal system on a compulsory basis, only six areas had organized themselves.[1]

The decade beginning in 1880 was a crucial period in Manitoba's municipal development. The province was divided into 26 areas and inhabitants of each were required to choose a council and accept responsibility for certain local works. An attempt was also made to transfer the Ontario county system to Manitoba, for some form of organization midway between the provincial and the municipal was necessary since there could not be a courthouse, gaol, and land registry office for each of the municipalities. The system proposed, in the words of the minister who introduced the legislation in 1883, was

... the organization of county councils in their most simple and workable form. The councils are to be composed of a presiding officer, and the reeve of each of the local municipalities, and mayor of each incorporated town

[1]These were Sunnyside-Springfield, Kildonan, St. James, Rockwood, Portage la Prairie, and Westbourne.

in the county. The counties are generally divided into from five to seven and sometimes eight municipalities. . . . There will not be less than five and in most cases no more than seven. This will give an efficient body to legislate on inter-municipal questions—such as bridges, drainage, roads, etc. Further these councils have the power of making provision for the procuring of a convenient place in the county as a site for the erection of the county court house, jail, registry office and other necessary buildings.[2]

But in only three areas, Selkirk, Portage la Prairie, and Brandon, was more than a paper existence achieved for the county system, which proved totally unsatisfactory partly because of the sparse population and partly because of the great distances involved. In many instances the proposed county seat was not even connected by road with some of its outlying municipalities. In addition, a large number of the municipalities that were grouped into counties were completely incapable of giving the senior body any financial support.

Before arriving at the system which prevails today Manitoba experimented briefly with the judicial district board. In 1884 the province was divided into three judicial districts, in each of which the board consisted of the mayors and reeves of every municipal corporation within the district. The original purpose of the boards was to decide the location and costs of courthouse buildings and raise the necessary money by a levy on each municipality. However, during the second year of their existence the boards took over the building of connecting roads and ferries and the appointment of district health officers. The difficulty with the system was that the municipalities were still incapable of meeting levies.

In 1886 a special committee of the legislature was struck to consider the whole question of provision of services that transcended municipal boundaries but which were still regarded as local in character. The committee recommended the abolition of the judicial district boards and "the appointment of a member or officer of the government to control the expense, connected with the maintenance of court houses, jails and administration of justice and to perform other duties now discharged by the Judicial Boards."[3] The committee also recommended that the capital cost of necessary public buildings be paid by the province and the cost of maintenance thereafter be levied against the municipalities. In short, the judicial districts were to be maintained only as convenient administrative units. The report of the committee was accepted and acted upon and in 1886 the office of municipal commissioner was created.[4] The

[2]Statement of C. P. Brown quoted in the *Winnipeg Free Press*, June 28, 1883.
[3]*Winnipeg Free Press*, April 15, 1886.
[4]*Statutes of Manitoba*, 1886, c. 52.

commissioner was made a member of the cabinet and charged primarily with the task of creating facilities for the administration of justice. The first levy was made in 1893 and since that time levies have been made for a variety of purposes including wolf bounties, sanatoria, mothers' allowances, wartime patriotic funds, soldiers' taxation relief, child welfare, and old age pensions.[5] In accordance with the report, any functions of an inter-municipal nature became the administrative responsibility of the province, no "second tier" (to use Professor Crawford's phrase) being added to the municipal structure. Though Manitoba's attempt to use Ontario's system had failed, its experience did prevent Saskatchewan and Alberta from making the same mistake.

The pattern of municipal organization established in 1886 is, in principle, the one prevailing at present and further consideration of history would be more tedious than enlightening. A more important consideration is the organization of the institutions of local government and the discharge of their functions.

Any area within a municipality in Manitoba may acquire separate existence as a village if 25 per cent of the householders so petition, if the petition comes from an area that has over 500 inhabitants, and if it has a taxable assessment of at least $300,000. In addition, the residents must be "sufficiently close together to form an incorporated village" which means that where the population is less than 2,000 the area must not exceed 640 acres.[6] However, as soon as the population reaches 1,500, the area may petition the cabinet for incorporation as a town, and after 10,000, as a city.[7]

In any institution of local government, whether it be a town, village, or rural municipality, the powers of the corporation are exercised through an elected council. The franchise is extended to all persons over twenty-one years of age whose residence in the area antedated the election by six months. Owners of real property of an assessed value of not less than $100 may vote whether resident or not. Only owners may vote on money by-laws requiring the approval of ratepayers.

[5]In 1952 the Municipal Commissioner's levy met the following expenses:

judicial district levy	$ 59,651
county court levy	19,833
soldiers' taxation relief	15,000
sanatoria	235,000
cancer research	29,000
institute for the blind	12,000
Total	$370,984

[6]R.S.M., 1954, c. 173, s. 9(c).
[7]Ibid., s. 12.

There are certain differences in the composition of the councils of these three different units. In a town the governing body consists of a mayor and two councillors for each ward with the provision that the maximum number of wards is six. In a village there are a mayor and four councillors who may be elected either on a ward system or at large. In a rural municipality the council consists of a reeve and not less than four or more than six councillors. Reeves and mayors are heads of their councils and chief executive officers of the corporations. As part of their general executive power they possess what is described in the Municipal Act as a veto power which applies only to by-laws and resolutions authorizing the expenditure of public money and must be exercised within twenty-four hours of passage. The veto power is simply a delaying action and a chance for a "sober second thought" on the part of the council because it "may be over-ruled and removed at any subsequent regular or special meeting of the council if a majority of the members of the whole council, not counting the mayor or reeve, are present and a majority of the members present vote in favor of over-ruling and removing the veto."[8]

In essence the functions of local governments offer certain protections for life and property through police and fire departments and inspections, provide such public works as streets, sidewalks, sewers, and local roads, certain health and welfare measures which come within their allocated jurisdiction, facilities for light and water, and, where appropriate, recreational and community services such as playgrounds and curling rinks. The most striking fact is the relatively narrow sphere of autonomous action given to the local governments of towns, villages, and municipalities in Manitoba. They have full control of fire departments except that the consent of the minister of municipal affairs is necessary before one corporation can make a contract with another for protection. All councils have the power to regulate the standards governing the installation and regulation of plumbing and may appoint inspectors for this purpose. Their power over other building trades in the interests of public safety is limited, however, in that any inspectors appointed must enforce only the provisions of the provincial Building Trades Protection Act. Zoning regulations are subject to the dual qualification that plans for new residential subdivisions must have approval of the Municipal Board and that all regulations made must be consistent with the Town Planning Act.

Councils may pass a number of by-laws in the interests of public safety and the general peace but compared with the Canada Criminal

[8]*Ibid.*, s. 338(2).

Code and the numerous provincial prohibitions they are relatively innocuous. For example, a council may compel the owners of a well to cover it or may prescribe general regulations for the handling of explosives (provided they are consistent with the Canadian Explosives Act) or may regulate on "the ringing of bells except church, blowing of horns, beating of drums, shouting and other noises calculated to disturb or annoy the inhabitants."[9]

The aid which municipalities may give to hospitals is limited to a rate not exceeding one mill on the dollar for taxable property in each year for five years. If the grant is less than this it may be made without prior approval by the ratepayers but not without the approval of the Municipal Board. Other grants in aid which municipal corporations may make are specified in the Municipal Act and cover the dependents of war veterans, support of boys' and girls' clubs, assistance in the maintenance of public cemeteries, agricultural societies, and the provision of seed grain or fodder to those unable to provide it.

The powers of municipal corporations to enter into contracts for light, heat, or water for the municipality are severely limited. All such contracts must be submitted to the electorate for approval, except those for light if they are under specified amounts in which case approval by the Municipal Board only is required.[10] Franchises granted to bus companies, street railways, or other forms of public transportation must have the approval of both the board and the ratepayers.

Councils may pass by-laws for the erection and maintenance of public rinks but if the expenditure requires an additional mill levy or if the debt incurred cannot be met in one year then permission of the Municipal Board is required. Exactly the same provisions apply to the creation of community centres.

Rigid financial controls indirectly restrict any autonomy that the units of local government do possess. In the first place they are permitted to use only the tax on property and a very carefully defined business tax. In rural areas the annual rate must not exceed three cents on each dollar of assessment exclusive of school rates and in towns and villages the figure is two-and-one-half cents. A council may borrow only for current expenses and the amount must not exceed the taxes levied for that year; any by-law for contracting debts of more than a one-year term is invalid unless approved not only by the ratepayers but also by the Municipal Board. If a municipality has a cash surplus and does not wish to estab-

[9]*Ibid.*, s. 907(a).
[10]Rural municipalities need board approval only if the amount of money involved is less than $3,000, villages if less than $1,500, and towns if under $6,000.

lish a reserve fund it must invest it in Government of Canada bonds. Finally, all financial records of the councils are subject to strict provincial supervision. All units must follow a standard system of bookkeeping and every municipal treasurer must make a detailed yearly statement of financial operations to the minister. A provincial auditor makes an annual inspection. If either report turns up any irregularities the minister may command the council to correct the situation and if it fails to do so he "shall deal with the matter in a manner best calculated to protect and further the interests of the corporation, and, for that purpose he may, if thought desirable, dismiss from office any treasurer or other officer of the corporation."[11]

Another indirect restriction is the very large fixed charges which the local councils have to meet and over which they have little or no control. Education expenses are the most important of these. Local school boards are independent of municipal councils and simply submit their budgets each year. The council has no alternative to raising its share of the money although it has no control whatever over how the money is spent. Education takes a substantial part of the budget; indeed, in Flin Flon in 1955, an extreme case, it consumed 60 per cent. On the average, education takes about one-third of available revenue.

In the last decade there has been strong pressure, particularly from the rural municipalities, for financial assistance from the province. The assistance that is given now takes the form of shared cost programmes and direct grants which total more than one-third of local government budgets. Provincial contributions have more than doubled in the past five years and if they continue to increase, as there is every reason to suppose, local governments will lose the small amount of power they now have.

A large number of the units of local government in Manitoba are too small to meet the demands made on modern government. As of June 1960, there were a dozen rural municipalities with a revenue over which the council had control (apart from school board levies and other fixed charges) of less than $50,000. If this figure is broken down according to the amounts normally spent on particular services, about $20,000 would be available for public works, which is not enough to buy the most efficient machinery for such things as snow removal, gravel loading, or road building. Only $2,000 could be devoted to the protection of life and property. Less than $5,000 would be available for hospital services and the welfare budget would be consumed if five children were maintained by a local children's aid society. Approximately $8,000

11*R.S.M.*, 1954, c. 173, s. 672.

would be available for administration out of which, by statute, the municipality must pay a secretary-treasurer and an assessor as well as meet printing and office expenses. The situation in some villages is even worse. Seventeen have controllable revenues of less than $30,000 and three have $5,000 or less. One village has a revenue of $2,500. It is inconceivable that any pretence can be made of providing a variety of services on such budgets. Surely such villages should be joined with the surrounding municipality.

School Boards

Until recently some 1,800 school districts in Manitoba were responsible for financing (through the municipality) and administering primary and secondary education within their boundaries. In 1959 a Royal Commission on Education reported in favour of creating larger units (40 or 50 instead of 1,800) to deal with secondary education and specified that each division should have a balanced assessment of at least 5 million dollars and should employ 80 to 100 teachers. This recommendation, which is being carried out, recognizes that from the points of view of both efficiency of operation and quality of instruction the larger unit is superior to the community school board. The larger unit will make possible a more diversified educational programme, will help to procure and retain competent teachers, and will encourage greater efficiency and economy through such practices as central purchasing.

The administration of the larger areas is entrusted to a board of five trustees (the number may under certain circumstances be increased to nine) elected for two-year terms. The division board has complete authority over secondary education, all powers formerly vested in city, town, or village boards being transferred to it. A notable and new power is that of floating debentures for capital purposes of up to $50,000 without obtaining approval of the ratepayers. Local school boards are left with authority over elementary education which includes hiring teachers and the general custody and regulation of school property.

The emphasis in financing the larger areas is on equality of opportunity for high school students. Each council levies taxes in accordance with a standard formula[12] and receives substantial provincial grants including free textbooks, 100 per cent of teachers' salaries up to an approved scale, 75 per cent of maintenance costs, 60 per cent of transportation, approximately 40 per cent of building capital, and 50 per cent

[12]The formula as stated by the Minister of Education is: "Five mills plus one mill on each additional $33,333 of balanced assessment per teacher up to $200,000 balanced assessment and, after that one mill for each $50,000." Man., L.A., *Deb.*, Oct. 27, 1958.

of administrative and library costs (maximums beyond which these percentages do not apply are established in the School Act). The financial relationship between the larger division boards and the local school boards was stated by the minister: "The local board would forward its requirements to the Division Board which has no authority here and is simply the receiving agency. Thus with the budget of the local districts before it, and its own budget, the Division Board determines the grants to which both the local board and the Division Boards are entitled and makes its requisition upon the municipalities concerned and notifies the Department of Education of the amount that will be required from the Provincial Treasurer."[13]

The importance of local government has been stressed by political scientists for generations. Several years ago Professor Clokie wrote:

There is good reason for the belief that local self-government is the cornerstone of democracy. From antiquity it has been observed that the existence of numerous semi-autonomous communities is a major protection against the rise of tyranny in a state. Under a stable democratic system, local self-government serves a most valuable educative purpose. It is through participation in the affairs of the immediate community that individuals can most easily be brought to perceive their public matters can most readily be awakened, maintained, and made effective. It is there, too, that the close connection between wise policy and sound administration is most evident for the electorate have constantly before them the consequences of their own decisions . . . in no other phase of government is there such an intimate contact between rulers and ruled as in rural and urban politics; no where else can the citizen be so completely identified with their own government.[14]

Manitoba's system could not be said even to approximate such an ideal. Except for the larger school areas, the present system of local government is antiquated and hopelessly out of touch with modern conditions, based as it is upon the concept that communications are difficult and that even the smallest local community will develop distinctive ways of carrying out particular services. Even if this were still true the range of autonomy which the councils are allowed is very narrow and in many cases their financial ability to cope with the functions they do perform is completely inadequate.

The City of Winnipeg

Winnipeg was first incorporated in 1873 under a provincial statute which provided that any district of more than 30 freehold residents might become a municipality if at least two-thirds of the freeholders so peti-

[13]*Ibid.*
[14]H. McD. Clokie, *Canadian Government and Politics*, p. 240.

tioned. From 1873 to 1902 the city remained subject to the general laws governing the powers of municipalities in the province. In 1902 a charter was granted which with periodic revisions and consolidations has remained as the basis of civic government.

Winnipeg is now governed by a council composed of a mayor and eighteen aldermen elected for two-year terms. The theory of government as stated in the charter is that the council is the legislative body and the mayor the chief executive. The charter does not mention the six standing committees (finance, public works, public utilities, public safety, health and personnel, and legislation) which are in effect the crux of the whole system.[15] The committees of council, like the cabinet, initiate policy and when it has been approved by the legislative branch, which is simply the members of the six committees sitting as a group, they exercise a general supervision over the officials who execute the legislation. The mayor presides at council but has no vote except in case of a tie and is *ex officio* a member of each committee. He has a veto over all by-laws and resolutions of the council authorizing the expenditure of money, which must be exercised within forty-eight hours of passage by a notice in writing to the city clerk. His veto may be overridden by a two-thirds vote of council.

In theory the six standing committees are equal and each has jurisdiction specified by by-law. In practice the committee on finance is dominant for it has jurisdiction over "all financial matters of the city . . . all contracts, orders, engagements, reports, recommendations and proceedings involving the expenditure of money, of all or any of the other committees . . . or of any officer of the city; and no contract, order, engagement, recommendation or procedure involving the expenditure of money of any of the said Committees . . . or of any officer of the city, shall have any legal effect or operation until the same shall have been recommended by the said Committee of Finance."[16] Because the committee of finance must review the recommendations of other committees where they involve expenditure is alone among the committees is in a position to acquire an over-all view of city operations and to act as a co-ordinating agency. Indeed, it often encroaches on work which might logically fall under the jurisdiction of another committee. For example, in 1953 when the city engaged a firm of management consultants to review the internal administration of civic departments it reported to an advisory committee

[15]In 1907 the committee system was abolished and executive functions were vested in a board of control, composed of a mayor and four controllers, elected annually by the city at large. In 1918 the committee system was restored following a referendum vote.

[16]City of Winnipeg by-law 15330.

of council which is responsible to the committee of finance and not to personnel and legislation.

There is a close relationship between each committee and the head of the civic department under its jurisdiction. In some committees, finance for example, the department head is an official adviser to the aldermen and entitled to attend all meetings. Whether the department head is officially recognized as a member of the committee or not his advice must be sought before a recommendation for an expenditure of money is approved.[17] Such a provision is, of course, only common sense. Laski's statement with reference to the English system is equally applicable to Manitoba:

Indeed, it may fairly be said that the more close the co-operation between them, the more effectively is its work performed. A committee relies upon its officials not only for expert information and advice, but for the shaping of plans, the guidance of policy, that discreet and tactful criticism of either excessive inertia or over-bold experiment which has been so largely responsible for orderly progress in English local government during the last century. . . . His [the head of a civic department] task, indeed, is a delicate one. He has to win the reality of power without seeming to secure it. He has to arrive at some *modus vivendi* not only with his chairman, to whom the exercise of personal power may be a precious experience, but of members who enjoy "teaching the officials their proper place." He cannot dominate them, since he thereby merely invites attack. He cannot intervene in debate with the hot, pungent argument which is often decisive in discussion. He has to hint, to persuade, to learn by trial and error the delicate art of letting facts speak for themselves. He has to learn to press advice without arousing antagonism and to invent policy without seeming to be its author.[18]

Winnipeg makes substantial use of special purpose boards which, while interlocked with the council through membership, have varying degrees of independence. The board of police commissioners, for instance, which is a statutory body in that its existence is provided for in the charter, has full control over the police force in the city and is made up of the mayor, two other aldermen, the senior judge of the county court of Winnipeg, and the police magistrate. One advantage of this type of board is that a specific and important function is singled out from the ordinary and routine business of the council, receiving instead the specialized attention of a smaller group. The presence of a senior judge and the police

[17]By-law 15330 (77–2) stipulates that before a committee recommends an expenditure it "shall first procure a report from such officer [i.e. the head of the appropriate department] as to how far the same is, in his opinion, necessary or expedient with reference to such of the general interests and requirements of the city as fall within the department."

[18]Harold J. Laski, W. Ivor Jennings, and William A. Robson, eds., *A Century of Municipal Progress 1835–1935* (London, 1935), pp. 92–3.

magistrate make it virtually impossible to use the administration of law enforcement for political ends. Nevertheless, the council retains ultimate control both by having the majority of the members and by having the power to change the annual estimates of the commission.

There are four boards with lay representation and two composed entirely of laymen. The auditorium commission, for example, is composed of five aldermen and four laymen appointed by council. Because the auditorium is completely devoted to public entertainment and is supported by a grant from the city it is entirely logical that representative citizens should join with the council in its administration. The trustees of the sinking fund are an example of a board made up entirely of laymen. Of the three citizens who sit on it one is chosen by council and two are appointed by the Court of Queen's Bench. The board is autonomous and, as its name indicates, has charge of the administration of all sinking funds.

The school board is quite different from the others in that its membership of 15 is elected by the same electorate that chooses the council. It is completely autonomous vis-à-vis the council and derives its authority not from the city charter but from the Public Schools Act. Although its financial support comes from taxes collected by the council, the council has no authority whatever to lower (or raise) the estimates which the school board presents to it. In many ways the adoption of this system in Winnipeg represents a rather unthinking imitation of the Ontario system. Egerton Ryerson once said that "to transfer the management of the schools . . . to the municipal bodies would doubtless result in their deterioration. To give these bodies power to limit the expenditure of the school trustees would tend in the same direction."[19] It is difficult to believe that the electorate which votes for a city council of such limited vision would choose the far-sighted school trustees that Dr. Ryerson envisaged. It is equally difficult to defend the proposition that one body can draw on another without having the responsibility for raising money. Understandably, the system has not always worked well in Winnipeg. In the 1930's there was almost continuous controversy between school board and council. In 1938 the legislature amended the charter and the Public Schools Act to provide machinery for arbitration in the form of two members of the council, two members of the school board, and a chairman selected by the Court of King's Bench. The one time this arrangement was tried it broke down completely. However, in more recent years there has been comparative peace between the two bodies, largely because of the party system that has developed in civic affairs.

[19]Nathaniel Burwash, *Egerton Ryerson* (Toronto, 1903), p. 197.

The casual observer of council or school board officers might easily conclude that the Co-operative Commonwealth Federation was the only party represented inasmuch as the other members bear no obvious labels. Nevertheless, there is behind the scenes a group known as the civic election committee which is dominated by owners of valuable real estate in the city and whose primary interest is reasonable economy of operation. This group will sponsor candidates, who agree with its philosophy, by open endorsement and provision of campaign funds. In recent years the committee has secured control of the significant committees in both the school board and the council and has thereby ensured that both are dominated by a conservative philosophy.

TABLE V
POPULATION OF WINNIPEG AND SUBURBS
1926–56

	1926	1931	1941	1946	1956
Winnipeg	191,431	218,875	221,960	229,045	255,093
St. Boniface	14,187	16,305	18,157	21,613	28,851
St. James	12,510	13,868	13,892	14,903	26,502
St. Vital	7,785	10,402	11,993	14,674	23,672
East Kildonan	8,415	9,047	8,350	9,071	18,718
West Kildonan	6,078	6,132	6,110	6,579	15,256
Fort Garry	3,168	3,962	4,453	5,200	13,592
Transcona	5,218	5,747	5,495	6,132	8,312
Charleswood	971	1,226	1,934	2,688	4,982
North Kildonan	1,019	1,347	1,946	2,338	4,451
Brooklands	2,489	2,628	2,240	2,728	3,941
Assiniboia	1,200	1,675	1,968	2,160	3,577
West St. Paul	614	790	1,032	958	1,623
East St. Paul	744	815	1,055	1,052	1,504
Tuxedo	717	*	735	677	1,163
Old Kildonan	451	647	704	666	1,011

*Census figures for this year not comparable with other years.

Special purpose boards, with all interested municipalities represented, until recently provided the only method of dealing with problems requiring inter-municipal co-operation.[20] In the past decade it has become evident that the problem of governing metropolitan Winnipeg cannot be solved by *ad hoc* boards. As shown in Table V, suburban growth has

[20]Seven of these have administered projects dealing with the whole of the Greater Winnipeg area. They are: the administrative board of the Greater Winnipeg water district, the administrative board of the Greater Winnipeg sanitary district, the Greater Winnipeg transit commission, the St. James Winnipeg airport commission, the metropolitan town planning commission, the metropolitan civil defence board, and the board of the Greater Winnipeg mosquito abatement district. Four other boards administer matters which are inter-municipal but not concerned with the whole area: the Winnipeg and St. Boniface joint bridge committee, the Winnipeg and St. Boniface harbour commission, the Winnipeg and St. Boniface harbour control board, and the rivers and streams protection authority no. I.

been very rapid, especially during the past ten years when some of the suburbs nearly tripled their population. In 1952 the provincial government appointed a committee of the legislature to review the question of provincial-municipal financial relations. This committee struck a sub-committee to consider the special problem of Greater Winnipeg and as an interim solution recommended the creation of a single metropolitan board to take over the services of all existing inter-municipal boards. As a long-term solution the committee stated that "Only the establishment of a single metropolitan authority, equipped with sufficient powers, would ensure that all necessary metropolitan facilities were constructed, that all metropolitan services were properly coordinated, and that the costs of such services were equitably shared."[21] As a result of this report the units of Greater Winnipeg moved to set up an inter-municipal study group but could not agree upon a basis for apportioning the cost among themselves. In 1955 the provincial government set up and financed the Greater Winnipeg Investigating Commission which, after four years of study, hearings, and travel recommended the creation of a metropolitan authority. The commission reported that:

No organization exists which is responsible for the welfare of Greater Winnipeg and which has the authority and capacity to deal with new problems which affect the Metropolitan area. When new problems arose, they were handled, belatedly, by ad hoc organizations created by the Provincial Government or through the tardy, unwilling, suspicious co-operation of the Municipal councils.

Thus in 1950, when a substantial area of Greater Winnipeg was flooded, the municipalities fought the flood independently and ineffectively; the necessary centralized organization came into being only when the Provincial Government called upon the Army to take charge. During the 1956 flood threat, the Provincial Government was obliged to establish the organization needed to build up Greater Winnipeg's flood defences.

In another sphere, it was not possible to build the Disraeli Freeway, partly because no Inter-municipal organization existed which had the authority to undertake the project, and to distribute the cost equitably among the residents of Greater Winnipeg. Arterial highways approaches to Greater Winnipeg are unkempt and unattractive, partly because no authority exists which could assume responsibility for beautifying them, levying the cost over the whole metropolitan area.[22]

The provincial government acted promptly on the report of the investigating commission. Less than a year after its presentation the Premier

---

[21]"Report of the Exploratory Sub-Committe on the Organization of Local Government Services in the Greater Winnipeg area," *Manitoba Provincial-Municipal Committee Report*, Appendix C (Winnipeg, 1953), p. 93.

[22]*Report of the Greater Winnipeg Investigating Commission* (1959), p. 224.

introduced legislation which laid the foundation for a metropolitan authority. In October 1960 a ten-man council took over certain designated functions within the metropolitan area as well as exercising jurisdiction over planning (the substitution of a carefully prepared rational plan of urban growth for the previous unco-ordinated urban sprawl) and river pollution in an additional zone five miles beyond the metropolitan boundaries. In general terms the new council has, "within the metropolitan area and the additional zone, sole and full responsibility for, and authority and jurisdiction over, the planning and development . . . including the design, lay-out, and plan of highways and public places, the creation and placing of buildings and other structures . . . and generally the uses to which land and buildings in the metropolitan area and additional zone may be put . . ."[23]

Other services and functions to be brought under control of the metropolitan council at such intervals as the cabinet may decide are assessment, arterial roads including bridges and regulation of traffic, the transit system, water except for local distribution lines, sewage and garbage disposal, major parks, flood protection, civil defence, mosquito abatement, and weed control. The council will be able to make a levy against the appropriate area for the necessary money and may also, after cabinet approval, require municipalities affected to contribute a part of their business and commercial tax revenues. It may also issue debentures without the usual referendum proceedings.[24] There is no mention in the bill of centralizing police and fire protection services. The government's strategy is obviously to transfer at first only services about which there is a large measure of agreement and thereby to prove in practice the virtues, so apparent in theory, of a metropolitan authority.

[23]*Statutes of Manitoba*, 1960, c. 40, s. 78.
[24]The act also provides that the present municipalities and school districts included in Metro, although still possessing the financial structure and powers that they have always had, will be asked to refer their proposals to borrow to the Municipal Board. When such proposals are presented the metro council may lodge an objection. If it does so the Municipal Board must make the decision.

A DISCUSSION OF THE JUDICIARY in any Canadian province is of necessity limited in scope. The Canadian constitution, unlike the American, does not make a neat and clear separation between provincial and federal courts. Under the British North America Act Canada is given control over the selection, appointment, tenure, and salaries of judges in the superior, district, and county courts. The provinces have jurisdiction over "the administration of justice in the province, including the constitution, maintenance and organization of provincial courts, both of civil and criminal jurisdiction, and including procedure in civil matters in those courts." For juvenile and family courts and magistrates' courts, the provinces have both the power of appointment and the responsibility of organization. Despite the fact that, as in every other province, part of the court structure in Manitoba is federal, there are some aspects of the development of the judiciary that are directly related to local circumstances.

It is somewhat paradoxical that although the area that is now Manitoba has enjoyed a long unbroken connection with the British Crown many of the British institutions of government developed very late. British common law was assumed to be applicable to any area settled by British people but if the area had been conquered it became a privilege to be sought and could be obtained only by special dispensation. The Canadian Northwest had, of course, been settled and hence the transfer of common law was, in theory, automatic.

When it sat as a court the Council of Assiniboia decided all cases that came before it in accordance with British practice. The question is whether the law applied was that of May 1670 (the date the Hudson's Bay charter was granted) or whether the improvements and changes made in Britain found their way into the court. Adam Thom, the first recorder of Rupert's Land, always maintained that he was applying the laws of 1670. The first mention of the adoption of a revised code is found in the Minutes of the Council of Assiniboia for April 1862 where the 53rd article provides that "In place of the laws of England of the date of the Hudsons Bay Company's Charter, the Laws of England of the date of Her Majesty's accession [1837] so far as they may be applicable to the condition of this Colony shall regulate the proceedings of the General Court till some higher authority or this Council shall have expressly provided either or in whole or in part to the contrary."[1] Two years later the Council passed the following amendment to remove "all doubts as to the true construction of the 53rd Article of the Code of 11th April, 1862 . . . the proceedings of the General Court shall be regulated by the Laws of England, not only of the date of Her present Majesty's accession, so far as they may apply to the condition of the Colony, but also by all such laws of England, of subsequent date as may be applicable to the same: in other words . . . the proceedings of the General Court shall be regulated by the existing Laws of England . . . in as far as the same are known to the Court."[2]

The intent of these ordinances is clear, and until 1870 practice followed intent despite the lack of precision in the language. The phrase "to regulate the proceedings of the General Court" which appears in both could be interpreted to mean that only the court proceedings were to be modernized. In a report on the laws in force in Assiniboia prior to Confederation, F. G. Johnson observed: "It is obvious that the language of either or both these enactments is inadequate to extend the laws of England . . . both being restricted to the regulations and proceedings of the court."[3] The Court of Queen's Bench created in Manitoba after Confederation followed Johnson's interpretation and decided all cases whose origin was prior to July 15, 1870, in accordance with the laws of England of 1670. In *Sinclair* v. *Mulligan* Chief Justice Killam held that "a mere verbal bargain for the sale of lands was sufficient to pass the title in both law and equity. It was not for some seven years after the date of the Company's charter that the statute of frauds was enacted. Before its enactment a verbal agreement was valid and enforceable in

[1]E. H. Oliver, ed., *The Canadian North-West*, I, 500.
[2]*Ibid.*, pp. 534–5.
[3]F. G. Johnson, a judge of the Superior Court of the Province of Quebec, was made a special commissioner of the federal government in 1870 to report on "the state of the laws, regulations and ordinances lawfully in force in Manitoba up to the 15th of July, 1870."

Assiniboia."[4] His judgment was upheld by Chief Justice Mathers in 1912 in the case of *Larence* v. *Larence* which had also originated in the pre-Confederation period. In his decision Chief Justice Mathers held that the English laws of probate of 1670 must apply.[5] Both judges based their decisions on a literal interpretation of the ordinances of 1862 and refused to take intent into account.

British common law, statute law, and judicial procedures began to come into use only after July 15, 1870. The early statutes creating the Manitoba courts were, in the main, so worded as to leave the judges free to adopt such precedents of court procedure as were applicable. By a statute of 1871 the newly formed legislature of Manitoba provided for the creation of a supreme court[6] and conferred jurisdiction on it by the simple statement that it was to be the same as a corresponding British court of law, equity and probate. The statute also stated that "as far as possible consistently with the circumstances of the country, the laws of evidence and principles which govern the administration of Justice in England, shall obtain in the Supreme Court of Manitoba."[7] Similar phrases are found in Manitoba statutes relating to the Court of Queen's Bench in 1880, 1891, and 1913. Their over-all effect has been to leave the judges free to adopt as much of the British body of rules, procedures, and precedents as has been found applicable.

For a considerable period after its creation Manitoba borrowed more than court precedents and legal principles. The province also obtained most of its lawyers and all of its judges from the Eastern provinces. The first superior court judge who was trained and articled in Manitoba was Thomas Graham Mathers who was made a member of the Court of King's Bench in February 1910. Of the twelve previous members of the Bench seven received their training in Ontario, three in Quebec, one in Nova Scotia, and one in England. An attempt to form a law society of Manitoba to certify candidates for the local bar was made in 1871 but the statute creating it contained the provision that no person who was not a member of the local bar could be made a judge. This bill, as previously noted, was reserved by the Lieutenant Governor. At the next session a new act was passed stating that candidates could be admitted to the bar of the province either by certification of the law society or by order-in-council. Until 1875 the common practice was for candidates to apply to the cabinet. In 1871, for example, Attorney General Clarke

[4]*Manitoba Law Reports*, 1886, p. 481.
[5]*Ibid.*, 1912, p. 145.
[6]The term Supreme Court was changed to Court of Queen's Bench in 1872.
[7]*Statutes of Manitoba*, 1871, c. 2, s. 38.

examined and admitted James Ross, who had taken two years of law at Toronto but had never completed his studies, and Marc Girard, a notary from the province of Quebec.[8] Immediately after they had been admitted Clarke asked them to join him in forming a committee to examine other candidates.

The example of British precedent, the adoption of British rules of evidence, and the chance to draw experienced personnel from the older provinces were all of incalculable value in the creation of an orderly provincial society from primitive frontier conditions. The comparative rapidity with which a highly creditable judiciary was organized was astonishing. Only in the first years of provincial existence was there any widespread lawlessness. In 1872 the cabinet declared that preservation of law and order had gotten beyond them and requested federal help, the Minute explaining that "the position of the town of Winnipeg owing to its proximity to the American frontier, exposes the province to frequent additions to its population of American desperados who are forced to flee from their own land."[9] Another request for federal support was made in 1876 because of "the presence of a large body of American Sioux Indians who have committed murder, robberies and thefts of cattle"[10] and because of "the construction of the railway which brings in men from the American side of the line where, in the new Territories, the law is very weak."[11]

There were numerous instances of a rough and ready frontier justice being dispensed by Manitoba judges and many other cases where no justice at all was dispensed because of the distances involved or the lack of personnel. In March 1877 a magistrate at Norway House reported to Lieutenant Governor Morris that "Murder was committed here about the month of November last," but added, "the Indians are opposed to any further action in the case that may involve the death by hanging of the guilty parties."[12] The justice of the peace did his duty in suggesting that a judge be sent immediately but no trial was ever held. In 1903 in the same district an Indian was killed, allegedly by a Lake Winnipeg fisherman, John MacKay. Chief Justice Dubuc proceeded to the district by boat, picking up a jury as he went, and also picked up the prisoner about 50 miles south of Norway House. A violent storm came up, the Captain was drunk, and the Chief Justice was forced to call upon the

[8]Minutes of the Executive Council, no. 30, May 8, 1871.
[9]*Ibid.*, no. 84, Nov. 6, 1872.
[10]*Ibid.*, no. 224, Jan. 15, 1876.
[11]*Ibid.*
[12]P.A.M., Morris Papers (Ketcheson Collection), Roderick Ross to A. Morris, March 29, 1877.

prisoner to take charge of the boat. He was credited with saving the lives of both the judge and the jury and was acquitted at the trial on the grounds that the jury could not be sure whether the Indian died as a result of MacKay's blow or as a result of a subsequent blow by an unknown party.[13]

Although the early proceedings of the Manitoba judiciary show a certain independence and colour, characteristic of the American frontier as well, it was largely free of political control in contrast to earlier judiciaries in various parts of the United States. In Ohio in 1810 the entire state judiciary was dismissed in what came to be known as the "sweeping order" and replaced by appointees more acceptable to the controlling parties in the legislature.[14] The judges who were dismissed had offended by nullifying an act of the legislature on the grounds that it was contrary to the state constitution. Although the action in Ohio was more dramatic and drastic than in most, there was, prior to the Civil War, a vigorous struggle in many states between the judicial and legislative branches.

Political affiliation, of course, played a part in Manitoba as in other provinces but, as Jackson stated, "The pressing of political claims . . . does at least end when the appointment is made; the debt is paid and the political account closed."[15] In more than eighty years of provincial history only two judges have been formally accused of malpractice or misbehaviour. In March 1881 a petition praying for the removal of E. B. Wood, the Chief Justice of Manitoba, was pressed in the House of Commons and a special committee of the House was subsequently set up to investigate.[16] E. B. Wood, shortly after he had become chief justice, accepted a commission from the legislature of Ontario to distribute five thousand dollars in prize money which had been offered by that body to the citizen of Manitoba who had done most to bring Louis Riel to justice. In reporting on his commission Wood went far beyond what was asked, which was dubious enough, and proceeded to criticize the Manitoba government in very strong language for the benefit of the Ontario legislature, writing, in part, "there seems to be no question that from the origin of the government of Manitoba in the summer of 1870, down to the autumn of 1873, the Executive head and officials not only systematically opposed any proceedings being taken against Riel, and directly or indirectly warned all peace officers to entertain no applica-

[13]A full account of this incident is in the *Winnipeg Free Press*, Nov. 29, 1929.
[14]Wm. Utter, "St. Tammany in Ohio," *Mississippi Valley Historical Review*, XV (1929), p. 321.
[15]R. M. Jackson, *The Machinery of Justice in England* (Cambridge, 1941), p. 210.
[16]Can., H. of C., *Deb.*, March 4, 1881, p. 1213.

tion to proceed against him, but also threw around him the shield and defence of the whole executive authority."[17] The report went on to accuse the Lieutenant Governor of being a dictator and to suggest that the other members of the government were wanting in common sense. Both the cabinet and the Lieutenant Governor objected to his action but the Minister of Justice promised only to let the Chief Justice know that he disapproved.

In 1877 the cabinet again objected to Wood's behaviour on the grounds that he had been drunk on duty. The cabinet passed and forwarded to Ottawa the following Minute:

It is with deep regret that the Executive Council feel it their duty to represent to the Privy Council that the Chief Justice of the Court of Queen's Bench in this province has when proceeding to discharge his duties in connection with the county courts and while being at the county sites in connection therewith, on two different occasions within the last twelve months, fallen into acts of public intoxication thereby bringing discredit upon the judiciary of the Dominion and creating a want of confidence in the administration of justice.[18]

The Minister of Justice took no official action though apparently Wood was asked to explain the charge and defend his conduct before the Governor General.

In 1880 Wood edited a consolidation of the laws of Manitoba to which he contributed a preface. With reference to several laws pertaining to the courts he stated that he had had the greatest difficulty in persuading the government that the laws were necessary. One year later formal charges against Wood, drawn up by a former attorney general, were presented in Ottawa. He was charged with partiality on the Bench, favouritism for his own relatives, introduction of political polemic in his charges to juries, acting as a private attorney for a person being tried before him, and use of abusive language on the Bench. Wood wrote a detailed reply to these charges but died before any conclusion was reached.[19]

The second case was that of Lewis St. George Stubbs who was removed from his office as a county court judge in Manitoba in 1933 because of certain actions he had taken in the Macdonald will case. Alexander Macdonald died on August 23, 1928, leaving an estate of nearly two million dollars. His only daughter produced a will in her favour and applied to Judge Stubbs for probate. The judge refused on the grounds that the will was not properly witnessed (a claim later proved false)

[17]Ontario, Sessional Papers, 1875, vol. 4, Paper 58.
[18]Minutes of the Executive Council, Jan. 4, 1877.
[19]His reply was published in Canada, Sessional Papers, 1882, Paper 106.

and then proceeded to do persistent private detective work which turned up an unsigned draft of a new will leaving the entire estate to charity. Judge Stubbs claimed that the signed copy of this will had been destroyed and refused all further applications for probate. Eventually the daughter applied for and was granted a writ of mandamus from the Court of King's Bench. The judge succeeded in having the decision reviewed by the Court of Appeal but it was confirmed. The matter would probably have ended there except that Judge Stubbs attacked the integrity of the judges of the higher court and denounced them at a public meeting. The Attorney General of Manitoba filed a complaint with the Minister of Justice that the administration of justice was being brought into disrepute. The federal government accordingly created a commission of inquiry under Mr. Justice Ford of the Court of Appeal of the Province of Alberta who concluded that "There is no doubt that the conduct of Judge Stubbs in respect to matters which I have dealt with has done great harm to the judicial institutions of Manitoba. . . . I am clearly of the opinion that such conduct on the part of a Judge amounts to misbehavior within the meaning of Section 31 of the Judges Act."[20] Judge Stubbs was removed by order-in-council.

The court structure in Manitoba is similar to that in the other provinces. At the bottom of the hierarchy are the magistrates sitting in magistrates' courts, and justices of the peace. In June 1960 there were 147 justices of the peace and 32 magistrates appointed and controlled entirely by the province. Justices of the peace have a very limited jurisdiction confined largely to issuing search warrants and summonses. In some instances of petty theft the Criminal Code gives them power to prescribe punishment if two of them sit together and agree. A magistrate, on the other hand, has all the power of two justices of the peace sitting together and other jurisdiction as conferred by statute. Under the revised Criminal Code of Canada a magistrate may be appointed by the province to have either ordinary or extended jurisdiction.[21] Ordinary jurisdiction involves theft, attempted theft, obstruction of a peace officer, common gaming or betting houses, assaults, and frauds in relation to fares provided that the sum involved does not exceed fifty dollars. If a magistrate is given extended jurisdiction he may hear a wide variety of offences of a much more serious nature if the accused elects to be so tried. If the accused does not so elect then the magistrate's power is restricted to a preliminary inquiry for commitment. The general practice in Manitoba is to confer extended jurisdiction only on those magistrates who are members of the

[20]*Enquiry into Matters Relating to the Macdonald Will Case* (Winnipeg, 1933).
[21]*Statutes of Canada*, 1955, c. 51.

bar and practising lawyers. In five instances a man not a lawyer has been given extended jurisdiction but all cases have been in remote areas where facilities for local trial are essential but where no qualified lawyers have settled.[22]

Immediately above the magistrates' courts are the county courts. There are nine county court judges in Manitoba, four in the judicial district which includes Greater Winnipeg and one in each of the other five districts. County courts are, in terms of jurisdiction, inferior. They have no inherent jurisdiction; that is, unless authority is specifically conferred by statute it does not exist. Furthermore, the jurisdiction of county courts is limited in two ways. They are not qualified to hear cases involving more than eight hundred dollars and secondly they are specifically denied jurisdiction in cases of malicious prosecution, false imprisonment, criminal conversation, seduction, injunction, foreclosure, ejectment, administration of estates, and alimony. Subject to the above limitations they are competent to hear actions arising out of contract and personal actions for the recovery of personal property. Despite their limited jurisdiction, however, the county courts are among the most important in the structure. As a past minister of justice said: "A County Court judge has a greater opportunity of impressing his personality upon the public than other judges . . . it is he of whom the people think when they speak of the courts rather than those more remote dignitaries who arrive from time to time to try Supreme Court cases on circuit. A good County Court judge has an unequalled opportunity of creating respect in his district for the courts and of leading his people to a realization of the true meaning of justice. If there is confidence in the County Court judge there is confidence in the courts."[23]

County court judges in Manitoba also act in the capacity of surrogate judges as there has never been enough probate business in the province to warrant the creation of a separate division. When a judge acts in a surrogate court he is under provincial rather than federal jurisdiction and is always given a separate appointment. Until 1934 remuneration was confined to fees, a method of payment which proved to be very inequitable and unsatisfactory. Since 1934 an appointment as a surrogate judge has carried with it a salary of $1,200 a year, paid by the province and supplementary to the salary received as a county court judge. All fees go to the provincial treasurer.

[22]The places are Bissett, Snow Lake, Wabowden, Matheson Island, and Norway House.

[23]J. L. Ilsley in an address to the County Court Judges' Association of Ontario, April 30, 1948.

The Court of Queen's Bench, the Court of Appeal, and the Admiralty Court, the three superior courts of the province, may be considered together. The Court of Queen's Bench is composed of a chief justice and five associate judges and its jurisdiction extends to "all manner of actions, suits, and proceedings, cause and causes of actions . . . whether at law, in equity or probate as well as criminal as civil, real, personal and mixed or otherwise howsoever."[24] Prior to 1906 the only machinery for hearing appeals, within the provincial structure, was through the judges of Queen's Bench sitting *en banc*—that is, any two hearing an appeal from a fellow judge. In 1906 a separate Court of Appeal was created for both civil and criminal cases. In criminal cases its decision is final if unanimous but if not the accused may appeal to the Supreme Court of Canada. The Admiralty Court was established in 1952 with the chief justice of the Court of Queen's Bench as the only judge. The question of admiralty jurisdiction has been debated at periodic intervals ever since Manitoba's boundaries were extended to the shores of Hudson Bay in 1912. For a time it was thought that the jurisdiction of a British Court of Admiralty resided in the Queen's Bench but the weight of opinion was that in the event of a collision between two ships the Queen's Bench could hear an action against the owners but not against the ships as legal persons. This loophole has now been plugged, but as yet no cases calling for a decision of the Admiralty Court have arisen. Should they occur, the chief justice of the Court of Queen's Bench is now equipped to hear them.

[24]The Queen's Bench Act, *R.S.M.*, 1954, c. 52, s. 50.

FINANCIAL
RELATIONSHIPS
BETWEEN
MANITOBA AND
THE FEDERAL
GOVERNMENT

11

WHEN MANITOBA WAS CREATED in 1870 little thought was given to the question of the financial relationship between the new province and the federal government. It was simply assumed that the pattern which had been established in 1867 would apply. This involved a *per capita* subsidy of 80 cents, a debt allowance, and a grant in support of government. The *per capita* subsidy was paid on an estimated population of 17,000, a figure presumably on the generous side, for no one at the time knew the exact figure. The debt allowance was fixed at $27.77 *per capita* or a total of $472,000 but because there was no debt the province received interest on this sum at 5 per cent or $23,604 per year.[1] The grant in support of government was fixed at $30,000 per year, making the grand total of subsidy payments $67,204 per annum.

As far as the original provinces were concerned the *per capita* subsidy was to compensate, in some measure, for the loss of import duties which had been a major source of provincial revenue. The debt allowance was made because much of the provincial debt had been contracted for assets that were to be transferred to the Dominion at Confederation, railways being perhaps the best example. The grant in aid of government was not contemplated in the Quebec Resolutions but was inserted later primarily in an attempt to reduce some of the Maritime acrimony.

The application of these provisions to the new province of Manitoba made little sense. Only minor sources of revenue had existed prior to

[1]The original figure in 1867 had been $25 *per capita*. In 1869 Nova Scotia and New Brunswick obtained better terms through an increase in the debt allowance and these terms were extended to Manitoba. For a full account see J. A. Maxwell, *Federal Subsidies to Provincial Governments*, particularly chap. IV.

Confederation and there were no assets to transfer. The problem was not transferring assets or authority but creating them. The delegates from Red River, inexperienced as they were, were willing to accept such provisions, but it is difficult to understand how men of such wide experience as Cartier and Macdonald could have believed that a full-fledged provincial administration could be created out of a primitive society on a yearly grant of less than $70,000. Manitoba's independent revenue was just over $10,000 in 1870 and the tax potential remained very low until after the turn of the century. The first attempt at a direct tax on corporations was made in 1891 and yielded $2,708.13. Succession duties began in 1893 and in the first year of their operation brought slightly more than $3,000 into the provincial treasury.

For the first ten years of its existence Manitoba had barely enough revenue to operate the machinery of government. It was as if a bank with headquarters in Ontario had established a fifteen-storey branch office in Winnipeg in 1870. Obviously a great deal of the operating revenue would have to come from the parent company and a disproportionate amount would be devoted to overhead expenses. This is precisely what happened in the case of the provincial government. In 1875, 88 per cent of the total revenue was in the form of a federal subsidy. The local revenue of 12 per cent was made up almost entirely of fines, fees, and licences. The "postage stamp province" with a population of approximately 15,000, a large percentage of whom were Métis of uncertain abode, had twenty-four members in its Legislative Assembly and seven in its Legislative Council, each paid $300 a year, plus an Executive Council of five, each receiving $2,000 a year. Only the Legislative Council was expendable and its abolition lowered the overhead by only $2,100 per annum.

Ottawa, having created the new province prematurely, was morally bound to prevent its financial collapse, though anxious to avoid the dangers of preferred treatment. Between 1870 and 1885 Manitoba leaders attempted to get better terms and in almost every instance the federal government exerted itself to oblige. In a rescue operation in 1875 Ottawa allowed Manitoba's deficit of $25,000 to be charged against the debt allowance. But its needs were insatiable and in 1879 the province made a further appeal based on the simple fact that bankruptcy was approaching. Part of the memorandum submitted read:

By carrying out [since 1875] a most energetic system of economy some times incompatible with the dignity of our institutions, and by ignoring persistently the ever increasing requirements of the Province filling up by immigration, it was possible for the Executive Council of Manitoba, to keep public expenditure within the limits of its revenue. But after four years, it is found impracticable to carry out any longer the administration of public affairs with a fixed and unelastic income and a population increasing steadily, and in great numbers every year.[2]

The result was that Ottawa agreed to increase the *per capita* subsidy to $105,650 through the device of assuming the population to be 70,000 when it was actually 39,069. In 1881 another delegation from Manitoba went to Ottawa and presented an estimate that the year's minimum expenditure would be $228,000 of which about $25,000 could be raised locally. The federal cabinet granted a loan of $50,000 and made a promise of a complete revision after the decennial census of 1881. The revision more than doubled the subsidy ($105,650 to $286,730) and the method employed illustrates the federal dilemma of the necessity to assist Manitoba yet keep within the pattern established for other provinces in 1867. For if monetary first aid were to be administered to Manitoba it had to be in such a way as to forestall claims for similar treatment by the other provinces. The population was assumed to be 150,000 when it was actually 69,800, an assumption said to be justified by the exceptional rate of population increase in Manitoba. A new grant was instituted to compensate the province in part for the federal retention of the public domain. The same provision was extended to Prince Edward Island, the only other province which could claim such compensation. Finally, the central government agreed to recommend a vote of money for "plain but sufficient" housing for the assembly and the lieutenant governor but warned the Manitoba delegation that it would have to find ways of furnishing them. The capital was advanced ($267,000) but was charged to the debt allowance, reducing by almost half the interest Manitoba received. Provincial officials insisted that they had been double-crossed and maintained that charging the capital grant to debt allowance was directly contrary to the understanding reached in the negotiations. The reduction continued to be a bone of contention in every subsequent negotiation for nearly twenty years. Finally in 1898 the federal administration restored the debt allowance and absorbed the cost of the buildings from its own budget.

A more fundamental misunderstanding between Manitoba and Ottawa concerned the duration of the settlement of 1881. The Minister of Finance stated in 1882 that "The very object of this bill is to close the question, so far as we can, and we gave the government of Manitoba to understand, as stated in this resolution, that this agreement was to

[2]*J.L.A.*, 1879, Appendix, p. 174.

stand as a contract until 1891."[3] A few days later Premier Norquay announced in the Manitoba legislature: "It will be found that the arrangement effected is not of a permanent character . . . that it is only to meet a temporary emergency, and that it is perfectly understood by the government [at Ottawa] that they will meet the exigencies of the province as circumstances warrant."[4] It is now abundantly clear, of course, that there was then no method of ending Manitoba's demands on the federal treasury. The piecemeal adjustments that took place were only an unsatisfactory, and at times unpleasant, method of meeting a situation that should have been anticipated.

The main result of the settlement of 1881 was to open up a new avenue for demands. The subsidy in lieu of lands inevitably led to a demand for full compensation in lieu of possession. Though Ottawa was unable to grant this request certain minor adjustments were made. All the swamp lands were transferred to the province in 1882 on the theory that they could be drained, and substantial blocks of other land were set aside for educational endowment. The process of making yearly claims on the federal treasury finally ended in 1885 when the total subsidy was increased to $441,000 and an agreement was made to adjust the *per capita* part every five years instead of every ten to allow for the rapidly increasing population.

During the whole period from 1870 to 1885 Manitoba was little more than a financial ward of the federal government and provincial fiscal autonomy was non-existent. In the negotiations of 1881, for example, when the province presented its budget to the federal cabinet for approval the Minister of Finance stated: "We took up the different items of expenditure [i.e. provincial] and estimated that the sum of $225,000 would, with the greatest economy on the part of the Manitoba Government and Legislature, enable them to pay the necessary expenses for the next ten years."[5] Edward Blake protested that the opposition was unable to judge the truth of the minister's statement without seeing the figures. The reply was, "If Blake wishes it, I will bring down a statement showing the exact expenditures under the heads of education and judiciary . . . and the mode at which we arrive at that."[6] Sir Richard Cartwright, who had been a partner to the settlement of 1875, stated that he was satisfied that Manitoba had used the federal money prudently but added that Parlia-

[3]Can., H. of C., *Deb.*, May 10, 1882, p. 1423.
[4]Quoted by Edward Blake in Can., H. of C., *Deb.*, May 16, 1882, p. 1568.
[5]Can., H. of C., *Deb.*, May 10, 1882, p. 1421.
[6]*Ibid.*

ment had a perfect right to know how the money it was now voting would be spent.

No major changes were made in subsidy arrangements between 1885 and 1907. In 1907 the main change as far as Manitoba was concerned was that the grant in support of government was put at $190,000 instead of $50,000. The conference of 1907 is remembered largely because of Laurier's unsuccessful attempt to make the settlement "final and unalterable." Manitoba played little part in opposing him and pressed no particular demands, however, because the provincial delegates believed their case lay in the favourable financial treatment given Alberta and Saskatchewan in 1905. They preferred to argue their case privately rather than at a general conference and continued to do so every year until 1912 when the newly elected Borden government gave the province financial equality with its western neighbours.[7]

The statutory subsidy as finally adjusted in 1912 accounted for 25 per cent of provincial revenue and was in dollar value worth twice as much as the yield from direct taxes in the form of succession duties and corporation taxes. The other main sources of revenue were interest from the school lands fund and fines and fees. Gasoline taxes and personal income taxes were first imposed in 1923 and automobile licences began to yield about $500,000 a year in 1921. Current account revenues were reasonably adequate for the fifteen years following 1912. The main financial problem arose from the rapid growth of population and the youthfulness of the province. The "plain but sufficient" public buildings that the Dominion had provided in 1879 had to be replaced and the province borrowed nearly $10 million to build an unnecessarily ornate home for the legislature. Between 1914 and 1921 another $6 million was spent on judicial buildings, hospitals, educational buildings, and mental institutions. In public utilities, too, the government found it necessary to supply most of the capital. In 1907 the province purchased the Manitoba assets of the Bell Telephone Company for $3.3 million and at the same time issued forty-year debentures for $3.5 million for development. The telephone system did not become self-supporting until after 1920 by which time the province had put up about $20 million of capital. Figures for hydro-electric development were even larger. In short, the public debt

[7]The debt allowance was recalculated at the Alberta and Saskatchewan rate of $32.43 *per capita*, the compensation in lieu of public lands was increased to $409,000 per year (to be adjusted upward), and the whole settlement was made retroactive to 1908 resulting in a lump sum payment of just over $2,000,000. This settlement is the basis of the statutory subsidy which in 1960 was as follows: (a) *per capita* subsidy at 80¢; (b) grant in support of government; (c) interest in lieu of debt; and (d) compensation for public land.

increased from $40 million in 1914 to $82 million in 1921. No attempt was made to create a sinking fund for any of this debt until the mid-twenties.

The depression dealt a shattering blow to the provincial financial structure which was based on continuous prosperity. The total cost of relief in Manitoba from October 1, 1930, to April 30, 1940, was $85,706,893, of which the province paid $32,849,020 and in addition loaned $4,566,580 to the municipalities.[8] Gross dollar figures are perhaps not as meaningful in these days of astronomical budgets as figures for unemployment. For example, unemployment in the winter of 1954–55 caused considerable alarm but the total number drawing unemployment insurance and on relief in Manitoba in March 1954 was approximately one-tenth the number who were on relief in March 1936. In the winter of 1937 there was not enough money in the provincial account to pay civil servants. In fact Premier John Bracken's statement that the province was about to default set in motion an inquiry by the Bank of Canada which resulted in the Royal Commission on Dominion-Provincial Relations.[9]

In presenting its case to the Commission Manitoba proposed a reallocation of responsibilities between the Dominion and the provinces, arguing that the federal government should take over unemployment relief in its entirety and should become responsible for the total cost of old age pensions. In addition it urged that the two jurisdictions share equally the cost of mothers' allowances, hospitalization, care of the mentally ill, public health services, highway construction and maintenance, and technical education. In return the provinces were to transfer to the Dominion the sole power to collect succession duties. The province was bitterly disappointed when discussion of the Rowell-Sirois recommendations was postponed at the Dominion-Provincial Conference of 1941.

The change in Manitoba's financial position since 1940 has been remarkable. The province once on the brink of default now has one of

[8]These figures were supplied by the Manitoba Department of Public Works.
[9]The Royal Commission on Dominion-Provincial Relations (commonly known as the Rowell-Sirois Commission) was appointed by the federal cabinet in August 1937. Its terms of reference included an examination of revenue sources and legislative responsibilities of the federal and provincial governments, the equity and efficiency of the systems of taxation prevailing, and the subsidies paid by Ottawa. The main recommendations of the Commission were that the federal government should take over unemployment relief and assume responsibility for provincial debt charges and that the provinces should receive national adjustment grants calculated to make possible a minimum level of social services throughout the country and in turn should transfer their rights to collect personal income taxes, corporation taxes, and succession duties.

the highest credit ratings in Canada. In 1936 the public debt charges accounted for 42 per cent of the total provincial expenditure; in 1951 the figure was 22 per cent. The great bulk of the 1936 percentage was interest on dead weight debt; the 1951 figure included a repayment programme that will leave the province completely free from non-self-sustaining debt by 1965. Several factors have, of course, produced the change. The most important are the rapid growth in Canada's gross national product, a relatively high level of farm income particularly from 1940 to 1952, a rapid increase in industrial production within the province, strong efforts on the part of provincial authorities to keep provincial expenditures at the lowest possible levels, and, finally, a substantial increase in federal grants.

Since 1940 a series of federal-provincial agreements and purely federal measures have greatly strengthened Manitoba's financial structure. They may be classified roughly but conveniently as stabilizing and equalizing measures which have tended to reduce provincial disparities of income and resource, have absorbed part of the rapidly increasing burden for welfare services, and have had an indirect but beneficial effect on provincial finance.

The federal-provincial tax-rental agreements, which have been operating since 1940, have both stabilized the revenues of provinces with low or fluctuating tax potentials and equalized provincial disparities although they were not originally adopted for either of these purposes. The genesis of these agreements was the necessity for the federal government to raise more revenue to fight the war. The provinces were, in effect, forced to vacate the income and corporation tax fields, the Minister of Finance announcing in his budget speech of 1941: "We have reached the conclusion that the rates of personal and corporation income taxes should be raised by the dominion to the maximum levels which would be reasonable at this time, if the provinces were not in these fields."[10] In return the provinces were offered a choice of a payment equal to the interest on the provincial debt less inheritance taxes collected by the province in the federal fiscal year ending nearest to December 31, 1940, or an amount equal to the revenue received in the preceding year from tax fields that were to be left in the hands of the federal government for the duration. In addition, Ottawa agreed to guarantee the existing level of revenue from gasoline taxes and when liquor was rationed in 1942 the guarantee was also extended to revenues from it.

In introducing these proposals the Minister of Finance stated that the arrangements would be discontinued and federal taxes reduced propor-

[10]Can., H. of C., *Deb.*, 1941, p. 2345.

tionately within one complete fiscal year after the end of the war. However, when the alternate proposals[11] of Ottawa at the 1946 Dominion-Provincial Conference on Reconstruction were rejected the cabinet showed no disposition to return to the rather chaotic system of pre-war taxation. If it did so, the yield in some provinces would be too low to enable the government to discharge its responsibilities and might force the use of regressive taxes. Moreover, the Minister of Finance and his advisers were convinced that central control of taxation policy was essential if the budget were to be the balance wheel of the economic machine. In the end Ottawa induced the poorer provinces to transfer their rights in the direct tax field by the simple process of paying them more than they would have received had they retained them, and in 1946 Nova Scotia, Prince Edward Island, New Brunswick, Manitoba, Saskatchewan, and Alberta signed five-year agreements.

Since 1946 these agreements have become more and more favourable to the provinces. Indeed, in the last decade Manitoba has derived an average of 45 per cent of its revenue from them. Because the federal government wanted to have the richer provinces in the agreements it was forced to sweeten the pill considerably. In 1947 British Columbia was attracted by an agreement stipulating that federal payments would increase in proportion to increases in both the gross national product and the provincial population but would not fall below a minimum figure. This provision was automatically extended to provinces that had previously signed because each individual agreement contained a "most favoured nation" clause. The same process was repeated when Ontario came into the scheme in 1952.

The basis of federal-provincial financial arrangements was changed in 1957, largely on behalf of Quebec. The revised system, unlike the one prevailing prior to 1957, made a clear distinction between payments for rental and those for equalizing provincial disparities in income. The legislation contained three operative words—rental, equalization, and stabilization. In 1957 Manitoba rented income, corporation taxes, and succession duties to the federal government for five years and received back 10 per cent[12] of the federal personal income taxes in the province, 9 per cent of the taxable income of corporations, and 50 per cent of the suc-

[11]The 1945 proposals which were considered at a Dominion-Provincial conference in 1946 assumed federal control of income, corporation, and succession duties and were, in outline: (a) old age pensions on a national basis; (b) federal responsibility for relief of unemployed employables; (c) a joint federal-provincial health insurance plan; and (d) a joint federal-provincial public investment plan.

[12]Raised to 13 per cent for all provinces by an amendment in 1959 (*Statutes of Canada*, 1959, c. 26).

cession duty collections.[13] In 1960–61 this amounted to $25,000,000.

Equalization and stabilization payments were quite different. All provinces received automatically, and without signing any agreement whatever with Ottawa, a yearly payment amounting to the difference between the *per capita* yield of the same percentages (that is 13, 9, and 50) of the standard taxes in the particular province and in the two provinces with the highest yield. The *per capita* yield in Manitoba for 1960–61 was $25.55 while in Ontario and British Columbia it averaged $43.07. Manitoba, therefore, received the difference between these two figures multiplied by its population of $15,000,000 (in round figures). Stabilization payments would be made if the combined total of rental and equalization payments were less than the amount the province would have received if the agreement made in 1952 and replaced in 1957 had been maintained. Such payments have not, so far, been necessary.[14]

Both the old and the new systems have greatly increased provincial revenue. Prior to 1957 Manitoba received substantially more money by renting the tax fields than it could have collected by retaining them, and all the financial benefits of the old system are guaranteed under the new. Finances will continue to be protected from revenue losses resulting from regional or local conditions. For example, in 1954–55 the gross national product for Canada fell by 2 per cent and at the same time farm income in Manitoba fell by an estimated 30 per cent. The decrease in the tax-rental payment was of course governed by the former percentage and

[13]The federal-provincial relations division of the Department of Finance at Ottawa has provided the following explanatory note: "the personal income and succession duty payments are a percentage of the federal collection in those fields, whereas the rental for corporation income is based on the taxable income of the corporations. In order to ensure that the rental payments for personal income and sucession duty do not fluctuate with changes in the federal rate of taxation, these two rental rates are based on the federal tax rates that were in existence on January 6th, 1956, that is, the province gets a rental for personal income and succession duties equivalent to 10%, 13% and 50% on federal collections that would have been made if the federal tax rates of January 6, 1956, had remained unchanged during the five years."

[14]The tax-rental agreements were substantially altered when they expired on March 31, 1962. The rental system was discontinued and each province levies its own rates in the fields of income and corporation taxes. However, the central government will, if requested, make the collections for any province that adopts federal definitions of taxable income. Ottawa has also agreed to a progressive rise in the percentages the provinces may levy (without double taxation) so that by 1966 they will have 20 per cent of the personal income taxes, 9 per cent of corporation taxes, and 50 per cent of succession duties. The equalization system is maintained but with modifications. The national *per capita* average yield of the standard taxes replaces the average of the two highest provinces but the calculation of the payments takes into account the yields from natural resource taxation whereas it has previously been based on personal income, corporation and succession duties only. Provisions for stabilization of provincial income remain substantially unchanged.

amounted to something under half a million dollars. The words of Premier D. L. Campbell, spoken in 1950, are just as applicable now: "We have had the assurance that in times of difficulty the revenues of the province would not fall below minimum amounts. The result has been that our province has been placed in a position to offer some assistance to our municipalities. In addition we have been able to undertake new programs of provincial services to the people of Manitoba which would not have been possible if we had not been sure of a relatively steady source of income."[15]

Health services have provided relief for provincial finances which ranks next to the tax-rental agreements in importance. These services have become a constitutional responsibility of the provinces but not through any specific statement in the British North America Act. The services that contemporary governments are called upon to provide in public health and welfare were not contemplated in 1867 and did not significantly affect provincial budgets until after the turn of the century.[16] The first attempt in Manitoba to provide a comprehensive plan for preventive and diagnostic medical services plus greatly increased hospital facilities is found in the Health Services Act of 1945. This provincial plan was put in statutory form before the federal programme was begun and before the Dominion-Provincial Conference of 1945 when the central government announced its willingness to enter the health services and welfare fields. In any event, it seems unlikely that the Act would have been fully implemented without the federal assistance which began in 1948.

Federal health services grants have been made for a variety of purposes and have had the dual result of reducing provincial financial

[15]*Proceedings of the Dominion-Provincial Conference 1950* (Ottawa, 1951), p. 33.

[16]Statistical evidence is set forth in the table below:

	Public welfare *per capita* costs	Public welfare expenditure as a percentage of provincial budget
1875	.04	1.74
1891	.23	5.16
1901	.30	7.81
1911	.85	13.00
1921	2.41	14.15
1931	4.24	22.18
1936	3.71	20.02
1941	4.39	21.67
1946	5.24	22.98
1951	10.87	23.52

burdens and of laying the foundations for a comprehensive hospital insurance scheme. Many of the grants were outright and did not require the province to match the sum put up by the federal government while others required the province to maintain a certain level of activity related to a base year. For hospital construction the cost of approved projects was shared equally. All projects for which grants were made have had to have approval of the federal Department of Health and Welfare but administrative jurisdiction has remained entirely with the province. The net result has been that the general level of services and facilities was raised enough to permit the introduction of a hospital insurance scheme on July 1, 1958, towards the cost of which the federal authority pays approximately 50 per cent.[17]

In addition to taking part of the financial burden for a variety of health services the federal government has, since 1951, been solely responsible for old age pensions for all persons over 70 years of age. It also matches provincial expenditures in pensions for those from 65 to 70 under terms of eligibility set by the province. The same holds true for allowances for blind persons. Total federal expenditure in pensions and allowances has in the past two years averaged nearly $22 million, almost one-quarter of the entire provincial budget.

The tax-rental agreements and federal social welfare measures have had a direct and measureable effect on provincial finances. One other measure, the benefit from which though indirect is important, must be mentioned.[18] The system of unemployment insurance inaugurated in 1941 has had the effect of reducing provincial and municipal expenditures for direct relief to very small figures which relate to a "hard core" of unemployables. The total provincial and municipal expenditure for these cases in 1954 was just under two million dollars; in the same year the Unemployment Insurance Fund paid out $240,722,456 within the province.[19] The responsibility for those not covered by insurance has been and still is a bone of contention between the provincial and federal governments, however. In 1955 the two authorities signed an Unemployment Assistance Agreement whose main provision was that if more than 0.45 per cent of the population of the province were receiving welfare assis-

[17]The actual formula is 25 per cent of the average *per capita* cost for hospital services in Canada as a whole plus 25 per cent of the average *per capita* costs in Manitoba multiplied by the number of insured persons.

[18]No attempt is made here to describe all the areas where costs are shared between Manitoba and the federal government. Only those that have a major effect on the provincial budget are treated. Others are vocational and apprenticeship training, farm labour service, 4-H clubs, soil erosion and water control, forest inventories and reforestation.

[19]Department of the Bureau of Statistics, *Statistical Report on the Operation of the Unemployment Insurance Act, 1954–58* (Supplement), Monthly 73–001.

tance of an approved kind, Ottawa would meet 50 per cent of the cost of those recipients above the 0.45 floor. In 1957 the Diefenbaker government announced that the floor had been abolished and that costs would in future be split evenly for the whole group. Manitoba has consistently maintained since 1921 that the federal government ought to bear the whole cost. Ottawa, provincial leaders have argued, has control over the basic tools of fiscal, tax, and interest policy by which depressions or recessions may be controlled and should therefore accept full responsibility for any failure or partial failure of its policies.

Provincial leaders have never viewed the tax-rental agreements or the shared costs schemes as threats to provincial autonomy. They have, in fact, done their best to see that the agreements were reached.[20] Few provincial functions conferred by section 92 of the British North America Act are associated in Manitoba with distinctive local customs as they often are in Quebec or Nova Scotia. The great battles over provincial rights prior to 1900 were not to protect non-existent local traditions but to rectify specific grievances.

Manitoba and Saskatchewan were the only provinces to give whole-hearted approval to the recommendations of the Rowell-Sirois Commission and would gladly have traded their permanent rights in the direct tax field for suitable yearly cash payments.[21] Manitoba had no objection to the proposal of national adjustment grants calculated by an independent commission even though, if Australian experience is any guide, such a system would seriously restrict provincial autonomy. The 1945 proposals, which assumed federal control over direct taxation, also were warmly welcomed by Manitoba; in addressing the plenary session of the Dominion-Provincial Conference of that year Premier Garson said: "the presentation [of these proposals] is tremendously gratifying to my province in the light of our position of the past eight years. During that time we have never been able to develop anything like the hope which the proposals now laid before us give us."[22] Garson's view contrasts sharply with that of Premier Duplessis, who said:

A federal system involving an allocation of public powers among different federated states must equally provide for a correlative allocation as to revenue sources. How could the possession of the widest legislative powers

[20]Mr. Harris, the Minister of Finance, was quoted in the *Winnipeg Free Press* March 23, 1956, as follows: "In 1937 Mr. Garson, as provincial treasurer of Manitoba, took the initiative which was the real beginning of all the activities which have resulted in our present federal-provincial proposals."

[21]See *Report of the Dominion-Provincial Conference 1941* (Ottawa, 1941), p. 23, for Manitoba's point of view as expressed by John Bracken.

[22]*Proceedings of the Dominion-Provincial Conference 1945* (Ottawa, 1946), p. 130.

profit the Provinces if, on the other hand, they were restrained from levying the funds required to exercise such powers . . . ? It would be an easy matter to show that a Province deprived of all revenue except subsidies . . . would become an inferior governmental organization under the tutelage of the authority on which it depends.[23]

In Manitoba experience with financial independence on the basis of revenue and responsibility, as allocated by the British North America Act, was never a happy one and turned into near tragedy during the depression. The province has shown no desire to assume a proud but poor status. Indeed, pride, in terms of deep-rooted local tradition, has never been present and the poverty of the past was scarcely compatible with dignity.

[23]*Ibid.*, p. 355.

*Lieutenant Governors of Manitoba Since Confederation**

	Date of Appointment
A. G. Archibald	May 20, 1870
Alexander Morris	Dec. 2, 1872
J. E. Cauchon	Nov. 7, 1876
James Aikins	Sept. 22, 1882
Sir John Schultz	July 1, 1888
J. C. Patterson	Sept. 2, 1895
Sir D. H. McMillan	Oct. 15, 1900
Sir Douglas Cameron	July 22, 1911
Sir J. A. M. Aikins	Aug. 5, 1916
Theodore A. Burrows	Oct. 25, 1926
James D. McGregor	Jan. 25, 1929
W. J. Tupper	Dec. 1, 1934
R. F. McWilliams	Nov. 1, 1940
John S. McDiarmid	Aug. 1, 1953
Errick Willis	Jan. 15, 1959

*SOURCE: *Parliamentary Guide.*

APPENDIX B

*Premiers of Manitoba Since Confederation**

	Date Office Attained
A. Boyd	Sept. 16, 1870
N. A. Girard	Dec. 14, 1871
H. J. H. Clarke	March 14, 1872
N. A. Girard	July 8, 1874
R. A. Davis	Dec. 3, 1874
John Norquay	Oct. 16, 1878
D. H. Harrison	Dec. 26, 1887
T. Greenway	Jan. 19, 1888
H. J. Macdonald	Jan. 8, 1900
Sir R. P. Roblin, K.C.M.G.	Oct. 29, 1900
T. C. Norris	May 12, 1915
John Bracken	Aug. 8, 1922
S. S. Garson	Jan. 8, 1943
D. L. Campbell	Nov. 7, 1948
Dufferin Roblin	June 16, 1958

*SOURCE: *Parliamentary Guide.*

Declaration of the People of Rupert's Land and the North-West, 1869

WHEREAS, it is admitted by all men, as a fundamental principle, that the public authority commands the obedience and respect of its subjects. It is also admitted, that a people, when it has no Government, is free to adopt one form of Government, in preference to another, to give or to refuse allegiance to that which is proposed. In accordance with the above first principle the people of this country had obeyed and respected the authority to which the circumstances which surrounded its infancy compelled it to be subject.

A company of adventurers known as the "Hudson Bay Company," and invested with certain powers, granted by His Majesty (Charles II), established itself in Rupert's Land, and in the North-West Territory, for trading purposes only. This Company, consisting of many persons, required a certain constitution. But as there was a question of commerce only, their constitution was framed in reference thereto. Yet, since there was at that time no Government to see to the interest of a people already existing in the country, it became necessary for judicial affairs to have recourse to the officers of the Hudson Bay Company. This inaugurated that species of government which, slightly modified by subsequent circumstances, ruled this country up to a recent date.

Whereas, that Government, thus accepted, was far from answering to the wants of the people, and became more and more so, as the population increased in numbers, and as the country was developed, and commerce extended, until the present day, when it commands a place amongst the colonies; and this people, ever actuated by the above-mentioned principles, had generously supported the aforesaid Government, and gave to it a faithful allegiance, when, contrary to the law of nations, in March, 1869, that said Government surrendered and transferred to Canada all the rights which it had, or pretended to have, in this Territory, by transactions with which the people were considered unworthy to be made acquainted.

And, whereas, it is also generally admitted that a people is at liberty to establish any form of government it may consider suited to its wants, as soon as the power to which it was subject abandons it, or attempts to subjugate it, without its consent to a foreign power; and maintain that no right can be transferred to such foreign power. Now, therefore, first, we, the representatives of the people, in Council assembled in Upper Fort Garry, on the 24th day of November, 1869, after having invoked the God of Nations, relying on these fundamental moral principles, solemnly declare, in the name of our constituents, and in our own names, before God and man, that, from the day on which the Government we had always respected abandoned us, by transferring to a strange power the sacred authority confided to it, the people of Rupert's Land and the North-West became free and exempt from all allegiance to the said Government. Second. That we refuse to recognize the authority of Canada, which pretends to have a right to coerce us, and impose upon us a despotic form of government still more contrary to our rights and interests as British subjects, than was that Government to which we had subjected ourselves, through necessity up to recent date. Thirdly. That, by sending an expedition on the 1st of November, ult., charged to drive back Mr. William McDougall and his companions, coming in the name of Canada, to rule us with the rod of despotism, without previous notification to that effect, we have acted conformably to that sacred right which commands every citizen to offer energetic opposition to prevent this country from being enslaved. Fourth. That we continue, and shall continue, to oppose, with all our strength, the establishing of the Canadian authority in our country, under the announced form; and, in case of persistence on the part of the Canadian Government to enforce its obnoxious policy upon us by force of arms, we protest beforehand against such an unjust and unlawful course; and we declare the said Canadian Government responsible, before God and men, for the innumerable evils which may be caused by so unwarrantable a course. Be it known, therefore, to the world in general, and to the Canadian Government in particular, that, as we have always heretofore successfully defended our country in frequent wars with the neighbouring tribes of Indians, who are now on friendly relations with us, we are firmly resolved in future, not less than in the past, to repel all invasions from whatsoever quarter they may come; and, furthermore, we do declare and proclaim, in the name of the people of Rupert's Land and the North-West, that we have, on the said 24th day of November, 1869, above mentioned, established a Provisional Government, and hold it to be the only and lawful authority now in existence in Rupert's Land and the North-West which claims the obedience and respect of the people; that, meanwhile, we hold ourselves in readiness to enter in such negociations with the Canadian Government as may be favourable for the good government and prosperity of this people. In support of this declaration, relying on the protection of Divine Providence, we mutually pledge ourselves, on oath, our lives, our fortunes, and our sacred honor, to each other.

Issued at Fort Garry, this Eighth day of December, in the year of our Lord, One thousand eight hundred and sixty-nine.

JOHN BRUCE, Pres.
LOUIS RIEL, Sec.

E. H. Oliver, ed., *The Canadian North-West*, II, 904–6.

APPENDIX D

*Comparison of Section 93 of the British North America Act, 1867,
and Section 22 of the Manitoba Act*

BRITISH NORTH AMERICA ACT

93. In and for each Province the Legislature may exclusively make Laws in relation to Education, subject and according to the following Provisions:—

1. Nothing in any such law shall prejudicially affect any Right or Privilege with respect to Denominational Schools which any Class of Persons have by Law in the Province at the Union:

2. All the Powers, Privileges, and Duties at the Union by Law conferred and imposed in Upper Canada on the Separate Schools and School Trustees of the Queen's Roman Catholic Subjects shall be and the same are hereby extended to the Dissentient Schools of the Queen's Protestant and Roman Catholic Subjects in Quebec:

3. Where in any Province a System of Separate or Dissentient Schools exists by Law at the Union or is thereafter established by the Legislature of the Province, an Appeal shall lie to the Governor General in Council from any Act or Decision of any Provincial Authority affecting any Right or Privilege of the Protestant or Roman Catholic Minority of the Queen's Subjects in relation to Education:

4. In case any such Provincial Law as from Time to Time seems to the Governor General in Council requisite for the due Execution of the Provisions of this Section is not made, or in case any Decision of the Governor General in Council on any Appeal under this Section is not duly executed by the proper Provincial Authority in that Behalf, then and in every such case, and as far only as the Circumstances of each Case require, the Parliament of Canada may make remedial Laws for the due Execution of the Provisions of this Section and of any Decision of the Governor General in Council under this Section.

THE MANITOBA ACT

22. In and for the Province, the said Legislature may exclusively make Laws in relation to Education, subject and according to the following provisions:—

(1). Nothing in any such Law shall prejudicially affect any right or privilege with respect to Denominational Schools which any class of persons have by Law or Practice in the Province at the Union:—

(2.) An appeal shall lie to the Governor General in Council from any Act or decision of the Legislature of the Province, or of any Provincial Authority, affecting any right or privilege of the Protestant or Roman Catholic minority of the Queen's subjects in relation to Education:—

(3.) In case any such Provincial Law, as from time to time seems to the Governor General in Council requisite for the due execution of the provisions of this section, is not made, or in case any decision of the Governor General in Council on any appeal under this section is not duly executed by the proper Provisional Authority in that behalf, then, and in every such case, and as far only as the circumstances of each case require, the Parliament of Canada may make remedial Laws for the due execution of the provisions of this section and of any decision of the Governor General in Council under this section.

BIBLIOGRAPHY

I. *Primary Sources*

UNPUBLISHED DOCUMENTS

Canada: Public Archives (P.A.C.)

Bulger Papers
Dafoe Papers
Hudson Papers
Laurier Papers

Macdonald Papers
Selkirk Papers
Sifton Papers

Manitoba: Public Archives (P.A.M.)

Archibald Letter Books
Archibald Papers
Cauchon Letter Books
Crerar Papers
Greenway Papers
Macdonald Letters
Minutes of the Executive
   Council of Manitoba
Morris Papers, Ketcheson
   Collection

Morris Family Papers
Morris Letter Books
Norris Papers
Records of General
   Quarterly Court of
   Assiniboia
Red River Papers
Roblin Papers
Taylor Papers

PUBLISHED DOCUMENTS

Great Britain

House of Commons

Report from the Select Committee on the Hudson's Bay Company (1857).
Report of Select Committee on House of Commons Procedure (1914).
Report of Select Committee on Procedure in Public Business (1931).

Colonial Office

Papers Relating to the Red River Settlement (1819).
. . . Correspondence . . . between the Colonial Office and the Hudson's Bay Company, or the Government of Canada . . . on the Affairs of the Company . . . (1858).
. . . Correspondence between the Colonial Office, the Government of the Canadian Dominion, the Hudson's Bay Company, Relating to the Surrender of Rupert's Land by the Hudson's Bay Company . . . (1869).
Correspondence Relative to the Recent Disturbances in the Red River Settlement (1870).

Canada

Province of Canada, *Sessional Papers.*
Parliament, *Sessional Papers.*
House of Commons, *Debates.*
Report of the Select Committee on the Causes of the Difficulties in the North-West Territory in 1869–70 (1874).
Report of the Royal Commission on the Transportation and Shipment of Grain (1899).
Report of the Royal Commission on Dominion-Provincial Relations and Appendices (1937).
Proceedings of Dominion-Provincial Conferences.
HODGINS, W. E., comp., *Correspondence, Reports ... on the Subject of Dominion and Provincial Legislation, 1867–1895* (Ottawa, 1896).
LA FOREST, G. V., *Disallowance and Reservation of Provincial Legislation* (Department of Justice, Ottawa, 1955).
OLIVER, E. H., ed., *The Canadian North West: Its Early Development and Legislative Records* (Publications of the Canadian Archives, no. 9, 2 vols.; Ottawa, 1914 and 1915).
OLMSTED, R. A., ed., *Decisions of the Judicial Committee of the Privy Council Relating to the British North America Act, 1867, and the Canadian Constitution, 1867–1954* (Department of Justice, Ottawa, 1954).
Statutes of Canada.

Ontario

Legislative Assembly, *Sessional Papers.*

Manitoba

Provisional Government, 1870, *Journals.*
Legislative Assembly, *Journals.*
Legislative Assembly, *Sessional Papers.*
Legislative Assembly, *Debates.*
Rules, Orders and Forms of Proceeding of the Legislative Assembly of Manitoba (1954).
Manitoba Grain Growers and the United Farmers of Manitoba, *Annual Reports,* 1910–35.
Report of the Manitoba Assessment and Taxation Commission (1919).
Report of the Royal Commission Appointed to Inquire into Certain Matters Relating to the New Parliament Buildings (Winnipeg, 1915).
Report of the Royal Commission Appointed to Investigate the Charges Made in the Statement of C. P. Fullerton, K. C. (Winnipeg, 1915).
Report of the Commission Constituted to Enquire into and Report on All Expenditures for Road Work during the Year 1914 (Winnipeg, 1917).
Report of the Special Select Committee on Education of the Manitoba Legislative Assembly (Winnipeg, 1945).
Manitoba Provincial-Municipal Committee Report, Appendix C (Winnipeg, 1953).
Report of the Royal Commission on Education (Winnipeg, 1959).
Report of the Greater Winnipeg Investigating Commission (Winnipeg, 1959).

Statutes of Manitoba.
Manitoba Law Reports.

Hudson's Bay Company
Charters, Statutes, Orders in Council, etc. Relating to the Hudson's Bay Company (London, 1931).

II. *Secondary Sources*

NEWSPAPERS AND PERIODICALS

Bison (1941–   )
Canadian Annual Review (1901–38)
Commercial (1890–1910)
Grain Growers' Guide (1908–38)
Labour Gazette (1901–   )
Manitoban (1870–87)
Morning Call (1887–89)
New Nation (Jan. to Sept. 1870)

Nor'Wester (1859–72)
Patrons' Advocate (1879–1900)
Single Taxer (1914–15)
Statesman (1913–18)
Tribune (1890–   )
Winnipeg Free Press (1872–   )
Voice (1909–18)

UNPUBLISHED MONOGRAPHS

CLAGUE, R. E., "The Political Aspects of the Manitoba School Question," M.A. Thesis, University of Manitoba, 1939.
JACKSON, J. A., "The Disallowance of Manitoba Railway Legislation in the 1880's: Railway Policy as a Factor in the Relations of Manitoba with the Dominion, 1878–1888," M.A. Thesis, University of Manitoba, 1945.
MILLIGAN, F. A., "The Lieutenant-Governorship in Manitoba, 1870–1882," M.A. Thesis, University of Manitoba, 1948.
ORLIKOW, L., "A Survey of the Reform Movement in Manitoba 1910 to 1920," M.A. Thesis, University of Manitoba, 1955.

PUBLISHED WORKS

BEGG, ALEXANDER, *History of the North West* (3 vols., Toronto, 1893).
BUCK, A. E., *Financing Canadian Government* (Public Administration Service, Chicago, 1949).
CLEVERDON, CATHERINE LYLE, *The Woman Suffrage Movement in Canada* (Toronto, 1950).
CLOKIE, H. McD., *Canadian Government and Politics* (2nd. ed., Toronto, 1950).
CREIGHTON, DONALD, *John A. Macdonald: The Young Politician* (Toronto, 1956).
DAFOE, J. W., "Economic History of the Prairie Provinces, 1870–1913" in

Canada and Its Provinces, vol. XX, *The Prairie Provinces* (Toronto, 1914).
—— *Clifford Sifton in Relation to His Times* (Toronto, 1931).
DAWSON, R. MacG., *The Civil Service of Canada* (London, 1929).
FRANCIS, E. K., *In Search of Utopia: The Mennonites of Manitoba* (Altona, 1955).
GEIGER, T. R., *The Philosophy of Henry George* (New York, 1933).
GIRAUD, MARCEL, *Le Métis canadien: son rôle dans l'histoire des provinces de l'Ouest* (Paris, 1945).
GLAZEBROOK, G. DE T., *A History of Transportation in Canada* (Toronto, 1938).
GRISWOLD, A. W., *Democracy and Farming* (New York, 1948).
HANSEN, M. L., and J. B. BREBNER, *The Mingling of the Canadian and American Peoples* (New Haven, 1940).
HEDGES, J. B., *Building the Canadian West* (New York, 1939).
HILL, R. B., *Manitoba: History of Its Early Settlement, Development and Resources* (Toronto, 1890).
HIND, HENRY Y., *Narrative of the Canadian Red River Exploring Expedition of 1857* (London, 1860).
HOPKINS, CHAS. H., *The Rise of the Social Gospel* (New Haven, 1940).
McCLUNG, NELLIE, *The Stream Runs Fast* (Toronto, 1945).
MacKAY, DOUGLAS, *The Honourable Company: A History of the Hudson's Bay Company* (Toronto, 1949).
MACKINTOSH, W. A., *Prairie Settlement* (Toronto, 1934).
McNAUGHT, KENNETH, *A Prophet in Politics: A Biography of J. S. Woodsworth* (Toronto, 1959).
MARTIN, CHESTER, *The Natural Resources Question* (Winnipeg, 1920).
MAXWELL, J. A., *Federal Subsidies to Provincial Governments* (Cambridge, Mass., 1937).
MILLIGAN, F. A., "Reservation of Manitoba Bills and Refusal of Assent by Lieutenant-Governor Cauchon 1877–1882," *C.J.E.P.S.*, XIV (1948).
MORTON, A. S., *A History of Prairie Settlement*, and CHESTER MARTIN, *"Dominion Lands" Policy* (Toronto, 1938).
MORTON, W. L., "The Western Progressive Movement and Cabinet Domination," *C.J.E.P.S.*, XII (May, 1946).
—— *The Progressive Party in Canada* (Toronto, 1950).
—— ed., *Alexander Begg's Red River Journal and Other Papers Relative to the Red River Resistance 1869–70* (Toronto, 1950).
—— *Manitoba: A History* (Toronto, 1957).
NYE, RUSSELL B., *Midwestern Progressive Politics* (East Lansing, Mich., 1951).
PATTON, H., *Grain Growers' Co-operation in Western Canada* (Cambridge, Mass., 1928).
POPE, SIR JOSEPH, ed., *Correspondence of Sir John Macdonald* (Garden City, N.Y., and Toronto, 1921).
ROSS, ALEXANDER, *The Red River Settlement* (London, 1856).
SAYWELL, J. T., *The Office of Lieutenant-Governor* (Toronto, 1957).
SKELTON, O. D., *Life and Letters of Sir Wilfrid Laurier* (2 vols., Oxford, 1921).

STANLEY, G. F. G., *The Birth of Western Canada: A History of the Riel Rebellions* (London, 1936).

WOODSWORTH, J. S., Strangers within Our Gates (Toronto, 1909).

YOUNG, CHARLES H., *The Ukrainian Canadians: A Study of Assimilation* (Toronto, 1931).

YUZYK, PAUL, *The Ukrainians in Manitoba: A Social History* (Toronto, 1953).